HIGH UNEMPLOYMENT

A CHALLENGE FOR INCOME SUPPORT POLICIES

·33/13 Hig.

ORGANISATION FOR ECONOMIC CO-OPERATION AND DEVELOPMENT

Pursuant to article 1 of the Convention signed in Paris on 14th December, 1960, and which came into force on 30th September, 1961, the Organisation for Economic Co-operation and Development (OECD) shall promote policies designed:

- to achieve the highest sustainable economic growth and employment and a rising standard of living in Member countries, while maintaining financial stability, and thus to contribute to the development of the world economy;
- to contribute to sound economic expansion in Member as well as non-member countries in the process of economic development; and
- to contribute to the expansion of world trade on a multilateral, non-discriminatory basis in accordance with international obligations.

The Signatories of the Convention on the OECD are Austria, Belgium, Canada, Denmark, France, the Federal Republic of Germany, Greece, Iceland, Ireland, Italy, Luxembourg, the Netherlands, Norway, Portugal, Spain, Sweden, Switzerland, Turkey, the United Kingdom and the United States. The following countries acceded subsequently to this Convention (the dates are those on which the instruments of accession were deposited): Japan (28th April, 1964), Finland (28th January, 1969), Australia (7th June, 1971) and New Zealand (29th May, 1973).

The Socialist Federal Republic of Yugoslavia takes part in certain work of the OECD (agreement of 28th October, 1961).

Publié en français sous le titre:

L'EXTENSION DU CHÔMAGE :
UN DEFI POUR LA POLITIQUE DE
GARANTIE DE RESSOURCES

A national expert's meeting on "Unemployment Insurance Issues and Alternative Uses of Unemployment Benefit Funds", jointly sponsored by the OECD and the Bundesanstalt für Arbeit, was held in Nuremberg, Germany, on 8 and 9 November 1982. Six papers presented at this meeting are included in this volume. They include analytical studies on factors underlying the growth of expenditure on unemployment insurance, the statistical documentation and commentaries on the papers. Four important topics discussed at the meeting were:

1. The "Costs" of Unemployment;
2. Major issues in Unemployment Compensation policy in the present labour market situation.
3. The Wage-Replacement function of unemployment compensation programmes;
4. OECD Member countries' practices in alternative uses of unemployment insurance funds.

The conference led to two days of debates about the costs of prolonged unemployment, alternative uses of unemployment insurance funds, and general policy prescriptions. Broadly, there were two schools of thought. One argued in favour of restrictive policies being continued to combat inflation. The rationale behind this view was that the ultimate benefits of such policies would eventually outweigh the costs attached to long periods of low or zero economic growth. According to the other school of thought, the importance of stabilizing or lowering unemployment has risen relative to that of pursuing anti-inflation efforts with vigour. Two reasons were cited: the sharp fall in inflation and the non-linear rise of economic and social costs flowing from protracted unemployment.

There was general agreement that the structural component of unemployment has increased over time largely reflecting demographic trends, higher female participation rates, continued advances in real total labour costs, and accelerated obsolescence of the capital stock due to feeble economic growth. Cuts in real wages relative to productivity were seen as desirable to improve profitability. Given the initial deflationary effects of such cuts, restrictive policies needed to be eased, at least temporarily as a bridging operation.

In other respects policy conclusions diverged sharply. Proponents of the first school of thought showed little inclination to consider the costs of prolonged unemployment in all of their dimensions. In

3

their view, special labour market policies create economic problems because of their expenditure-raising character. Adherents to the second one viewed such policies as increasingly important, given prospects of low medium-term growth and the attendant danger of skill erosion and lack of job experience.

According to this latter group, there are various avenues other than unemployment compensation through which unemployment tends to raise public spending: prolonged unemployment adversely affects physical and mental health; given the strong concentration on low paid employees, it increases poverty over time, and with it, crime and family disorder; and through the erosion of skills and the obsolescence of the capital stock unemployment tends to raise the full capacity unemployment rate weakening the cyclically adjusted public sector's financial position. Furthermore, through capital shortages and skill mismatches, protracted unemployment affects the cyclical behaviour of inflation in periods of expansion - a point often overlooked by those who assign a high priority to bringing inflation under control through pronounced economic slack.

Most participants were ready to agree that the quantification of the above effects presented formidable theoretical and empirical problems. They also tended to share the view that judging from circumstantial evidence they were important and growing in strength over time, especially in countries with a high proportion of long-term unemployment.

Placed into the above context, the alternative use of unemployment insurance funds was regarded as a means of avoiding some of the public expenditure-raising effects of prolonged unemployment, i.e. skill erosion is attenuated, and the health consequences are mitigated. Member countries' experience in this area, however, was found to be limited and, often, lacking in coherence. In general, scepticism tended to prevail among some participants as to possible generalisations concerning which alternatives, for whom, at what net cost for governments and with what effectiveness and economic efficiency implications. All countries appeared to be well aware of the problems of balance they were facing between the fiscal side of government worries about costs and how to reduce growing spending, and social concerns about the impact of government programmes and services to people. It was, however, felt that the cost/benefit sides of the various labour market programmes alternative to unemployment compensation were not sufficiently explored and results not yet firmly established. This area of research was indeed suggested as a major area of work for the Secretariat. But, apart from clarifying the questions involved, it was obvious that because of the state of the art, the meeting could not yet produce

4

the answers policy-makers would need for more effectively and efficiently integrating income and active labour
market policies.

Opinions expressed are those of the authors and do
not commit OECD or its Members.

Also available

OECD EMPLOYMENT OUTLOOK – SEPTEMBER 1983 (September 1983)
(81 83 03 1) ISBN 92-64-12487-X   104 pages   £4.50   US$9.00   F45.00

THE CHALLENGE OF UNEMPLOYMENT: A REPORT TO LABOUR MINISTERS (June 1982)
(81 82 04 1) ISBN 92-64-12332-6   166 pages   £7.60   US$17.00   F76.00

THE WELFARE STATE IN CRISIS (September 1981)
(81 81 01 1) ISBN 92-64-12192-7   274 pages   £7.00   US$17.50   F70.00

UNEMPLOYMENT COMPENSATION AND RELATED EMPLOYMENT POLICY MEASURES. General Report and Country Studies: Canada, France, Germany, Sweden, United Kingdom, United States. "Document" Series (September 1979)
(81 79 03 1) ISBN 92-64-11909-4   288 pages   £8.50   US$17.50   F70.00

Prices charged at the OECD Publications Office.

*THE OECD CATALOGUE OF PUBLICATIONS and supplements will be sent free of charge
on request addressed either to OECD Publications Office,
2, rue André-Pascal, 75775 PARIS CEDEX 16, or to the OECD Sales Agent in your country.*

TABLE OF CONTENTS

Part Three

BACKGROUND DOCUMENTATION

INTRODUCTION

by
W.R. Dymond

    Unemployment compensation concerns people: people
made vulnerable and insecure by an indefinite loss of
employment and, consequently, their main if not only
source of income; but also people suffering a temporary
interruption in employment, such as seasonal workers,
or a reduction in hours worked, or who are in the process of changing jobs. In some Member countries, even
first time job-seekers may be covered.

    In OECD Member countries, cash payments to unem-
ployed workers for unemployment compensation have risen
over the years 1970-81, on average from about 0.39 per
cent to over 1.2 per cent of GDP and from 1.03 per cent
to $2\frac{3}{4}$ per cent of public expenditure.

    In spite of its high annual growth rate since the
first oil shock, unemployment compensation cannot be
regarded as a large expenditure area compared to other
income-maintenance programmes. Yet, behind the relatively low expenditure figures for unemployment compensation there is a programme whose effects are spread
widely throughout the population and the economy.

    Available statistics for the seven largest OECD
Member countries put the number of weeks of compensated
unemployment at about 330-380 million in 1980; and at
well over 20 million the number of unemployed workers
whose income was supported. Including dependents, the
number of persons relying on unemployment benefit can be
estimated in the region of 40-45 million persons.
Clearly, few other government programmes affect the life
of as many people as unemployment compensation. Indeed,
if financing arrangements were to be taken into account
and employers and employees paying contributions to UI
funds are included, the number of persons and groups
affected by what governments decide on unemployment
compensation is much greater than the 40-45 million
figure.

    In this context, the array of views concerning the
role, functions, effectiveness and impact on the economy
of unemployment insurance is bound to be wide and diver-
gences to be sharp. A corollary of this is that to reflect in unemployment insurance programmes the needs of
the existing economic and social environment; and the

9

view of governments, of workers (as beneficiaries as well as contributors), and of trade union and business representatives is a major and difficult task - as indeed many governments have discovered.

Reforms of unemployment insurance programmes of one type or another have been advocated and tried, often on a piecemeal basis, over a number of years now in several Member countries, e.g. United States, United Kingdom, France, Canada and Finland. The reasons have been many and varied. Changes which were easy to implement when systems were liberalised in the early '70s have, however, met with increasing resistance as greater stringency and less generosity have come to be required. Two conclusions seem to emerge from these attempts in Member countries. The first is that it is important to recognise that insistence on maintaining policies developed at a time of low and mainly frictional and cyclical unemployment is not only ineffective and inefficient but also leads to compounding the budget problem facing UI systems. The second is that the implementation of successful reforms requires an effort to reach public consensus by expanding the area of discussion of economically necessary and politically feasible options.

Two fundamental questions require careful analysis and review as a basis for thinking about the nature of the reform problem and to expand the area of public debate:

. the original role and functions of unemployment compensation programmes;
. changed labour market conditions and needs and how unemployment compensation schemes could be improved by adapting them to new conditions within the limits imposed by present economic prospects and public sector financial constraints.

a) Original Role and Functions of Unemployment Compensation Schemes

Three quarters of a century have passed since the first scheme of unemployment compensation was enacted in an OECD country. This event signalled the beginning of a new trend in industrial countries: away from the dole method of relief, with its pauper stigma, towards compensation as a right for all persons unemployed through no fault of their own.

By the end of the 1940s, practically all Member countries had adopted a programme of unemployment compensation although the proportion of covered workers remained limited - often to no more than half of those in the labour force. Only in the late '60s and early 1970s did programmes expand to reach coverage figures of over 70 per cent (1).

10

Unemployment compensation developed as an alternative to "relief work" which had begun to be criticised, to quote from William Beveridge, on grounds:

> "...of the expense; as involving interference with independent labour; as weakening the incentive to self-help and individual or collective thrift; as demoralising men by accustoming them to earn only half their wages".(2)

The failure of "relief work" as a policy for poverty had become evident as events shook the belief that any man who really wanted employment could always obtain it. The steady, if gradual, growth of the sense of public responsibility for the unemployed led at first to the removal, in their special case, of most of the disqualifications of the Poor Law until then attached to relief work (e.g., in the United Kingdom, with the 1905 Unemployed Workmen's Act) thus leading to the inclusion of unemployed workers among the "deserving" poor. Later on, as relief work showed its limits, such as the cost of unemployed labour and its productivity being much above and much below, respectively, that of ordinary labour (3). Events gradually led to a recognition that unemployment and not the unemployed is the problem, the income support and job provision policy functions of government were separated: employment and the creation of jobs became an economic policy aim; income maintenance a social policy objective.

By the end of the 1930s, this separation between economic ministries' responsibility for the level of unemployment (i.e. the full employment goal) and social ministries' responsibility for a more equitable distribution of the economic risk of unpredictable unemployment had already been established in a number of Member countries. For instance, in 1935 a U.S. President's Committee on Economic Security report described the role of unemployment insurance in the following way:

> "There is considerable misunderstanding as to what unemployment insurance can be expected to do in solving the problem of unemployment. Unemployment insurance will not furnish jobs for idle workers, nor will it eliminate unemployment. The primary function of unemployment insurance is to distribute more equitably the economic risk of unemployment ... in this respect (it) is analogous to fire insurance"(4)

and a 1937 pamphlet published by the U.S. Social Security Board emphasized that:

> Unemployment compensation is a method of safeguarding individuals against distress for a short period of time after they become unemployed. It

is designed to compensate only employable persons who are able and willing to work and who are unemployed through no fault of their own. Instead of making the individual get along on a steadily descending level of living until he has exhausted the last shred of his savings, credit, and the generosity of his relatives and friends, thus reaching a point of destitution at which he is eligible for relief, unemployment compensation sets aside contributions during periods of employment and provides the individual with benefits as a legal right when he becomes unemployed. During the periods of prosperity a fund is built up, to be available for the payment of benefits in the periods when industry fails to maintain employment. Unemployment compensation is not a system under which every unemployed person is assured of benefits for any and all unemployed time. It provides protection primarily for the persons who normally are steadily employed"(5).

Originally, therefore, unemployment insurance was only intended to alleviate the distress consequent on unemployment; not to prevent unemployment nor to be a welfare programme for minimum income. In general terms, then, it was introduced to perform two explicit functions:

a) an aggregate income maintenance function or inter-temporal redistribution of aggregate purchasing power. Reserves are accumulated in time of full employment and used to pay out partial compensation in time of unemployment. Contributions and benefits are negatively and positively related, respectively, to unemployment and should, in principle, function as an automatic stabilizer steadying fluctuations in the economy;

b) an insurance against personal losses function or between groups' redistribution of purchasing power. The risk of unemployment being widely shared and unpredictable, an analogy exists with private insurance principles of pooling of personal risk.

Subsequently, however, especially in the post-World War II period, other functions have been attributed to unemployment insurance, such as:

i) improving the functioning of labour markets, and
ii) employment stabilization at enterprise level.

Some would argue that these are not functions intrinsic to unemployment insurance but specific functions or effects dependent upon a number of institutional aspects such as financing methods, interaction with other welfare

programmes, eligibility requirements, level and duration
of benefit and so on. It is, however, clear that in
today's systems all these various objectives are inter-
twined no matter how implicitly or explicitly they are
stated. Their balance can change across countries and
over time, but nowhere can the important connection
between the income protection and the labour market roles
of UI be denied.

b) Changed Labour Market Conditions

Even to a casual observer it is obvious that
labour market conditions have been changing dramatically
since the early 1970s.

Unemployment which was generally low and mostly
frictional and cyclical until the late 1960s, is now
high and has an important structural component. Even
with the resumption of economic growth, unemployment will
still remain substantially above the levels prevailing
before the first oil shock, for at least some time.

In the post-World War II period and in the '60s
the greatest proportion of unemployed came from the rank
of workers with low education and skills. Nowadays
white-collar workers and workers with higher education
also suffer unemployment. Bread-winners as well as
secondary or other earners are found among the unemployed.
The proportion of women and youth among those looking
for a job is substantial. Redundant workers are
increasingly numerous(6). Also characterising today's
labour markets is the development of a number of additional income support schemes, such as redundancy pay
schemes and an array of selected labour market
programmes.

What do these changes mean for unemployment insurance systems? Labour market conditions, as well as
policies, have clearly grown in complexity and become
more diversified. When unemployment was low and mainly
frictional and cyclical, providing money and thus time
to find another job also helped to bring about a better
match between workers and jobs. Now that unemployment
is high and has a substantial structural component this
complementarity of income support and labour market
functions of unemployment insurance schemes is no longer
clearly apparent. Indeed, the balance between these
two functions in current unemployment insurance schemes
can be questioned as it seems it is not doing enough to
promote employment and the efficient functioning of
labour markets. In the present juncture of economic
conditions, therefore, an imbalance has developed in
unemployment insurance schemes between income support
and labour market functions; thus the need for a reconsideration of the unemployment insurance systems in
terms of their basic function, design, target groups and
levels and duration of benefit.

The reform task ahead will not be easy. Maintaining the status quo, however, needs to be set against issues such as:

i) higher payroll taxes for unemployment insurance which in various Member countries are required to ensure correspondence between contributions and benefit or to avoid increases in unemployment insurance fund deficits. Can, however, industry and business sustain higher payroll taxes with their adverse effects on employment?

ii) possible effects of unemployment insurance on the rate of money/wage inflation and on real wage flexibility. Current research does not lead to a firm conclusion on whether unemployment benefits affect the reservation wage. Nevertheless, this very important question cannot be ignored.

iii) great disparities amongst the unemployed, some of whom have their income maintained through unemployment insurance, redundancy payments, etc., and some not (e.g. many youth and females); some get very high wage replacement rates and some very low ones.

iv) respective role of unemployment insurance and labour market services. Can present relationships be considered satisfactory? Are there co-ordination problems?

v) Does paying cash out of unemployment insurance funds best serve the interest of unemployed workers? Is this the only option permitted by current unemployment insurance systems? Or, if more effective and efficient alternatives are possible, what are they? What is implied by them in terms of integrating cash and services, identifying qualifying people, policing for availability for employment and so on?

Processes of questioning current unemployment schemes can, and sometimes rightly so, be feared in that they may hide attempts to put the clock back and thus seriously undermine social protection programmes which took over fifty years to be universalised to the working population. The intent, however, can be quite the opposite, namely to search for indications and ideas throughout the industrialised world in order to help policy makers improve on current systems so that the tasks assigned to unemployment insurance schemes can be implemented better and possibly at a lower cost and without seriously sacrificing human welfare.

FOOTNOTES

1. See Chapter I, Table 3.

2. See W.H. Beveridge, Unemployment: A Problem of Industry, Longmans Green and Co., London, 1917, p.191.

3. On this point see W.H. Beveridge, op. cit., Chapter VIII, especially pp. 176-180.

4. See Toward Economic Security, quoted in C. Warden, Jr., "Unemployment Compensation in Massachusetts", in O. Eckstein (ed.) Studies in the Economics of Income Maintenance, The Brookings Institute, Washington, D.C. 1977, p.26.

5. U.S. Social Security Board, Unemployment Compensation, What and Why? Publication No. 14 (1937) p.7.

6. See OECD Employment Outlook, Paris, 1983.

CONTRIBUTORS

I.C.R. Byatt
: Deputy Chief Economic Adviser,
H.M. Treasury,
United Kingdom

J.C.Y. Charlebois
: Executive Director,
Benefit Programs,
Employment and Immigration Canada,
Canada

J. Due
: Deputy Director General,
Directorate of Labour,
Denmark

W.R. Dymond
: Deputy Director,
Directorate for Social Affairs,
Manpower and Education,
OECD
France

A. Holen
: Economist,
Office of the Assistant Secretary
for Policy,
Department of Labor,
United States

D. McBain
: Administrator,
Manpower Policy Division,
Directorate for Social Affairs,
Manpower and Education,
OECD
France

A. Mittelstadt
: Principal Administrator
Economic Growth Division,
Department of Economics and
Statistics,
OECD
France

B. Rehnberg
: Director General,
Swedish Labour Market Board,
Sweden

L. Reyher	Institut für Arbeitsmarkt und Berufsforschung, Germany
P. Roberti	Principal Administrator Social Affairs Division, Directorate for Social Affairs, Manpower and Education, OECD France
A. Sinfield	Professor, Department of Social Administration, University of Edinburgh, United Kingdom
C.H. Smee	Senior Economic Adviser, Department of Health and Social Security, United Kingdom
F.O. Sørensen	Deputy Director, Ministry of Labour, Norway
E. Spitznagel	Institut für Arbeitsmarkt und Berufsforschung, Germany
L. Voogd	Director for Social Insurance, Ministry of Social Affairs, The Netherlands
R. Zeppernick	Director, Ministry of Economic Affairs, Germany

Part One

HIGH UNEMPLOYMENT, ITS COSTS AND WIDER IMPACT

I

THE COSTS OF UNEMPLOYMENT

by
Axel Mittelstadt
and Paolo Roberti

INTRODUCTION

The events surrounding the two oil price shocks in
1973/4 and 1979 entailed sharp increases in unemployment,
from 9.2 million in 1970 to nearly 30 million persons in
1982 for the OECD area as a whole, corresponding to a
standardized rate of unemployment of 3.0 and an estimated
$8\frac{1}{4}$ per cent, respectively. These figures, even though
perceived as the inevitable consequence of efforts to
establish conditions for a return to sustained non-
inflationary economic growth, reveal both an enormous
waste of human resources and huge output losses. Given
the scale of the problem it is imperative to look beyond
the sheer figures of numbers unemployed and examine the
costs of high unemployment for the economy, for the
individual and for societal life.

Three major categories of "costs" can usefully be
distinguished(1):

i) <u>macro-economic costs</u> which can be defined as
   loss of output i.e. goods and services which
   unemployed members of the labour force could
   have produced, had they been employed, as well
   as additional real income and output losses
   consequent on low activity levels.
ii) <u>costs for public sector budgets</u>. Social
   security and assistance money are paid to the
   unemployed while revenue is lost due to unemployment, reflecting a smaller tax base and,
   thus, smaller revenues from direct and indirect
   taxes and social security contributions.

iii) <u>social and individual costs</u> leading to hardship for individuals and families and involving stress, ill-health and disruption of family life. Unemployment strains social life and community relationships (e.g. disorders and crime), and impedes progress towards societal goals (e.g. reduction of poverty and equal opportunity etc.).

These different types of costs are discussed in turn.

I. MACRO-ECONOMIC COSTS OF UNEMPLOYMENT

A. Main Components

Macro-economic costs of unemployment fall into three major categories:

i) <u>comparative-static costs</u> corresponding to the incremental output which could have been produced by the unemployed;
ii) <u>dynamic human capital costs</u> equivalent to potential output losses resulting from the erosion of skills and lower investments in human capital;
iii) <u>other dynamic costs</u> equivalent to potential output losses due to lower investment in capital equipment and slower implementation of technological progress.

Periods of unemployment typically depress investment. There are three reasons for this: first, there is the effect from unused capacity; second, a recession reduces profits and may also lower expectations of medium-term growth, especially when the period of weak demand is protracted and expectations of faster output growth have repeatedly been frustrated; third, prolonged recessions by pushing up budgetary deficits may have negative effects on inflation and interest rate expenditures. Additional adverse consequences may relate to tax increases and/or spending cuts (notably on investment) designed to limit or avoid a recession-induced rise in budgetary deficits.

B. Measurement Problems

Clearly, the <u>dynamic</u> costs are hard to measure, if at all. Computations of potential output growth are notoriously difficult to perform, and changes in the

structure of government revenues and expenditure and in
the method of financing budgetary deficits have a range
of macro-economic effects which escape precise measurement. Regarding comparative-static costs, measurement
problems also exist, but they are less formidable than
in the case of dynamic costs.

Recorded unemployment rates are known to be an inadequate measure of labour market slack. Some of the unemployed tend to withdraw from the labour force when overall
demand weakens ("discouraged worker effect"), even though
there may be some recession-induced new entrants. Moreover, short-time work typically rises in a recession,
and some of the foreign workers may be repatriated.
Mainly for these reasons, recorded unemployment rates
tend to understate the underutilisation of human resources.
On the other hand, market economies cannot be operated
at zero unemployment rates, and even the adjusted "full-
employment unemployment rate" fails to measure labour
market slack adequately, given unrecorded employment
("underground economy").

Besides the above measurement problems, it is open
to question which loss in primary income should be imputed to a genuinely unemployed person. A large portion
of the unemployed tend to have below-average skills so
that the imputed loss in real income should be lower than
the average real income accruing to the remaining employed. On the other hand, it is also true that the
recorded value added per employed person is below its
high employment level.

Consequently, any attempt to quantify the macro-
economic costs of unemployment are necessarily tentative.
The comparative static costs of unemployment may be
approximated in the following way: for any period of
high unemployment, recorded real value added per employed
person is multiplied by the number of unemployed persons
in excess of what may be viewed as a medium-term sustainable full-employment unemployment level. In the
absence of a generally agreed measure of the "full-employment unemployment rate", the average recorded unemployment rate of the 1960s may serve as a proxy. On this
basis, the comparative static costs of unemployment for
the OECD area as a whole amounted to as much as $460 bil-
lion in 1982 or 6.1 per cent of OECD output (lower bench-
mark estimate).

Another mechanical calculation indicates that a
hypothetical annual rise in OECD real GDP of 4 per cent
from 1973 to 1979(2) followed by a rise of 3 per cent a
year from 1979 and 1982 would have yielded a cumulative
gain in real GDP of 38 per cent in the 1973-82 period.

This compares with an actual rise of only 20½ per cent. The difference between actual and hypothetical economic growth amounted to as much as $1350 billion in 1982 (higher benchmark estimate).

II. PUBLIC FINANCE COSTS OF UNEMPLOYMENT

Macro-economic costs of unemployment inevitably affect the financial balance of the public sector. The dynamic costs of unemployment imply that reaching full capacity use (after a prolonged period of unemployment) leads to both lower government revenues and to higher expenditures than would have prevailed at full capacity use prior to the rise in unemployment. Unless offset by fiscal action, protracted unemployment therefore tends to generate budget deficits at full capacity use, if previously there was balance. Since the dynamic macro-economic costs of unemployment are virtually impossible to quantify, their effects on the financial balance of the public sector can hardly be traced.

As regards the comparative static costs, they impinge on public sector finance in a variety of ways, most of which are open to measurement. On the expenditure side, they relate to unemployment benefits and other income support for unemployed persons in excess of the level corresponding to the full-employment unemployment rate (including administrative costs). In addition, budgetary funds are devoted to cushioning the impact on employment of weak overall demand (payments for short-time work, training schemes and other support measures). Finally, higher government spending along with lower government revenues typically leads to higher budgetary deficits so that a rise in unemployment involves higher interest payments on an increased public debt.

On the revenue side, the public finance costs of unemployment arise from losses in revenue from direct and indirect taxes, and social security contributions. Obviously, for a given fall in employment, the public finance costs are high for countries with:

    i) high ratios of unemployment benefits to previous earned income (replacement ratios);
   ii) easy access to such benefits (eligibility provisions);
  iii) long entitlement periods;
   iv) high effective income tax rates; and
    v) high social security contributions.

As is evident from Table 1 expenditure on unemployment compensation as a percentage of GDP varies strongly across countries, partly reflecting differences in recorded unemployment rates. Dividing for the seven major OECD countries the payments for unemployment compensation as a proportion of GNP in 1980 by the standardized rate of unemployment reveals a comparatively high level of such payments for Germany and Canada, and a low one for Italy, the United States and the United Kingdom, with Japan and France occupying intermediate positions (Table 2)(3).

Part of the inter-country differences shown in Table 2 can be ascribed to unemployment insurance coverage. Another explanation lies in the replacement ratio which is high by international comparison in Germany and low in Italy, the United Kingdom and the United States /offsetting the effect of high unemployment insurance coverage (Tables 3 and 4)7.

In addition to expenditure on unemployment benefits and assistance, Governments have taken a number of measures designed to stabilize employment in periods of weak overall demand (outlays for short-time work, training schemes, etc.). The data in Table 5, which refer to 1978-79, show these expenditures per head of the labour force, with the average being set equal to 100. The importance of these outlays varies strongly across countries, with Sweden spending three times as much as the average and France only one-fourth of it. On the basis of the above calculation, the United States allocated significantly more budgetary funds to special labour market measures than European countries for which data are available (with the exception of Sweden). This contrasts with the relatively low level of expenditure for unemployment compensation (Table 1).

Turning to the revenue side, Table 6 presents estimates of losses in general government revenues from income and indirect taxes and social security contributions caused by a fall in employment by 1 million persons. Based on national accounts data for 1980 these estimates are expressed as a percentage of GNP. Comparatively strong losses are shown for Italy, France and Germany and smaller ones for the United States and Japan. Adjusting the estimates for differences in employment does not alter this ranking except for Canada, where, on an adjusted basis, the shortfall in revenue is relatively small. According to a hypothetical computation mentioned earlier, the cumulative loss in real GDP in 1982 was $1350 billion. On the basis of an estimated share of total tax revenue in GDP of some 33 per cent in 1982, this corresponds to an overall loss in government revenues of just under $450 billion.

It is of interest to examine the respective parts of revenue losses and expenditure increases in the deterioration of the public financial balance. Some, albeit highly incomplete, indications are provided by Table 7 which shows the weight of unemployment benefits, income tax losses, and the shortfall in social security contributions in costs of unemployment. In most countries the combined revenue element predominates, especially in Italy and the United States. By contrast, in Germany and Canada, the expenditure element is the prime force (partly reflecting comparatively high replacement ratios and high unemployment insurance coverage). It is possible, though, that including outlays for unemployment assistance and special labour market measures and, as well, losses from indirect taxes may lead to a different assessment(4).

III. COSTS OF THE INDIVIDUAL UNEMPLOYED AND THEIR FAMILIES

Costs for the individual unemployed and their families include wages and salaries not received plus non-wage pay elements (e.g. fringe benefits) and protection rights (e.g. health insurance coverage) cancelled or reduced as a result of loss of employment.

Wages and salaries are relevant in the determination of unemployment benefits. Non-wage elements of pay are not taken into account, although some of them are lost immediately upon lay-off, while others are suspended within a period of one to three months following lay-off (e.g. sickness and health insurance) or may no longer be accumulated (e.g. pension rights). Since non-wage fringe benefits have risen relative to wages and salaries, replacement ratios tend to overstate the role of unemployment compensation on a rising scale(5). Estimates of macro-economic costs of unemployment, however, mentioned earlier, include these non-wage elements.

Micro-replacement rates typically vary among individuals - from as low as zero to more than 100 per cent in isolated cases. The factors affecting replacement rates include duration of unemployment spells, family circumstances, previous earnings levels and, in the United States, inter-state differences in unemployment insurance programmes(6). Calculations of benefit entitlement for the OECD average production worker in 1980(7) (with earnings set at 66, 100 and 200 per cent of average earnings) show that the loss of disposable income was generally limited.

25

In addition to short-term income losses, there are adverse effects of unemployment on human capital and earnings over the life cycle. Unemployment may create a downward shift of the level of life-earnings(8) and a change in the shape of the life-earnings profile, e.g. earnings may grow at a lower rate (for young people) or fall faster (for older workers) after re-employment (9). Other losses include loss of job tenure and the erosion of skills or lack of job experience, stress and family disruption, a higher incidence of crime and rising morbidity and mortality rates, the latter including infant mortality and suicide(10). Evidence on the association with added health costs has led to unemployment, and in particular long-term unemployment, being regarded as a public health problem in some countries.

Table 1

TOTAL EXPENDITURE ON UNEMPLOYMENT
COMPENSATION(1) AS A PERCENTAGE OF GDP

$$\frac{UC}{GDP} \times 100$$

	1970	1975	1978	1979	1980	1981
Australia	0.03	0.69	0.89	0.81	0.76	..
Austria	0.29	0.39	0.44	0.47	0.44	0.53
Belgium	0.44	1.55	2.26	2.44	2.60	..
Canada	1.67	2.76	2.80	2.36	2.32	2.33
Denmark	0.42	2.38	3.19	2.73	3.03	3.90
Finland	0.21	0.21	0.84	0.63	0.41	..
France	0.32	0.78	1.17	1.23	1.46	1.92
Germany	0.40	1.49	1.06	1.05	1.12	1.52
Greece	0.19	0.35	0.32	0.31	0.31	0.44
Ireland	1.28	2.31	1.91	1.76	2.12	..
Italy	0.18	0.45	0.48	0.50	0.47	0.60
Japan	0.27	0.48	0.43	0.39	0.40	0.43
The Netherlands	0.23	0.70	0.41	0.47	0.57	0.89
New Zealand	0.02	0.07	0.31	0.32	0.49	0.54
Norway	0.09	0.11	0.16	0.20	0.23	0.27
Spain	0.14	0.48	1.23	1.65	2.11	2.48
Sweden	0.27	0.24	0.44	0.43	0.39	0.53
Switzerland	..	0.17	0.12	0.12	..	..
United Kingdom	0.47	0.70	0.85	0.72	0.94	1.38
United States	0.42	1.18	0.44	0.41	0.62	0.53

1. Figures include unemployment assistance, but exclude administrative costs. The latter can be substantial according to an estimate by the United Kingdom Treasury, a rise in the number of beneficiaries drawing unemployment benefits by 100,000 requiring 2,000 additional civil servants with a cost equal to about 8 per cent of total benefits paid.

Source: National sources.

Table 2

EXPENDITURE ON UNEMPLOYMENT COMPENSATION
(as a percentage of GDP) divided by
Standardized Unemployment Rate (1980 or nearest date)

United States	0.07
Japan	0.20
Germany	0.35
France	0.26
United Kingdom	0.13
Italy	0.07
Canada	0.31
Average (unweighted)	0.20

Source: authors' estimates.

Table 3

EMPLOYEES COVERED BY UNEMPLOYMENT INSURANCE
PROGRAMMES, 1950-1980(1)
(Per cent of total civilian labour force)

	1950	1960	1970	1975	1980 or nearest
Canada	50.2	63.6	64.6	89.7	89.6
France	n.a.	38.2	55.8	59.4	58.8
Italy	38.0(2)	38.2	46.6	45.5	47.7
Japan	21.9	33.5	45.6	50.2	50.4
United Kingdom(4)	88.9	82.4	76.6	73.8(3)	n.a.
United States	55.2	66.5	72.0	76.7	89.5

1. Excludes general social assistance coverage
2. Refers to 1957
3. Refers to 1974
4. Based on the analysis of contributions by type of benefit payable. No figure available after 1974 due to a change in the method of collecting contributions.

Sources: National statistics and official reports.

Table 4

UNEMPLOYMENT INSURANCE: AVERAGE UNEMPLOYMENT
BENEFITS AS A PERCENTAGE OF AVERAGE WAGES
(1980 or nearest date)

United States	36.3
Japan	68.9
Germany	67.4
France	42.9
United Kingdom	32.0
Italy	17.4
Canada	42.9
Average (unweighted)	44.0

Source: authors' estimates.

Table 5

INDEX OF GOVERNMENT EXPENDITURE ON
SPECIAL LABOUR MARKET MEASURES
IN EIGHT COUNTRIES(1)

Per capita of the labour force, 1978/79

	Expenditure on special measures Mean = 100
Sweden	317
United States	157
Germany	104
Denmark	59
Great Britain	38
Canada	37
Australia	31
France	25

Note: To some extent this index reflects the
relative wealth of the countries concerned. The first
four countries in the list have higher GDP per head
than the others, and all the countries listed have a
higher GDP per head than the United Kingdom. Sweden's
is about twice that of the United Kingdom.

Source: Calculated from data contained in
"Employment Creation", memorandum by the Department of
Employment, Employment Committee, Session 1980-81
HMSO, London 1981, Table 3, p. 39.

Table 6

LOSS IN GENERAL GOVERNMENT REVENUES ASSOCIATED WITH
A FALL IN EMPLOYMENT BY 1 MILLION PERSONS (1980)
(as a percentage of GNP)

	Social security contributions	Direct income tax	Indirect tax	Total
United States	0.09	0.17	0.09	0.35
Japan	0.27	0.19	0.19	0.65
Germany	0.65	0.58	0.59	1.82
France	1.05	0.37	0.84	2.26
United Kingdom	0.28	0.63	0.72	1.63
Italy	0.86	0.77	0.68	2.31
Canada	0.36	1.57	1.27	3.20

Source: Estimates based on OECD National Accounts and Labour Force Statistics.

Table 7

COMPOSITION OF COSTS OF UNEMPLOYMENT
TO THE PUBLIC PURSE (1980)
(in per cent of total costs)

	Unemployment benefit	Income tax loss	Social security contribution loss
Canada	56.6	32.7	10.7
France	43.2	10.9	45.9
Germany	56.5	18.1	25.3
Italy	9.6	35.8	54.6
Japan	48.3	21.5	30.2
United Kingdom	41.7	40.2	18.2
United States	25.2	45.6	29.2

Source: OECD, The Challenge of Unemployment, Paris, 1982, p.19

FOOTNOTES

1. A. Sinfield, "Social Policy amid High Unemployment", forthcoming; J. Stevenson (eds.) Yearbook of Social Policy in Britain, 1980-81, Routledge and Kegan Paul, 1982; V. Rys and R. Beattie, The Impact of Unemployment on Social Security, mimeo, Geneva, London 1981; H. Gibier, "Le Coût du chômage", Le Nouvel Economiste, November 1980; European Trade Union Institute, The European Economy 1975-1985: An Indicative Full Employment Plan, Bruxelles 1980; and Manpower Services Commission, Review of Services for the Unemployed, London, 1980. P Roberti, "Unemployment" in R. Klein, Inflation and Priorities, CSSP, London, 1975.

2. This is one percentage point less than the rate recorded in the 1960s, to make a notional adjustment for the loss in economic growth during the adjustment period. Higher oil and energy prices may directly curb potential output growth. If actual output thereafter rises less than new potential output, potential output growth is reduced further.

3. Table 2 provides no information about the speed with which payments for unemployment compensation would rise relative to GDP if unemployment were to rise by a given amount.

4. To the extent that the loss of employment reduces pension rights and the access to health insurance benefits for the unemployed potential outlays of social security schemes decline. In some countries, however, central government funds are used to maintain publicly funded pension and health insurance rights of the unemployed (e.g. France and Italy). This adds to central government outlays associated with increases in unemployment, but does not necessarily increase the future liabilities of the public sector.

5. Definitional as well as theoretical problems concerning replacement ratios are examined in Chapter V. See also, J.M. Becker, Unemployment Benefits, Should There be a Compulsory Federal Standard? American Enterprise Institute, Washington, D.C., 1980, Royal Commission on Income and Wealth, Higher Incomes from Employment, Cmnd. 6383, HMSO., London, 1976, Table 49.

6. J.M. Barron and W. Mellow, "Inter-State Differences in Unemployment Insurance" National Tax Journal, March 1981, pp. 105-113.

7. This is defined as "a male full-time manual worker in the manufacturing industry whose earnings are equal to the average earnings of such workers". See OECD, The Tax/Benefit Position of Selected Income Groups in OECD Member Countries, 1974-79, Paris, 1980.

8. In France, 41 per cent of those unemployed in October 1977 who had found a job by March 1978 were working for less money than in their previous job (see INSEE, Données Sociales, 1981, Paris, p.129).

9. F.J. Borjas, "Job Mobility and Earnings Over the Life Cycle" in Industrial and Labour Relations Review, vol. 34, No. 3, April 1981, pp. 365-376; and J. Mincer and H. Ofek, "Interrupted Work Careers: Depreciation and Restoration of Human Capital", The Journal of Human Resources, Winter 1982, pp. 3-24.

10. House of Commons, Third Report from the Social Service Committee, Session 1980-81; London 1981; D. Schnapper, Le Vécu du Chômage, Ministère du Travail, Paris, 1979; S. Ramsden and C. Smee, "The Health of the Unemployed: ADH 55 Cohort Studies", in United Kingdom Department of Employment Gazette, September 1981, pp.357-401.

II

THE WIDER IMPACT OF UNEMPLOYMENT

by
Adrian Sinfield

INTRODUCTION

The financial accounting of the costs of increased unemployment throws considerable light on its significance for those out of work and for the wider society. It is necessary to complement this with a review of other evidence on the nature of the experience of unemployment and the effects its increase has had on many other groups and on the policies and institutions of society.

The purpose of this chapter is to raise for discussion a variety of issues arising from increased unemployment, many of which do not appear to have been linked to the more specific and long continuing debates about the unemployed. A brief review of the experience of being out of work is followed by examination of the effects of higher unemployment on "the Welfare State" and its objectives, and on other goals generally accepted by society such as the promotion of equal opportunity for women and minority groups. The significance of increased unemployment for those who remain in work and the vexed question of its relation to crime and ill-health are considered in the later sections.

Much of the discussion cannot be supported with quantitative data, not only because many of the effects are not easily quantifiable, but also because there is a lack of regular and comprehensive data within countries which can be confidently used in comparison between countries. While attempts have been made to indicate variations across countries, the constraints of time and space have enforced greater dependence upon evidence from Britain.

IDENTIFYING THE IMPACT OF UNEMPLOYMENT

Assessing the impact, direct or indirect, of unemployment is made more difficult by the concurrent effect of many other factors, including changes in the demographic structure or the growth of inflation. A particular problem in attempting to isolate the impact of unemployment is the effect that society's responses, and especially those of government, have in shaping the impact. Political and policy responses both affect and are affected by public attitudes about unemployment and the unemployed - or, more precisely, particular forms of unemployment and particular groups of unemployed.

Public and policy reactions to unemployment differ according to the view taken of the main causes of unemployment and of its significance for society or the economy, the priority that should be given to tackling it and the most appropriate strategy that should be followed. The view that the major cause of increased unemployment is inadequate demand leads to a very different management of the economy and specific policies for the unemployed from the view that places emphasis on structural employment resulting from technological change. In the first, extra resources are likely to be pumped into the economy by tax cuts and/or increased benefits. The second view may lead to more effort being devoted to creating a labour force more flexible and able to respond to technological change with a particular emphasis upon training and retraining, and to giving special support for the new industries, helping them to develop more speedily to compete in international markets and protecting them from the full force of these until they are able to compete.

For the unemployed the first view may lead to increases in the value and duration of benefits especially amongst those worst hit by increased unemployment. The emphasis of policy is on changing factors external to the unemployed, apart perhaps from encouraging their own consumption to maintain demand.

The second strategy may include more substantial help for training and retraining together with removal and relocation allowances. It aims to make potential workers more adaptable and able to use the new technology which, it is hoped, will create extra jobs.

Both strategies differ sharply in their implications for the unemployed from the monetarist approach. With its emphasis on a firm control of the money supply, its "main proposals are for a reduction of public expenditure to levels which need not be financed by borrowing, for the removal of alleged imperfections in a labour market,

and for reduced expectations of real wages. The hope is
that the increased levels of unemployment which result
from this policy would be of a transitional kind /and7 ...
the existence of a less tight labour market will help to
induce a lowering of future wage expectations and even
real wage levels. In this way, workers will come to
realise that they must lower their 'supply price' and
'price themselves into jobs'". (H of L, 1982, I, p.32)

This summary by the all-party Select Committee of
the House of Lords on Unemployment in Britain indicates
how different policies are likely to be when real wages
are believed to be too high and creating inflation, and
this is seen to be the main cause of unemployment. The
increased demands on public expenditure that result from
the higher unemployment are themselves in conflict with
government policy. The fact that more people are out of
work is expected to have a sobering effect on trade unions
in their wage bargaining and the effect of this may be
accelerated if a government allows the value of benefits
to fall. Given the traditional importance attached to
the maintenance of occupational differentials, the reduction of the lowest wages may be seen as particularly
necessary in bringing down "reserve wages" even if those
on the lowest pay are the least organised and powerful in
bargaining. In consequence, the wish to support the
unemployed conflicts with the determination to increase
incentives to work by, for example, reducing benefits or
introducing special controls and restrictions.

National policies rarely combine in the single-
minded and unbending pursuit of one single philosophy,
escaping entirely from long-established commitments to
other approaches which have become institutionalised in
the laws and in the structures and working practices of
individual departments and agencies. In addition, strategies may be changed in response to unemployment remaining
high and in reaction to protests from groups influential
on, or threatening to, the party in power.

THE DIRECT IMPACT UPON THE UNEMPLOYED

Any analysis of the wider impact of unemployment
must take account of the immediate impact upon those most
directly affected, the unemployed themselves and those
dependent upon them. In addition, the ways in which those
out of work are affected by unemployment, and by its
increase, has significance for the less direct impact
upon the rest of the community and for its response to
higher unemployment.

The heterogeneity of the unemployed deserves particular emphasis because the experience of being out of
work can vary considerably. School leavers looking for
their first job have a very different experience from
those who are forced to leave the labour force early at
the end of their working lives. Unskilled labourers
vulnerable to constant short spells of unemployment, which
may become longer as the economy declines, face difficulties very different from those who become unemployed for
the first time in their early fifties: they will have
had little experience of finding work for themselves, or
of coping with the reduced income, tedium and uncertain-
ties of being out of work. Skilled craftsmen declared
redundant because their product is no longer needed or
their trade is now obsolete have to cope with very different problems from immigrant workers, whether from
rural areas or abroad, who have already had to learn to
survive on the margins of the labour market in the poorest
paid, least secure and lowest status jobs.

Obviously, also, the experience may be expected to
differ considerably from country to country given the
differences in incidence, rate of change, duration and
social and spatial distribution. Even if the level and
duration of unemployment is similar, the marked variations
in income support, other services and public reaction
affect the impact on those out of work and their families.

In this paper most evidence has had to be drawn from
one country, Britain, although attempts have been made
to indicate differences where these are known.

Despite the great variety in the experience of
unemployment in Britain, most studies have found financial
problems are given particular emphasis by the unemployed.
It is evident that many people entering unemployment
have been totally unprepared for the extent to which their
income falls and financial difficulties lead to many more
pressures and strains than material ones alone.   The
difficulties such people experience is a function not only
of the actual level of benefits but of the still persistent public mythology about the prodigal life enjoyed
by work-shy "scroungers" on state benefits. In work, many
of these people had probably helped to nourish this mythology: once out of work they have the additional strain
of having to live with themselves occupying a role that
they had previously joined in stigmatising.

The risk of financial hardship and thus the importance of the level of benefits available is very much a
function of the unequal incidence of unemployment in market economies. Rates of joblessness are generally much
greater for those without skills occupying the lower paid

jobs. The same workers are also more vulnerable to repeated spells out of work and to prolonged unemployment. These people and their families are likely to have very few savings or any other resources to fall back on when a job ends. They are particularly dependent therefore on state benefits, and even more so when unemployment is prolonged or recurrent. Although this unequal incidence of unemployment is probably common to all market econo- mies, the extent of it varies: Britain, for example, appears to have a higher concentration of unemployment among the low paid than the United States or Canada (Smee, 1980).

While the unemployment remains high, the number of people remaining out of work for very long periods in- creases. Whatever their initial resources and level of savings, more people become vulnerable to poverty as a result. During a recession, therefore, the level of benefits made available to the unemployed, particularly the long-term unemployed, becomes particularly important. This is underlined by the evidence which indicates that those who experience prolonged unemployment are likely to include a disproportionate number who have either always been in poorly paid jobs or have been slowly forced down the occupational hierarchy because of poor health, disability, obsolete skills, or simply previous experience of unemployment. While generous early retire- ment provisions do exist with occupational pensions inflation-proofed and paid at the same rate as if the employees had continued to the normal retiring age, these benefits are still the exception for those long out of work in most countries.

Of course not all the unemployed suffer poverty and deprivation. Even during periods of very high unemploy- ment some periods out of work are brief. Shipyard workers may have more overtime in their final weeks and additional bonuses for completion of work on time so that the company does not have to pay any penalty for late delivery. Their first weeks out of work may provide a holiday, especially if the chances of recall are high. Many, especially higher paid senior staff, may receive additional severance payments and may also be among the first to return to work or be able to opt for a generously-provided early retirement.

However the financial effects of unemployment seem to be understated in most research that depends on single interviews with the unemployed, still the most common form of unemployment and redundancy study. Surveys which follow over a longer period the experience of people becoming unemployed show that even better-off managerial staff made redundant may experience financial difficulties which are often greater than they themselves initially recognised or are prepared to acknowledge while they are

suffering them. In one study, most ex-managers said that
they had suffered little financially but it became evident
that many had sold their car or cashed life insurances.
Even if they return to work, the same level of insurance
protection becomes more expensive to obtain. Other
studies have shown that families are often more prepared
to discuss the full impact of unemployment on them once
the wage earner is back in work. Admission of some
difficulties during unemployment to friends and relatives,
let alone to a question-asking stranger from a different
class or background, can itself be demoralising (Sinfield,
1981).

The effect of persistent high unemployment is difficult to evaluate. Some point out that the greater
number out of work may reduce the sense of individual
failure and this appears true immediately following major
redundancies or plant shutdowns. However, even in these
situations, some people succeed in finding a new job
fairly quickly and the sense of failure or the doubts of
others, including the unemployed's own family, quickly
appear. Other evidence indicates that the average duration of unemployment lengthens with higher unemployment
and many more fail to get a job at all. The chance of
returning to a job that is better or even as good as the
previous one in terms of pay, status and security is
also very much less during times of high unemployment.

This evidence is very important for understanding
the wider impact of unemployment. The careers and other
ambitions of many people are set back by continuing high
unemployment. In addition, the fear that unemployment
may be prolonged can itself be demoralising. It is very
much easier to cope with all the problems of being out of
work when there is a reasonable hope of escaping from
these pressures quite soon. When the chance of obtaining
work appears increasingly bleak as more and more people
compete for the few jobs available, coping with the
pressures of unemployment demands very much more determination and resilience and places very much greater
strain on the unemployed and their families.

Evidence of the extent of the strain comes in the
increasing number of reports from social workers, doctors,
clergy and others of violence within the family, against
wives and children, when people snap under the multiple
pressures of unemployment and poverty. More children
are having to be taken into care for their own protection
by local social work departments. We do not know, however, how typical these reactions are to the cumulative
experiences of rejection and segregation which reinforce
the stigma of unemployment. And we do not know how much
more these and other effects will make themselves evident
if unemployment persists high for many more years. My

own impression based on the examination of many studies in the inter-war depression and more recently, including my own, is that there is likely to be more depression than agression, more marital collapse than marital discord, and more isolation than the overactive engagement with society that leads to confrontation and riots.

None of these responses, however, are inevitable results of increased unemployment. Its impact is very much influenced by the way in which the rest of society responds to the problem. There has tended to be more sympathy for craftsmen whose skills are no longer needed after many years of regular work than for school leavers, immigrants or married women. Concern over unemployed youth may express itself not so much in sympathy with programmes of support but anxiety that "idle hands make idle work" with fears of increased crime and violence and the loss of "the work ethic". And, similarly, the response to increased unemployment amongst married women is very different when many influential people believe the real problem is women out at work, not out of work.

The response of government does much to create the public climate in which the problems of the unemployed are viewed. What priority it gives to preventing any increase in the numbers out of work and what measures it brings in or expands to help those already unemployed and the others suffering from the impact of the recession are clearly extremely important. The adoption of policies to promote demand or respond to technological change encourages a very different perception of the causation of unemployment, and so the merits and needs of the unemployed, from policies aiming to reduce public expenditure, or contain it, and bring down real wages by reinforcing the incentive to seek work.

A government wishing to gain support for the first strategy may emphasize the social costs of unemployment and the need to help people out of work through no fault of their own. The second strategy is more likely to link reductions in benefit and tighter controls on its receipt with tacit or even explicit support for the view that much unemployment is voluntary or self-induced. This is particularly true of the non-interventionist monetarist argument which places great weight on the self-curing properties of the market and is often accompanied by the view that present problems are the consequence of too much interference by government in the past. "Jobs should be allowed to create themselves" as one minister of industry has declared.

At any level of unemployment the benefits available to those out of work and their families can very much influence the nature of the experience. At the same time expenditure on income support for the unemployed represents a significant proportion of the total on any calculation of the costs of unemployment to the Exchequer and society as a whole. It is particularly relevant that for most political debate this is the most visible and widely recognised part of the costs.

Without any changes in the programmes, increased unemployment leads to a rise in applications for benefits at the same time as a drop in contributions to the insurance funds. The extent to which this happens is affected of course by the groups most affected and the incidence and duration of unemployment. School leavers unable to find their first job, and re-entrants, such as women after childbirth, are likely to impose less of a demand on insurance programmes than a marked increase in company closures and shutdowns. A rise in unemployment due to more people remaining longer out of work than an increase in the number becoming unemployed will eventually result in a heavier burden on assistance programmes, and in many countries this cost is not as easily identifiable a part of the expenditure on the unemployed as insurance benefits.

The extent of insurance support varies considerably among OECD Member countries in terms of the level and duration of benefits, coverage and eligibility, and conditions and controls. Means-tested assistance programmes vary much more, and within most countries, but it is considerably more difficult to find out how the unemployed actually fare under these schemes. Given the increase in prolonged unemployment and the limited duration of insurance programmes, with the exception of the Belgian one, the support provided by assistance schemes warrants much closer attention from international agencies than it seems to have received (Etienne, 1956 and 1973; Blaustein and Craig, 1977; Sinfield, 1976, on the United States and Britain, and 1983, Austria, Britain, France, Germany and Switzerland).

At present the income maintenance response to increased unemployment appears to differ - and may increasingly - from what it was during the recession of the mid-1970s after the first sharp rise in energy prices. At that time the evidence of a severe rise in the numbers out of work led most countries - with some marked exceptions - to adopt a more sympathetic policy response in recognition that the unemployed were the victims of

external change and so deserving of help. The degree of
wilful idleness was accepted as insignificant when very
much increased numbers of workers with good working
records behind them were chasing a dwindling number of
jobs. The acknowledgement that these costs were social
and should not be left to be borne by those out of work
and their families led to attempts to improve and extend
compensation.

In many countries this extra help was deliberately
directed towards those with previously regular employment
by the introduction or extension of generous redundancy
schemes and the provision of unemployment insurance for
periods extended beyond the usual duration (France,
United States, Germany). This entailed a recognition
that, at the very least, prolonged unemployment damaged
workers' potential - a view expressed most vividly by a
major study of the 1930s: "the unemployed are not simply
units of employability who can, through the medium of
the dole, /employment service7 be put in cold storage
and taken out again immediately they are needed. While
they are in cold storage, things are likely to happen to
them" (Pilgrim Trust, 1938, p.67). Young people seeking
their first job or women seeking to re-enter the labour
force after childbirth received less support, reflecting
general views of the more deserving position and greater
needs of those made redundant.

However, the increase of unemployment in the current
recession and the sharp rise in costs have led many
governments to take a generally tougher stance, and many
of the extensions introduced a few years earlier have been
modified or removed. In France, for example, the high
degree of support for the redundant worker was substantially reduced in 1979 (Lion, 1983). In Britain the
earnings-related supplement which was paid over and
above the basic flat-rate unemployment insurance benefit
for the first six months has been abolished. It is worth
noting that this measure was introduced in 1966 shortly
after the introduction of the state redundancy payments
scheme as part of a programme to promote labour mobility
and reduce resistance to "redeployment" by unions and
management (see also on Germany, Furmaniak, 1983, and
Webber, 1982).

In a number of countries there have also been substantial cuts or modifications in the means-tested
assistance programmes, particularly those affecting the
unemployed. The changes have generally given governments
greater control over expenditure by reducing or restrict-
ing the rights of those out of work and curtailing discretionary supplements to support them in particular
difficulties.

These changes have very much wider significance in that they represent a clear shift away from previous traditions of compensation for social cost to a much more limited recognition of the needs of the unemployed. This becomes even more evident when account is taken of the increase in measures of surveillance and control of the unemployed. In Britain, for example, the doubling of the number of Unemployment Review Officers was explicitly linked by the Minister to a "crack-down on scroungers" as part of an anti-fraud and abuse drive.

In some countries the shift away from compensation and increased controls has been accompanied by a cut in services for those out of work. Sometimes this has simply meant that the staff and resources have not been increased in line with the rising number seeking work but elsewhere there has been an actual cut in staffing and facilities for particular groups.

In 1979 an OECD report acknowledged: "it must be recognised that beliefs about the financial benefits of unemployment, however mistaken, affect the attitudes of the working population and have an impact on policy makers" and pointed out that "the need to curb escalating fiscal expenditure" had an important influence (OECD, June 1979, p.41, on the interaction of policy and public perception, see also Deacon, 1978, and 1980; Golding and Middleton, 1982; on the United States, May, 1964. Chapter 2, and Feagin, 1975). Unlike most other recipients of social insurance, there is no clearly identified pressure group or lobby for the unemployed. Trade union concern for benefits has been both erratic and spasmodic, and reflects the views of the organised, generally better-paid workers who usually have a lower risk of unemployment, especially of a recurrent or prolonged type.

The development of many different benefits, each with its own level of support and form of control, has helped to foster an impression of wide generosity although the highest payments only reach a minority of those out of work. In 1930 in a very similar climate, Beveridge commented upon the problems created by the availability of higher benefits: "the danger to be avoided lies less in the demoralising influence of a generous plan ... upon the individual workman, than its effect on the minds of those in authority - government, trade unions, leaders of industry" (1930, pp. 408-9).

Growing concern over abuse and the erosion of work incentives has been exploited by some governments, particularly those committed to reducing public expenditure (e.g. Deacon, 1978; Golding and Middleton, 1982). The neglect of many unemployed by existing systems has received very little attention by contrast, and there has been much less energy given to exploring the full extent of their needs (Sinfield, 1983). While support remains relatively generous for some groups, others may only be eligible for programmes which appear to be less concerned to do something <u>for</u> the unemployed than <u>to</u> them. The difference in prepositions reflects a different perception of the causes of being out of work and so a different view of government's responsibility. In many countries, however, official as well as independent studies have continued to show that the link between unemployment and poverty has not been broken, especially for families and those long out of work. With increasing unemployment the need for adequate income support has become all the greater (Clark, 1978; Colledge and Bartholomew, 1980; Furmaniak, 1983; Lion, 1983).

THE THREAT TO "THE WELFARE STATE"

There has been increasing discussion of the costs of unemployment with particular focus on the financial burdens imposed on the Exchequer, especially by the benefits just discussed. The costs in terms of hardship, deprivation, loss of career, etc. borne by the unemployed themselves are not as easily quantified and receive much less attention. Yet they are not totally distinct. The costs borne personally may be increased by reductions or restrictions in benefits and services. These cuts make the official costs less than they would otherwise be, a fact neglected in most discussions of public accounting.

Nevertheless even a reduced level of benefit imposes heavy demands on public expenditure when the number of recipients has grown as fast as it has done in most Western economies (however much less it still is than the bill for pensions, despite public beliefs to the contrary). But the cost to the Exchequer includes not only the payment of benefits but the very much larger loss of revenue from direct or indirect taxation and insurance contributions. The closure of many factories, businesses and shops also reduces revenue, usually to local government, in the form of rates or property taxes.

Persisting high unemployment therefore is a threat to the continuing growth of that assorted collection of services, "the Welfare State". The dangers presented by high unemployment were well recognised by William Beveridge who is generally credited with being one of the architects of the post-war "Welfare State". In his 1942 report he emphasized that his proposals could not be provided without sustained low employment.

Today this problem is all the more difficult to cope with, given the many other pressures of increased needs and costs which have to be considered within the context of current debates on public expenditure. What has come to be regarded as an uncontrollable growth has resulted in widespread concern. Politicians on both the left and the right have attacked the growing power of an interfering or repressive bureaucracy, stifling entrepreneurial initiative and featherbedding the work-shy or tranquillising and controlling the working class in the interests of capitalism. In addition, many economists have also seen public sector growth as part of the cause of the present economic plight, including inflation and low productivity.

This has become an issue for wider debate as public concern has risen over levels of direct and indirect taxation during a period when increased inflation has meant a much slower rise, if not a decline, in the standard of living of many people. The dilemma has been made all the greater by the fact that other changes have been generating their own demands for increased public expenditure. Only a few examples need be given here. The most evident and general of these changes is the growing number of people reaching the age of retirement and so drawing state pensions or means-tested assistance. One obvious and acceptable way of reducing this demand on state expenditure is to allow older people to remain longer in the labour force, and even encourage them to do so by, for example, providing higher pensions for those who defer their retirement. Such practices which are now being debated in some countries were introduced by a number of countries in the past to counter problems induced by labour shortage, but they are likely to be less popular during high unemployment with campaigns for earlier retirement. By contrast, the exploration of more options to allow earlier retirement has to take account of the fact that this will only increase state expenditure, the more successful it is in reducing the scale of overall unemployment.

Another trend in many countries has been the increase of one-parent families, mainly women bringing up children on their own. This is a group especially vulnerable to poverty and very many of them are forced to depend, at least temporarily, upon state support. Expenditure is likely to be even greater, given that high unemployment makes it very much more difficult for many of them to obtain the work, either full-time or part-time, which enables them to support themselves.

The very growth of the "Welfare State" and its achievements, however limited, has encouraged higher expectations among many in the population and so increased

demand for more and better state services. The experience
of providing these services creates a certain additional
momentum: doctors or teachers become more aware of the
resources they need to maintain standards and could use
to improve them.

These factors, all increasing the demand for public
expenditure, have been set out here to underline the
acuteness of what O'Connor (1973) called "the fiscal
crisis of the state" even before the costs of unemployment began to rise with the deepening of the recession.
By this phrase he meant the simultaneous growth of
opposition to increasing taxation and demand for more
and better services meeting a wider range of need more
effectively and sensitively. This conflict is made all
the worse by the extra costs of the energy crisis and
inflation. To all these are now added the double pressures of increased unemployment, raising the demand for
benefits and services at the same time as it reduces the
revenue available to pay for them (see also OECD, 1981).

The worsening of the fiscal crisis of "welfare
states" beset by high unemployment means that cuts have
to be made in services that previously tended to respond
according to demand. Whether or how far this happens
depends, at least in part, on the prevailing views on the
causes of increased unemployment and the most effective
response to it. But, irrespective of philosophy, forms
of covert rationing have to occur to meet the increased
extent of need. In a sense the extra number of unemployed
will be "competing" with other dependent groups including
the elderly and the disabled for resources such as benefits, services and staff time. Because, for example, of
anxieties over child abuse said to rise with unemployment,
social workers may be visiting families of unemployed
men to the neglect of the physically or mentally handicapped. Pensions for the "more deserving" elderly may be
maintained at the expense of the unemployed.

The ideas of displacement and competition, however,
are too simple to explain the wider impact of unemployment.
As subsequent sections will show, higher unemployment
leads to increased needs and problems among many groups
besides the unemployed, including those in work and others
outside the labour force. This imposes even heavier
demands on the state welfare services. As more and more
urgent and acute demands are made, standards in many
services and areas are bound to fall unless adequate
staffing and other resources are made available. This
decline conflicts with the desires and expectation of
many better-off groups for a wider and better range of
personal and social services from the public system.
The result may be a widening in the "social division of
welfare" (Titmuss, 1958, Chapter 2). The increased

strain on the "Welfare State" provides a further incentive for those who have the economic resisting power or status to negotiate better services through (or subsidised by) their employer or union. Others with sufficient private resources may well also be encouraged to purchase their health, education and other services on the private market. This is likely to lead to a further growth in separate and unequal services - private or employer-subsidised welfare on the one hand, with residual care from the state for poorer groups on the other.

This brings additional problems for state social services and public expenditure which has received surprisingly little discussion. The reason is a further drain on public revenue because many services provided outside the public welfare system benefit from considerable but hidden state subsidies. The most common are exemptions or concessions in the payment of direct and indirect taxation for the recipients and/or providers of these services. These less visible subsidies squeeze public expenditure indirectly: the recipient of the "private" benefits may pay less in taxation and so reduce the revenue available to the government at any one time to meet its public expenditure needs. The scale of this reduction is receiving increasing attention in many countries; in the United States early efforts to quantify the extent of "tax expenditure" suggested that it was as high as "one-fourth of the regular budget" (Surrey, 1973; see also Pond, 1982; Graycar, 1983; and Owens, 1983).

The main recipients of occupational and private welfare tend to be found disproportionately among the better-off groups in society - those with private incomes, professionals and salaried groups in particular. Many manual workers are unable to obtain such benefits until they have been more than 3, 5 or even 10 years with the same company, so that a large proportion of women workers and unskilled and semi-skilled men never gain access to these benefits. With the growing insecurities brought by economic decline, the proportion of manual workers to qualify is likely to remain low or be further reduced. Evidence for Britain and the United States indicates that the value and number of benefits or services tend to grow as income, status and security rises. Growth in these sectors therefore leads to a more general widening of inequalities, for those who are left without access are concentrated among the poorer, marginal workers with little security, the unemployed and those right outside the labour force including those who have retired without any occupational pension, the many disabled who have never been able to gain work and the growing number of one-parent families. These are the same groups that suffer disproportionately from reductions in the benefits and services of the public "Welfare State".

THE SPREADING OF POVERTY

The importance of sustained high employment in both preventing and reducing poverty was more widely recognised in the decades after the Second World War. "Tight full employment is vital for an anti-poverty programme" (Minsky, 1965, p.177). Ironically during that period those concerned about the persistence of poverty had to challenge the conventional wisdom that sustained low unemployment was sufficient to combat poverty, especially when there was economic growth. The "trickling down" of economic growth and increased employment was not sufficient to bring the wages of many more marginal jobs up to an adequate level and did little to help those on low benefits or without any form of non-wage financial support. However, while trickling down by itself is not sufficient, it makes a major contribution in bringing more resources to lower income families. A high level of employment with adequate wage levels remains a vital part of any attack on poverty.

With prolonged high unemployment, therefore, poverty is bound to increase unless major measures are taken to combat it. The resources of those becoming unemployed generally fall well below what they would have been in work, and the risk of poverty and deprivation is all the greater because the lower paid are more vulnerable to unemployment, both recurrent and prolonged. The increased poverty resulting from higher unemployment lasts longer and bites more deeply since more of the unemployed are likely to be out of work for longer periods. It is even more severe in countries where benefits for those long out of work are reduced or restricted.

The double hardship of poverty and prolonged unemployment is likely to mean an increased demand for health and other services, increasing public expenditure costs as well as indicating the general decline in the lives of these people and their families.

Because of the unequal incidence of unemployment, its increase means a disproportionate reduction in the income and resources of working class families in particular. Irrespective of whether or not all family members are living in the same household, resources of the family as a whole are reduced even more when two or more members are unemployed or excluded from the labour force. When unemployment was half its present level in Britain, one study found that one in five unemployed teenagers had at least one other member of their household out of work. The writer's own research indicates how multiple unemployment within a family may severely affect its ability to cope with the strains and pressures of unemployment combined with deprivation.

Even the loss of one job can bring poverty to families with the main wage-earner still in work. In many households two wages are essential to lift the family income above the poverty line - in Britain, for example, it has been estimated that the number of families with the man in work but still in poverty would be increased by as much as one-half if the woman was not working as well. The importance of a second earner becomes all the more important during a recession with increased short-time working and reductions in overtime, especially when the basic wage is very low.

The increase in poverty with rising and prolonged high unemployment is not therefore confined to the unemployed. Many other groups also become more vulnerable. Women bringing up children on their own are unable to obtain part-time, let alone full-time jobs. People who are disabled or in poor health have less chance of finding less demanding jobs or getting back to work after illness.

The ways in which higher unemployment brings more old people into poverty illustrate the processes at work. Even those who have completely retired may suffer because the resources of the family as a whole are reduced by unemployment, whether or not they live in the same household. Research in Britain, for example, has shown the standard of living of retired people is higher when they are living with their children, in part because they have access to more consumer durables including washing machines and other facilities which also reduce the physical demands on them. Even old people living alone but in close contract with relatives tend to be better off than those completely isolated (Townsend, 1979, p.812). These advantages will be weakened when the standard of living of the younger members is reduced by unemployment.

Older workers have a very much poorer chance of returning to work once they are unemployed and this is recognised in the benefits systems of only a few countries. Many officially retire long after their resources have been reduced by years of unemployment. Others, who opt for early retirement or are cajoled into it, with the encouragement of unions, may lose most of the value of their pensions: yet there is very much less prospect of a part-time job to supplement a reduced pension during a recession. Some anyway volunteer because of poor health and are likely to have been on lower wages.

The support for early retirement varies considerably across and within countries. Unless it is generous, withdrawal early from the labour force greatly increases the chance of poverty. Research across a number of countries has documented the fact that the greater

incidence and depth of poverty amongst the very elderly
is not a function of their age but of the length of time
since they, or the wage earner in their household, last
received employment income (see especially Shanas et al.,
1968). Many people ceasing to work in their fifties or
early sixties may begin to experience the hardships now
suffered by many in their late seventies or eighties some
five or ten years earlier.

This problem has received surprisingly little attention, and yet it seems all the more serious when account
is taken of changing demographic trends among the elderly.
Far more old people are now living into their eighties
and nineties than even 20 or 30 years ago. In Britain,
those over 75 are the fastest growing group of the population and there is clear evidence of their demand for
health and personal social services with a cost per person 6 or 7 times the amount of someone of labour force
age and over twice that of people between 65 and 75.
This is particularly because residential care is disproportionately taken up by this group (Social Trends 1979,
Table 8.24).

We have been moving towards the four-generation
rather than three-generation family in Western society
over this century. Twenty years ago economists were
drawing attention to the financial advantages which one
might expect with two generations earning, one still in
school and one retired. During a recession, and especially if early retirement becomes a major strategy for
reducing unemployment, the shift is a more disturbing
one: in many families only one out of four generations
will be working. In addition, the third generation,
just leaving the labour force, may quickly become more
deprived than the fourth generation who were able to
build up some resources with both husband and wife
working and plan for their retirement, investing in
new household durables (e.g. bedding, cookers, carpets)
before their incomes dropped. The public expenditure
as well as personal costs of these differences are considerable, for poverty and poor housing are still major
factors forcing many elderly people into residential
care.

The discussion of unemployment and poverty has
moved from a consideration of those unemployed to
examining the effect on their wider families and on
groups remaining within the labour force or right outside
it but with reduced resources. Attention should also
be given to the impact on communities, especially where
there has been a major closure which is usually accompanied by a collapse in the smaller industries and
services that have grown up to serve the larger plant.
This is particularly visible with the closure of major

coal mines or steel works in small towns or villages. The effect may also be seen in larger industrial areas when the traditional working class end of a city loses the main traditional employer around which the community was built, often many decades ago. On many coastal locations, the concomitant rundown of shipbuilding, heavy engineering, fishing and marine transport has left many major ports with enormous problems of dereliction in addition to the hardships of individuals out of work. Without special support, these areas will not be able to prevent the growth of environmental poverty leading to an urban blight which is likely to discourage potential investors who could bring new jobs and the hope of re-expansion and revitalisation to the community.

More generally, housing standards and living con-ditions are seriously affected by high unemployment. In their major review of housing policy, Donnison and Ungerson conclude that "most housing problems are really problems of unemployment, poverty and inequality" (1982, p.287). Since higher unemployment tends to increase poverty and inequality, the impact can be considerable.

However, while unemployment is rising, there may be some immediate improvement to housing as skilled and other unemployed spend time repairing and improving their homes with single lump sums made as severance or redun-dancy pay by the employer or the State. Neverless, the persistence of high unemployment is much more likely to increase housing problems. The maintenance of rent, mortgage and rates payments becomes a major difficulty for many as incomes fall with unemployment, and bad debts, repossessions and evictions rise. The number of homeless in the larger cities is increased by those forced out of their homes and by others, especially young people, who have come in search of work. The demands on housing departments are made all the more urgent by the virtual disappearance of cheap private lodging houses and by the pressure on funds as unemployed tenants of public housing have more difficulty in meeting their rents.

The quality of housing suffers because, despite the exceptions noted above, unemployed people have less money to spare for repairing, let along improving, their accom-modation. In addition, the closure of major companies reduces the revenue from rates or property taxes to local government which is usually responsible for housing and other local amenities. Poorer housing estates are likely to suffer particularly high unemployment and experience the fastest deterioration unless special action is taken.

THE COSTS OF THE REDUCTION IN EMPLOYMENT OPPORTUNITY

Increased unemployment not only increases poverty but also weakens further the less powerful groups in society in their efforts to achieve more equal access to job, **career** and promotion opportunities. Measures aimed to reduce inequalities or protect the more vulnerable in the labour market have often originated during periods of economic growth and/or labour shortage. Even where this has not been so, their success has generally depended on sustained low unemployment when an adequate, even expanding, number of jobs can be opened up to groups or individuals that, for one reason or another, have not been regarded as acceptable by employers and fellow employees.

The structural widening of inequality which results from unemployment remaining high is a particular problem for equal opportunity policies. In market economies where employment is the main way by which most people are integrated into society, the improvement of access to paid work becomes a crucial part of any attempt to reduce discrimination and disadvantage. Without better opportunities in employment, gains in other areas, such as education, are jeopardised. When employment opportunities actually deteriorate, other problems of discrimination very often become worse.

Access to housing, for example, is very much affected by the level and security of income which is largely determined by people's access to and status in employment. This is perhaps particularly true of the private housing market so that the implications are all the more serious when there is only a small public sector, or access to that is limited by residence requirements and other factors which work against any group moving into an area including immigrants. The more unequal the access to employment the more these groups will be forced into the poorest housing, only exacerbating the problem of getting a job. With a surplus of labour, employers may be less willing to take workers from areas generally regarded as undesirable.

Such points seemed well recognised in policy debates and campaigns to improve employment opportunities when the economy was healthier. Amid a recession, however, there seems less acknowledgement that the decline in employment opportunities will lead to a set-back in these strategies unless specific measures are taken to promote the labour market position of vulnerable groups. Those already established in the labour force are concerned to hold on to the jobs they have and tend to see claims for equal opportunity from other groups as a further attack on their diminishing power. In that atmosphere married women in work come under criticism for taking "men's jobs" and are even accused of contributing to unemployment. The attack on their claim to employment becomes linked with the assault on public expenditure: the same married women are expected to take on the role of the "unpaid community carer", thus reducing the demand for paid jobs and the need for state-financed community care services at one and the same time.

In Britain women may have made significant gains in the labour market as the result of policy changes in the mid-1970s. However, the effect of the recession has been to destroy much of the advance (Hakim, 1981). The gains made by professional and salaried women are probably more secure than those of the lower paid white-collar and manual workers who are more vulnerable to increased unemployment.

Sustained high unemployment also widens inequalities between racial, ethnic or religious groups and reduces the value of previous advances. Society in recession is a fertile ground for those who wish to reverse previous achievements in tackling inequality, creating a particularly acute dilemma for governments. If they act to protect the gains achieved by minority groups, charges of "reverse discrimination" are used to gain support and strengthen resistance among majority groups increasingly fearful of their own job security. If they take no action, many years of slow advance may be lost and attacks on minority groups may appear to be sanctioned by an inactive administration.

The impact on minority groups is increased because their greater vulnerability to unemployment may isolate and segregate them even further. In a society where being out of work still tends to carry a stigma, the stereotyped media image of "young blacks" as unemployed and roaming the streets may only reinforce prejudices.

Many minorities have managed to survive in a relatively hostile host society by a combination of very hard work and strong family and community ties that provide employment opportunities within specific industries or occupations. In groups with a strong tradition of rapid upward social mobility with economic success, there may be less sympathy and a little institutionalised support within the group's welfare network for those who fail to find work. Rejected by the wider society, these unemployed may find themselves neglected or even more stigmatised in their own community. The blow to the group as a whole is greatly increased when the occupation or industry which it has succeeded in reaching is in decline: for example, major redundancies in the tailoring and clothing industry in the north of England have had a particular impact upon the Jewish community (Kosmin and Levy, 1982).

IMPACT ON WORK

The shadow of the recession stretches right over the labour force, including those members of it who remain employed: they also experience changes, both quantitative and qualitative, in their lives. There is more short-time and less overtime working and many jobs become temporary and/or part-time. The extent of these changes varies not only between countries but within them, by industry and occupation. In Britain, for example, there has been much less of a reduction in overtime than an increase in short-time working among manual workers, reflecting considerable differences in security and stability.

Less easily quantifiable changes are linked to these, reflecting the decline in opportunities, the increase in insecurity and the shift of power against the worker. A satisfactory working career generally depends upon chances of mobility and promotion, especially among professional, managerial, administrative and many other white-collar occupations. For most manual workers getting a better job tends to require changing employers and is less easy when job openings are reduced. Even given the opportunity, manual workers have to assess the risk of being made more insecure in the new job because of the prevalence of the "last-in first-out" formula for redundancies.

The recession therefore limits opportunities and makes taking those that do arise a risk. In consequence very many workers become trapped in jobs in which they had never expected to stay, poorer in pay, status or conditions of work. Their frustration, compounded by inflation and heavier taxation, makes them all the readier recipients of stories about a carefree life of luxury enjoyed by those out of work at their expense as taxpayers.

Policies to improve the quality of work or its rewards are liable to be frustrated by high unemployment. Wages in many jobs drop in real terms and attempts to maintain the lowest wages are especially vulnerable given the greater insecurity of these jobs and their low level of unionisation. Protection to the lowest paid is further reduced when the number of wages inspectors is cut, in part because of the decision to reduce public expenditure.

Protection to all workers against dangers to their health and safety is also jeopardised by high unemployment. Enforced public expenditure savings on factory inspectors mean less visits and inspections: the frequency of visits is said to have been reduced from five to seven years in Britain. The pursuit of safety standards laid down by law is also affected when "inspectors are under instructions to adopt 'a more reasonable attitude to all companies' ... because of the economic climate" (The Guardian, 28 January 1980).

"CRIME AS A SOCIAL COST OF UNEMPLOYMENT" (NACRO, 1982)

In many countries increases in recorded unemployment have been accompanied by rises in the amount of reported crime. The conclusion of one recent review that "unemployment provides the time, opportunity and ... in some cases the actual motive for crime" (Taylor, 1982) is supported by the Select Committee of the House of Lords on Unemployment, and would probably be endorsed by most people. But in the same week as that review was released the British Home Office published an analysis of 30 studies across a number of countries which decided that at best the relationship between crime and unemployment was "very unclear ... with no discernible pattern" and "no evidence of a significant relationship between the two factors". Rising crime was also "highly correlated with the consumption of ice-cream, the number of cars on the road and the gross national product" (Guardian, 2 October, 1982, my emphasis).

While the argument over the nature of the association has been raging for many years, it obviously becomes more of a public policy issue with increased rates of unemployment. The issue most in debate is whether more unemployment causes more crime, and more specifically, if it does, what sort of unemployment and what type of crime are involved. Those who identify a link believe that an increase in unemployment among young people, especially in inner cities, leads to more crimes, especially those against property (for example, shoplifting and taking and driving cars) and assaults against the person. In Britain anxieties have grown with an increase in the numbers of young people in the labour force and a disproportionate increase in their rates of unemployment. After the violence in some inner cities in mid-1981 there was a particular tendency to link increases in reported crime with the growth of unemployment among young people, especially young blacks, although the evidence provides little support (NACRO, 1982).

Less than a decade ago an increase in similar offences, then described as "crimes of affluence", was attributed to rising living standards. It may well be that economic growth can be as disturbing as decline and the explanation lies in the speed of change and its destabilizing impact, as a United Nations Report in 1976 argued. How far it is possible to see increased unemployment causing more criminal behaviour is not at all clear. Some have suggested that poverty or relative deprivation should be seen as the major cause, an issue which might be related to the level of benefits for young people, while others have placed the emphasis on the isolation, even segregation, of unemployed young people, especially young blacks, leading them to react against the society to which they have little attachment, and argued for increased services and better community facilities. The official enquiry into the "Brixton disorders" in south London took some account of these points, recommending more positive and coherent support for major policies to tackle the underlying problems of discrimination, poverty, unemployment and poor housing in contrast to the tougher policing which had exacerbated the problems (Scarman, 1982).

What is very much less in dispute is the increase in problems for offenders created by unemployment, in part because of the general lack of support or sympathy for the unemployed as well as those who commit crimes. A convicted offender out of work is more likely to be sent to prison than an employed one, especially if this is not the first conviction. This may be because judges accept that those out of work are less likely to be able to pay fines or that being sent to prison may cause the employed to lose their jobs. However, it seems that sentencers may feel prison is more likely to do an unemployed offender some good. In fact the unemployed are also less likely to get bail before their trial. Since the chance of acquittal is lower for those who have been kept in custody, it would seem that being out of work increases the chance of conviction.

Whatever the reasons, there is strong evidence that rising unemployment is accompanied by "rising rates of imprisonment and larger prison populations over and above any increase in crime rates" (NACRO, 1982, p.658). This is not only one more demand on public expenditure: in Britain it exacerbates an already alarming problem of overcrowding in the prison system which has caused considerable concern.

Prisoners are more likely to be awarded parole or early release if they can show that they have a job waiting for them, so that those who remain unemployed are more likely to spend a higher proportion of their original sentence in prison - and the longer the time spent in prison, the greater chance there is of a further conviction. Finally, with higher unemployment, the ex-prisoner has very great difficulty in finding work, even

during much lower unemployment, a detailed case study
nearly a decade ago by Apex (an employment service trying
to place white-collar ex-offenders) shows the extent of
the difficulty when even a court appearance, let alone
imprisonment, has resulted in job loss (Soothill, 1974).

Barely one-third obtained a job and at least 50 contacts were needed before a job was found for 1 in 3 of
these placings. Those who managed to stay in the same
job for a year or longer were very much less likely to be
reconvicted during the next 5 years (Soothill, 1981).
Organisations working with ex-offenders emphasize the
inadequate service provided by state employment agencies
and the almost total lack of any job preparation provided
within the prison before discharge. Probation officers
and social workers report that persisting high unemployment is reducing their ability to help ex-prisoners and
indeed threatens the whole philosophy underlying services
for the care and resettlement of offenders.

Once again "the way a society responds to the problems associated with unemployment" seems to be a critical
factor but "at times of economic hardship societies tend
to become less tolerant of deviance, become more punitive
and aggravate the problem" (Crow, 1982).

THE EFFECTS ON HEALTH

In recent years a debate similar to the one about
crime has flourished over the effect of increases in unemployment on the health, not only of unemployed people but
of the population as a whole. While criticising a
government report for the very cautious conclusion that
data on the relation of both crime and health to unemployment "are inadequate but a link is 'plausible'", the
House of Lords Select Committee on Unemployment remains
guarded in its conclusion that the evidence is "highly
indicative ... a reduction in the general level of
economic activity does appear to trigger off a sequence
of events leading to ultimately increased levels of ill-
health and death rates" (House of Lords, 1982, I, pp.54-6
and 59;   see also Popay, 1981).

Claims of increased mortality and mobidity have
emerged from studies of changes in rates of unemployment
or economic activity correlated with these factors over
long periods of time (see for example Brenner and
Mooney, 1983). Findings have been disputed with particular argument about the appropriate "lag" time to allow
for the effect of unemployment to be demonstrated on
health and vital statistics. Some who accept the link
argue the causes lie more in increased stress resulting

from economic instability, whether due to growth or
decline, or to increased poverty among those suffering
the impact of a recession. These would suggest that
policy responses to increased unemployment could have a
significant effect upon mortality or morbidity outcomes.
Indications that high infant mortality may accompany
increased unemployment in Northern Ireland would appear
to support those drawing attention to the growth of
poverty and the decline in available services and general
environmental standards with persistent high unemployment.

Suicide rates may also be related to increased
levels and longer duration of unemployment. The interpretation of statistics on suicidal behaviour is notoriously problematic, but "unemployed people constitute a
high proportion of suicides and attempted suicides"
(House of Lords, 1982, I, p.57). There are also indications that prolonged unemployment may be particularly
significant (Platt, 1982). Those vulnerable to some form
of mental disorder, especially reactive depression, may
have more difficulty finding and keeping a job as well
as coping with the lack of one. But it may also be that
some pressures of unemployment, including the isolation
and lack of status, are particularly unsettling, especially for many young people. Voluntary groups such as
the Samaritans report a marked increase in "phone calls
for help from teenagers in despair at trying to cope
with the problems of unemployment".

Poor health and disability are clearly linked with
unemployment, in part because people with these difficulties are more vulnerable to unemployment. It is less
clear to what extent and in what ways the stress of
redundancy or the persistence of unemployment leads to
a deterioration of health. Given the working conditions
and pressures of some jobs, unemployment allows a return
to better health for some, but it also has its own damaging effects especially when resources and living standards
fall, and isolation and stigma threaten self-respect.
Those with most involvement in their jobs may suffer
particularly and the likelihood of getting a job may be
another important factor. Recent evidence suggests the
scale of the health problem may be very much greater than
has so far been identified. A national survey of middle-
aged men, employed and unemployed, concluded that self-
assessment and family-doctor diagnosis may both "substantially underestimate the prevalence of major physical
illness in the unemployed" (Cook et al., 1982, p.1293).

It seems likely that health problems, both physical
and mental, may become more evident with unemployment
because people are better able to cope with these while
their job provides them with a daily routine, social
contacts, status and an income. When these are removed

and their existing problems compounded by poverty, isolation and stigma, it is difficult to see how their general state of health can fail to deteriorate.

Increased unemployment also brings an increased risk of disability, injury and damage to health in other ways. Workers often refuse to take sick leave during periods of minor illness for fear of increasing their chances of being made redundant if a firm has to reduce its workforce; and, when health is poor, the risk of an accident to workers and their colleagues is increased. Many doctors and specialists are noting that workers come to them with particular illnesses and strains which could in the past have been largely cured or removed by changing jobs, but this option is no longer as available, particularly to older workers (over forty years old in some areas). In addition, there is the risk of increased accidents as well as pressures within the worker's family. As well as the costs and losses to individuals and families, the pressures of unemployment on health have obvious public expenditure costs - higher disability pensions and sickness insurance, medical care, domiciliary and residential social services, etc. These become greater problems when health care and other resources are limited.

THE FRUSTRATION OF REHABILITATION SERVICES

Throughout this chapter there have been references not only to ways in which policies can help reduce the impact of unemployment but also to the inhibiting, blocking effect that increased unemployment can have on many policies and services. In consequence the potentially ameliorative effects of many programmes are frustrated by the lack of employment opportunities. This shows particularly clearly in the problems facing most forms of rehabilitation service.

Much of the work, for example, in the health and personal social services is concerned with helping people back to some regular or "normal" life after a particular crisis event - imprisonment or simply conviction for a crime, physical disability or a period of mental illness, whether in hospital or not, the collapse of a marriage, etc. Probably the main means of rehabilitation by which people become reabsorbed in the community is through becoming re-employed. A job not only provides a regular income and an accepted status in society, but a daily routine and range of social contacts which can help people to rebuild their health and confidence and involve them in the wider community. The considerable "therapeutic" value of employment in rehabilitation cannot be

made as easily available during periods of high unemployment. Many of those with difficulties find themselves
forced into the poorer jobs which will not bring them
the support of adequately paid and secure employment and
may only compound their problems.

In the majority of cases increased unemployment has
not caused the problems which handicap these people but
it does prevent the easing or resolution of them, and it
may also exacerbate them. Under better employment conditions these difficulties could often be overcome, or
at least reduced to more tolerable levels. The maintenance of high unemployment therefore means that the helping or caring professions have to find new strategies of
rehabilitation. There is so far little evidence that
they have been able to do so.

THE LEGACY OF HIGH UNEMPLOYMENT

Throughout this chapter there have been references
to long-term effects from higher unemployment both on
those who actually experience the higher risk of being
out of work and many others who may remain in work or
right outside the labour force. It has been argued that
increased unemployment is not only an outcome of other
events and changes but is itself a cause of major changes:
for example, the attacks on poverty and unequal opportunity for disadvantaged groups may be set back, previous
achievements reversed and the experience and understanding
acquired over many years lost.

In the same way perhaps, countries today are having
to relearn the harsh lessons taught by the 1930s about
the "profoundly corrosive experience" of prolonged unemployment (Department of Employment Gazette, 1976, p.34).

In many countries in the early 1980s there appears
a greater mood of pessimism about the persistence of high
unemployment than, it is claimed, was prevalent during
the inter-war depression. But this may simply reflect
the fact that the best-known accounts of that period
emerged as economies were showing signs of recovery.
Earlier discussions not only shared present gloom but
often displayed remarkably similar explanations and fore-
casts of the contemporary predicament. The accounts of
the impact are also often surprisingly recognisable despite great differences in the level of income support
and the general standard of living (Constantine, 1980;
Stevenson, 1977). "For many hopes were hammered thin by
unemployment and the necessity of living on relief" and
"the future is resisted as a threat" concluded one of

the classic studies of mid-depression America (Lynds, 1937, p.475; see also Bakke, 1933 in London and 1960 in New England). How much can be learnt from that depression about the long-term effects of prolonged high unemployment given the cataclysmic events that succeeded, it is hard to say. <u>The Children of the Great Depression</u> suggests a variable and limited effect (Elder, 1974).

Evidence from the late 1960s in Britain found that poverty persisted after unemployment "however short in the recent past" because of low pay, further unemployment or sickness (Townsend, 1979, p.614). Reinterviews in the mid-1970s with men who had been out of work in the industrial north-east of England some twelve years earlier revealed the human erosion resulting from labour force careers of insecure, poorly paid work and unemployment. Only a minority of a small sample of working class men had "fully escaped from poverty or low pay" (North Tyneside CDP, 1978, pp.245-7). Those with the longest or most frequent unemployment had the poorest chance of moving to a more secure position. A recurrence of unemployment can also be very undermining according to studies in the United States (Aiken et al., 1968, Chapter VIII) and Britain (Hill, 1978).

Work insecurity in the United States was found to "foster a retreat from both work and the larger communal society" (Wilensky, 1961, pp.523-4 and 539). "Unemployment is not forgotten with the passage of time and can lead to a misanthropic view of society and a pessimistic view of life" (Hyman, 1979, pp.290-3). Other evidence from American voting studies suggests that political views shaped by the recession may persist for decades.

The fear of insecurity may persist into higher employment years as a working class strategy or "folk-memory" that dominates contact between employer and worker, encouraging resistance to change and more militant collective bargaining (see, for example, Burkitt and Bowers, 1979, p.13; Blackaby, 1976, p.289; Bakke, 1933, pp.43-44).

CONCLUSION

A society with unemployment remaining high for many years is qualitatively different from one which provides adequate opportunities for all who want work. The unemployed bear a heavier burden as unemployment increases and becomes more prolonged, but the shadow of the recession is also cast over many more groups whose resources and ability to participate in society are reduced unless specific action is taken to protect them.

Many of the basic "Welfare State" policies require high employment levels for their success: the recession for example, is a major obstacle to any attempt to reduce or prevent poverty, and equal opportunity and rehabilitation programmes are likely to be frustrated. The widening of inequality is accelerated by the double pressures imposed on public social services by increased needs and diminished resources. The way in which government responds to high unemployment has particular significance for the more vulnerable, among not only the unemployed but all groups in society, as they are particularly dependent on the public services.

A successful response to current economic problems can only be achieved by change of many kinds, requiring adaptability and flexibility throughout society. However, "rising unemployment and pressure on living standards have hardened resistance to change, at a time when change is essential for the restoration of economic health and a return to better employment" (CEC, April 1981).

BIBLIOGRAPHY

Aiken, Michael: Ferman, Louis A; and Sheppard, Harold L. (1968) Economic Failure, Alienation and Extremism (Ann Arbor: University of Michigan Press).

Bakke, E. Wight (1933) The Unemployed Man (Nisbet).

Bakke, E. Wight (1960) "The cycle of adjustment to unemployment" in Norman W. Bell and Ezra F. Vogel (eds.) A Modern Introduction to the Family (Glencoe III: Free Press).

Beveridge, William H. (1930) Unemployment: A Problem of Industry (revised with additions) (Longmans Green).

Beveridge, William H. (1942) Social Insurance and Allied Services, Cmd 6404.

Beveridge, William H. (1944) Full Employment in a Free Society (Allen and Unwin).

Blackaby, Frank (1976) "The target rate for unemployment" in Worswick (ed.)

Blaustein, Saul J: and Craig, Isabel (1977) An International Review of Unemployment Insurance Schemes, W.E. Upjohn Institute for Employment Research, Kalamazoo, Mich.

Brenner, Harvey and Mooney, Anne (1983) "Unemployment and Health in the Context of Economic Change", Social Science and Medicine, vol. 17:16, pp.1125-1138.

Burkitt, Brian and Bowers, David (1979) Trade Unions and the Economy (Macmillan).

Commission of the European Communities (1981) "Problems of Unemployment - Points for Examination", Brussels, 29 April.

Clark, Marjory (1978) "The unemployed on supplementary benefit", Journal of Social Policy 7 : 4, October, pp.385-410.

Colledge, Maureen and Bartholomew, Richard (1980) "The long-term unemployed: some new evidence", Employment Gazette, January, pp.9-12 (summary of their report A study of the Long-Term Unemployed, Manpower Services Commission, February, 1980).

Constantine, Stephen (1980) Unemployment in Britain between the Wars, (London: Longmans).

Cook, D.G.; Cummins, R.O.; Bartley, M.J.; Shaper, A.G. (1982) "Health of Unemployed Middle-Aged Men in Great Britain", The Lancet, 5 June, pp.1290-4.

Crow, Iain (1982) "The Unemployment-Crime Link", Unemployment Unit Bulletin, 4 July.

Deacon, A. (1978) "The scrounging controversy", Social and Economic Administration 12.

Deacon, A. (1980) "Unemployment and Politics in Britain since 1945" in Showler and Sinfield (eds.).

Department of Employment Gazette (1976) "The demoralising experience of prolonged unemployment", April, pp.330-349.

Donnison, David and Ungerson, Clare (1982) Housing Policy (Harmondsworth: Penguin).

Elder, Glen H. (1974) Children of the Great Depression: Social Change in Life Experience (Chicago: Chicago University Press).

Etienne, Raymond (1956) <u>Administrative Problems of Schemes Providing Protection Against Unemployment</u>, ISSA, Geneva.

Etienne, Raymond (1973) <u>The Evaluation of Schemes of Protection Against Unemployment since 1955</u>, ISSA, Geneva.

Feagin, Joe R. (1975) <u>Subordinating the Poor</u> (Englewood Cliffs, NJ: Prentice-Hall).

Ferman, L.A. and Gordus, J.P. (eds.) (1979) <u>Mental Health and the Economy</u> (Kalamazoo, Michigan: W.E. Upjohn Institute for Employment Research).

Furmaniak, Karl (1983) "West Germany: Poverty, Unemployment and Social Insurance" in Walker et al. (eds.)

Golding, Peter and Middleton, Sue (1982) <u>Images of Welfare: Press and Public Attitudes to Poverty</u> (Oxford: Martin Robertson).

Graycar, Adam (ed.) (1983) <u>Retreat from the Welfare State</u> (Sydney: Allen and Unwin).

Hakim, Catherine (1981) "Job segregation: trends in the 1970s", <u>Employment Gazette</u>, December.

Hill, M.J. (1978) "Unemployment: an isolated experience or a recurrent event in a disadvantaged life?" in RCDIW.

House of Lords Select Committee on Unemployment (1982) <u>Report</u>, House of Lords Papers 142, Vol. I, Vols. II and III, Minutes and Evidence (London: HMSO).

Hyman, Herbert H. (1979) "The effects of unemployment: a neglected problem in modern social research", in Robert K. Merton, James S. Coleman and Peter H. Rossi (eds.) <u>Qualitative and Quantitative Social Research: Papers in Honor of Paul F. Lazarsfeld</u> (New York: Free Press).

Kosmin, Barry and Levy, Caren (1982) "Unemployment: The Hidden Problem", <u>Jewish Chronicle</u>, 6 August.

Krafchik, Max (1983) "Unemployment and Vagrancy in the 1930s: Deterrence, Rehabilitation and the Depression", <u>Journal of Social Policy</u>, Vol. 12:2, April, pp.195-213.

Lion, Antoine (1983) "Poverty and work in France", in Walker et al. (eds.).

Lynd, Robert S. and Lynd, Helen Merrell (1937) Middletown in Transition, (New York: Harcourt Brace).

May, Edgar (1964) The Wasted Americans (New York: Signet).

Merritt, Giles (1982) World Out of Work (London: Collins).

Minsky, Hyman P. (1965) "The role of employment policy", in Margaret S. Gordon (ed.) Poverty in America (San Francisco: Chandler).

NACRO (National Association for the Care and Resettlement of Offenders) (1982) "NACRO and its work with unemployed offenders", in House of Lords (1982), Vol. III, pp.657-668.

North Tyneside Community Development Project (1978) In and Out of Work (Home Office).

O'Connor, James (1973) The Fiscal Crisis of the State, (New York: St. Martin's Press).

OECD (1979) Manpower and Employment Measures for Positive Adjustment, Manpower and Social Affairs Committee (Paris: Organisation for Economic Co-operation and Development), document for general distribution.

OECD (1981) The Welfare State in Crisis (Paris: Organisation for Economic Co-operation and Development).

Owens, Jeffrey P. (1983) "Tax expenditures and direct expenditures as instruments of social policy", in S. Crossen (ed.) Comparative Tax Studies (North Holland).

Pilgrim Trust (1938) Men Without Work (Cambridge: Cambridge University Press).

Platt, Steve (1982) "Unemployment and suicidal behaviour: a review of the literature", MRC Unit, Department of Psychiatry, University of Edinburgh, unpublished paper.

Pond, Chris (1982) "Taxation and Public Expenditure", in Alan Walker (ed.) Public Expenditure and Social Policy (London: Heinemann).

Popay, Jennie (1981) "Unemployment: a threat to public health", in Louie Burghes and Ruth Lister (eds.) Unemployment: Who pays the price? (London: Child Poverty Action Group).

Scarman, Lord (1982) The Scarman Report: The Brixton Disorders, 10-12 April 1981 (Harmondsworth: Pelican)

Shanas, Ethel et al. (1968) The Old in Three Industrial Societies (New York: Atherton).

Showler, Brian and Sinfield, Adrian (eds.) (1980) The Workless State: Studies in Unemployment (Oxford: Martin Robertson).

Sinfield, Adrian (1968) The Long-term Unemployed (Paris: Organisation for Economic Co-operation and Development).

Sinfield, Adrian (1976) "Unemployment and Inequality", Social Administration Association Conference paper, Exeter.

Sinfield, Adrian (1981) What Unemployment Means, Martin Robertson, Oxford.

Sinfield, Adrian (1982) "Social policy amid high unemployment", in Catherine Jones and June Stevenson (eds.) The Year Book of Social Policy in Britain 1980-81 (London: Routledge and Kegan Paul).

Sinfield, Adrian (1983) "Unemployment", in Peter A. Köhler and Hans F. Zacher (eds.), Beiträge zu Geschichte und aktueller Situation der Sozialversicherung (Berlin: Dunker and Humblot).

Smee, Clive (1980) "Unemployment and poverty: some comparisons with Canada and the United States". Paper presented to the SSRC Research Workshop on Employment and Unemployment, June 1980.

Social Trends 1979 (London: HMSO).

Soothill, Keith (1974) The Prisoner's Release: A Study of the Employment of Ex-Prisoners (Allen and Unwin).

Soothill, Keith (1981) "Employing white-collar ex-offenders", British Journal of Social Work.

Stevenson, John (1977) Social Conditions in Britain Between the Wars (Harmondsworth: Penguin).

Surrey, Stanley (1973) Pathways to Tax Reform (Cambridge, Mass: Harvard University Press).

Taylor, Laurie (1982) Unemployment, Crime and Young People (London: Keep Out).

Titmuss, Richard M. (1958) "The Social Division of Welfare", in Essays on "the Welfare State" (London: Allen and Unwin).

Townsend, Peter (1979) Poverty in the United Kingdom (London: Allen Lane Press).

United Nations (1976) Economic Crises and Crime (Rome: UN Social Defence Research Institute).

Walker, R.; Lawson, R. and Townsend, P. (eds.) (1983) Responses to Poverty: Lessons from Europe (London: Heinemann).

Webber, Douglas (1982) "Between programmatic claim and political practice - the development of Labour Market Policy in the Federal Republic of Germany 1974-1982", unpublished paper, Bonn.

Wilensky, Harold L. (1961) "Orderly careers and social participation: the impact of work history on social interpretation in the middle mass", American Sociological Review, pp.521-39.

Worswick, G.D.N. (ed.) (1976) The Concept and Measurement of Involuntary Unemployment (Allen and Unwin).

THE WIDER IMPACT OF UNEMPLOYMENT

A comment
by
I.C.R. Byatt

Many figures are quoted on the cost of unemployment to public budgets. We have done our own calculations covering both public expenditure and taxation "costs" and published them in the February 1981 Economic Progress Report. This showed "costs" of £3 400 per additional person on the unemployment register in 1980-81.

We have not updated this figure because we have become increasingly aware of its limitations. Costs are usually calculated to help decision-makers. What decision are these "costs" meant to illuminate? Presumably because unemployment costs the government money, it might be better to spend the same money on reducing unemployment. But this suggests that the unemployment arises because demand is inadequate. Some unemployment may well arise in this way, for example, as a result of a reduction in external demand. But not all of the secular increase in unemployment which we have observed in our economies in recent years can be explained in this way. Some of it, particularly in Europe, may result from excessive wage costs. If unemployment resulted from an increase in wage costs, this would be associated with increases in tax receipts as wages rose, followed by reductions in tax receipts as employment fell. The net result might be either to increase or reduce public sector receipts. This example shows that in order to calculate the costs to the public sector of additional unemployment, it is necessary to determine first what caused the higher unemployment.

The view that unemployment results from demand deficiency alone is extremely difficult to sustain. Poor economic performance and higher unemployment in the Seventies resulted from a host of factors whose relative importance is difficult to determine. The wage explosion beginning in Paris in 1968, a progressive slowdown in productive potential even before 1973, a

breakdown of the Bretton Woods payments system, the syn-
chronous boom of 1972-73 and its effect on raw material
prices, especially oil, may be the major factors, but
they are not the only ones.

In a world where inflationary tendencies still pose
major problems for output and employment, it is misleading to argue that a reduction in unemployment is an over-
riding priority and therefore simple-minded to document
the costs of unemployment as if the establishment of such
costs was a sufficient reason for action.

We were careful to stress the assumptions underlying
the figures. They related only to changes in private
sector jobs. The results depended on assumptions about
registration, as well as the personal characteristics of
the unemployed. But in view of the way the figures were
subsequently used, we should perhaps have stressed even
more that the figures were simply a static statistical
snapshot: also no second round effects were allowed for.
On this basis there is nothing wrong with the figures
themselves. But the use that can be made of them is
inevitably limited.

They were misused in two ways. First, the figure
was grossed up by the number on the register to derive
what was termed "the total cost of unemployment". This
misuse is also apparent in the Secretariat report. This
is misleading because it suggests that unemployment could
be reduced to very low figures quickly with a benefit
to public budgets. But to what low figures? We have
experienced rising levels of unemployment and persistent
slack in our economies. Nevertheless, we have little
idea what a non-inflationary full employment level is
like. In thinking about policy, we are more concerned
with the effects of changing the level of unemployment
- on inflation, balance of payments, etc. - than on aiming in any short period of time at a particular level
of unemployment.

Secondly, it was assumed that £3 400 per person
was "available" to be spent on ways of relieving unemployment without cost to the public finances. Un-
fortunately it is not as simple as this.

In order to ensure zero net costs, unemployed workers given public sector employment could only be paid
at the level of their social security benefits grossed
up for any tax and employees' National Insurance contributions they would pay on such a wage. Pay more than
this and the flowbacks would not be sufficient to cover
the wage. The point is simple really - it's a zero sum
game. If the employee is to be left better off after
taxes etc. than he was on benefit, then the government
must be worse off. Moreover, even community programmes
which pay benefit only (or just a bit above to cover

expenses) will have a significant net cost because of overheads.

It is easier to think of "recovering" the £3 400 if the new employment is in the private sector - since in this case the public sector does not have to pay the wages. But there is a number of reasons why zero net cost is unlikely:

i) the £3 400 includes tax receipts from 1.3 people (basic sums refer to 100 000 registered and 33 000 unregistered unemployed); thus if one new person is employed the tax receipts will be less than assumed;

ii) private sector wages would have to equal (or exceed) those assumed in the sum;

iii) no deadweight or displacement, i.e. the subsidy must be accurately directed and should assist neither those who would have been employed in any case nor those whose employment is at the expense of other people.

The result is that it is very difficult to get a private sector scheme which yields zero net cost after flow-backs.

This is not to say that calculation of flow-backs is not useful when considering specific employment measures. We do this in the United Kingdom. But we try to relate the size of these flow-backs to particular policy initiatives, allowing for deadweight displacement, financing costs, etc. in the context of a particular measure rather than attempting to use an overall ready reckoner.

In conclusions, there are four points I would like to make:

a) Figures which purport to show the "cost" of unemployment are of very limited value.

b) In considering job creation policies, more attention should be paid to the resource costs and benefits of employment rather than the Exchequer costs. Special employment measures may have low Public Sector Borrowing Requirement (PSBR) costs but they have a poor resource profile. They may make sense in a short but deep recession but be no way to restore economic growth.

c) Wage and non-wage labour costs are important in explaining unemployment in many parts of the OECD - especially in Europe. It would be worth considering how social security policy could affect these costs, either through their effect on wage bargaining or on social security contributions.

d) As an extension of (c), the effect of labour
   market and social security policies on the economy needs further examination. We need to look
   at their contribution to labour market rigidities
   and not simply to ask how particular sums of
   money could be spent in different ways.

THE IMPACT OF UNEMPLOYMENT ON GOVERNMENT BUDGETS

A comment
by
Fred-Olav Sørensen

Let me first say that the opinions expressed here are my own and not necessarily those of my Minister.

The impact of unemployment can be seen from many different points of view. The following list contains what I feel are the main ones. Distinctions can be made between consequences for:

1. The individual
   Consequences for revenue and expenditure
   Psychological and social consequences
   Effects on attitudes and behaviour

2. Government finance
   Central government expenditure and revenue effects, including social security
   Local government expenditure and revenue effects

3. The firm
   Revenue and expenditure effects
   Effects on expectations,
   planning and investment

4. Society as a whole
   Macro-economic effects
   Effects on the social and political
   structure and stability

In this note the task is primarily to focus on the effects of unemployment on government finance. However, it is crucial to bear in mind that this is a partial viewpoint. It is necessary to extend the analysis in order to clarify the links between this limited viewpoint and the broader viewpoint of society as a whole. I will say a few words about this in the second part of my short intervention.

The general analysis regarding the effects on both
society as a whole and on the government budget needs -
as its point of departure - a specification of the possible alternatives. It may in this connection be important to remember that the status quo is almost never a
possible alternative. Initially, it seems to be necessary to specify the following alternatives:

Alternative 1: A given increase in unemployment is
in process, and is allowed to develop.
Alternative 2: One or several policy responses
are made to check the increase in unemployment or to prevent the increase from taking place.

This initial specification is necessary because an
assessment of the costs of unemployment needs to be made
with reference to something else.

I will now take a brief look at some figures drawn
from work we have done in Norway. Such figures have by
now been computed in many countries, and generally give
very similar results. The following table gives the net
increase in central and local government deficits as a
result of an increase in unemployment of selected persons. It also shows the individual's loss of disposable
income as a result of unemployment, as well as the gross
income before unemployment. Let us take the example of
a male worker in manufacturing industry with an annual
income of about 92 000 Norwegian kroner, becoming unemployed. Increased expenditure on unemployment benefits
and reduced tax and social security revenue amount in
total to about 70 000 Norwegian kroner for the central
government on an annual basis. Add about 10 000
Norwegian kroner of local government budgetary losses,
and you get a total net increase in government deficits
of about 80 000 Norwegian kroner. This is not very far
from the gross income received by the worker prior to
unemployment. I should add that these figures do not
include costs incurred by health and social authorities
when unemployed persons ask for economic help to make
ends meet or because of deterioration in physical or
mental health. Neither do they include additional costs
incurred by labour market authorities when an increased
number of unemployed have to be helped.

The table shows how these figures vary according to
the person's level of income prior to unemployment. I
shall not go through all these examples in the text.
The main message of this table is that the financial effects of unemployment are surprisingly high. The table
also indicates how much you could alternatively spend
(as a minimum) to avoid unemployment, without incurring
budgetary losses.

This latter statement, however, is a controversial
one and it needs elaboration. This leads me to consider

72

CHANGES IN REVENUE AND EXPENDITURE (ANNUAL BASIS)
AS A CONSEQUENCE OF AN INCREASE IN UNEMPLOYMENT

EFFECTS ON GOVERNMENT BUDGETS AND THE INDIVIDUAL'S BUDGET (Norwegian Kroner)

	Male worker in manufacturing industry	Woman worker in manufacturing industry	Male supporting wife and two children	Youth	Part-time female worker
Central government(1)	70 095	57 421	69 840	12 344	27 204
Local government(2)	10 122	8 358	9 592	1 470	3 948
Sum central and local government	80 217	65 779	79 432	13 814	31 152
Reduction in disposable income for the individual	27 552	24 584	28 466	7 228	14 088
Income prior to unemployment	92 300	77 300	92 300	18 000	38 700

1. Increased central government expenditure consists of unemployment benefits. Reduced revenue consists of reduced social security payments from employers, reduced tax payments of different kinds.

2. Consists of reduced tax revenue. Increased social budget expenditure is not included.

73

the broader perspective of the costs of unemployment to
society as a whole. Let me then move back to the specification of alternatives 1 and 2 above. If we look at
these alternatives from the point of view of society as
a whole, the consequences might be arranged as follows:

Alternative 1: A given increase in unemployment
which is allowed to develop

Consequences on:

a) the individual's income, health, attitudes and
behaviour
b) the social and political structure and stability
(dependent on time perspective and magnitude of
unemployment)
c) demand pressure on public health and social
services
d) the pressure on public labour market services
including management of unemployment benefit
schemes
e) loss of human capital and learning on the job
f) capital and labour mobility
g) wages and prices, through expectations,
negotiations and market mechanism

Alternative 2: Policy responses to meet the
increase in unemployment

Consequences on:

h) investment and operating costs, public and private, of given measures. Less public "operating
costs" of unemployment, i.e. unemployment benefits and the like
i) production value of given measures
j) differences regarding the consequences outlined
in alternative 1

Two important points need to be made before I
quickly run through the list of consequences.

First, unemployment is - at the moment it arises -
a consequence of earlier actions and decisions which
must be taken as given (sunk cost). Possible costs or
benefits arise with reference to our actions or lack of
actions when facing such a development. Secondly, this
discussion aims at unemployment of a level and duration
which exceeds what one could reasonably associate with
frictional unemployment.

Turning now to the list of consequences, it is primarily the consequences on the individual's income,
health, attitudes and behaviour (see point a) which mo-
tivate the fight against unemployment. Professor
Sinfield's invervention gives a deeper insight into the
kinds of consequences that arise here. The consequences

of high levels of long duration unemployment on social
and political structure and stability (see point b) are
not extensively documented, but there seems to be widespread agreement that these consequences are also of an
entirely negative nature. Point c), demand pressure on
public health and social services as a result of increased unemployment, is relatively easy to identify but
harder to quantify. There is, however, no doubt that
such demand pressure increases significantly and thereby
represents an increased cost to society. The same holds
for point d), regarding labour market services. Point e),
loss of human capital and learning on the job, covers
several elements. Learning on the job ceases by definition when unemployment starts. Loss of human capital
is more drawn out in time as it is connected with loss
of relevance of knowledge and loss of professional self-
confidence. There are relatively few examples, among
the long-term unemployed, of persons who have been able
to build up their human capital while unemployed. Examples of the contrary seem far more numerous. It is
therefore a reasonably safe assumption that this also
represents a cost to society.

Point f), the consequences of unemployment on capital and labour mobility, also covers several aspects.
The general assumption is that such mobility increases
when unemployment increases. This is probably right as
regards unemployed labour and unemployed capital. However, the effect of high unemployment on the mobility
of those people who are employed is likely to be negative. This is because the risks connected with job
changes are higher and people are generally averse to
risk. More empirical work is needed to assess the relative importance of these two counteracting factors.
As regards the assessment of whether increased labour
mobility is a benefit or a cost to society, it seems
clear that it is a benefit from an economic point of
view. The issue is more complex from the point of view
of individual welfare. National attitudes and practice
differ. Frequent changes of jobs and location of jobs
seem to be a natural and accepted way of life in the
United States, whereas this seems to have negative con-
notations to most people in Norway. Due to insufficient
evidence, I find it difficult to conclude on this point.

The effects on wages and prices (point g) act
through reduced demand pressure in markets, lowered income expectations, and increased emphasis in the bargaining process on keeping the number of jobs intact.
All these factors contribute to reduced growth in wages
and prices. Reduced inflation is a target in all OECD
countries and thus a clear-cut benefit. Reduced growth
in nominal and real wages is a question of changes in
relative income between different groups and the judgement of costs and benefits is thus linked more clearly to
what group it is seen from. Many governments have seen

75

this as a target in relation to improved competitiveness. From this point of view reduced wage growth would therefore be considered as a benefit.

The alternative to allowing unemployment to develop is to make policy responses to avoid this development (see alternative 2). According to point h) this leads to investment and operating costs associated with the given measures. If these costs replace the central and local government "operating costs" of unemployment (see the table above), the government costs of unemployment can be deducted from the costs of implementing measures. To the extent that these measures do not reach those unemployed who for instance get unemployment benefits the government's operating costs of unemployment cannot be deducted. Numerous measures are conceivable and it will lead us too far to go into them now. The costs of some measures will not exceed the operating costs of unemployment, whereas others are more expensive.

Point i) refers to the fact that most policy measures that are set up to combat unemployment lead to an immediate or future increase in production, compared with alternative 1. In some cases the increase may be negligible and in other cases it may be substantial. None of these measures are in themselves such that they are likely to lead to a reduction in production. This is on the condition that the measures do not entail crowding out of activities with higher productivity. Point j) refers to the point that if the policy measures of alternative 2 lead to lower unemployment, this will give benefits and costs related to the differences obtained on points a) - g) under the two alternatives.

Overall decision criterion

On the basis of what is said above, one could establish a decision criterion from the point of view of society as a whole:

If the net costs of point h) are considered to be smaller than the total net benefits of points i) and j), then policy measures should be taken. This may be specified further. It is mostly with respect to mobility, wages and prices that costs of reducing unemployment may arise. If measures are implemented specifically designed to avoid problems of reduced mobility or increased pressure on wages and prices, the net costs of point h) can be weighed directly against the more clear-cut benefits that then remain under points i) and j).

Part Two

<u>MAJOR POLICY ISSUES IN UNEMPLOYMENT
COMPENSATION POLICY AND THE ALTERNATIVE
USES OF UNEMPLOYMENT BENEFIT FUNDS</u>

III

MAJOR POLICY ISSUES IN UNEMPLOYMENT COMPENSATION

by
P. Roberti

I. OVERVIEW

The events of 1973-1974 triggered a sharp increase
in unemployment rates, in many Member countries, un-
equalled since before World War II. By early 1983 unemployment in the OECD area as a whole stood at about
33 million persons, or 9¼ per cent of the labour force.
This figure was 10 million higher than in 1980, three
times the level recorded in 1973, and 21 million above
the 1970 level. In 1983, in spite of some employment
recovery in North America, unemployment in OECD countries
is still growing and expected to continue to rise, reaching perhaps 9½ per cent in the first half of 1984, or
nearly 35 million people.(1)

All this, it is acknowledged, adds up to a loss of
potential output and an enormous waste of human resources
to which should be added individual sufferings (such as
psychic costs, stress, ill health and family disruption)
and social costs (such as crime and disorders) associated
with unemployment.(2)

In OECD Member countries, unemployment insurance and
(specific or general) assistance programmes are the usual
methods of safeguarding individuals against distress after
they become unemployed. Additionally, Member countries
rely on a varied mix of labour market policies and programmes aiming at preventing the condition of unemployment from arising, or at reducing both the number of jobless and the duration of unemployment.(3) Reliance on
cash expenditure, subsidies and labour market services
varies in different countries. However, only expenditure
on income maintenance can be readily documented.(4) In
1981 their cost averaged, for the OECD area as a whole,
about 1.2 per cent of GDP (over three times as much as in

1980), or $2\frac{3}{4}$ per cent of total public expenditure (as against 1 per cent in 1970) and just over 9 per cent of total transfers to households (as against 4.4 per cent in 1970).

The extremely high rates of unemployment and the long term growth in the full-employment unemployment rate has revealed the protection afforded by compensation systems to be inadequate. Since then, measures have been taken by governments, often on an ad hoc basis under the pressure of events, with the object of providing compensation for a growing number of unemployed over a longer period of time. Above all, these measures tended to ease the conditions of entitlement to benefits for the most vulnerable categories, to extend the period of payment of benefits and to maintain, if not increase, the real value of benefits. Also ad hoc programmes to provide training or jobs for specific groups (e.g. youths) or to encourage withdrawal from the labour market (e.g. early retirement schemes) have multiplied.(5)

Policies since the first oil shock have been characterised by two main features. First, they have been expensive, and this at the very time when unemployment was increasing rapidly, potential revenue was lost, and the financial positions of insurance funds and public sector budgets were worsening. Simulations by the OECD(6) of the additional costs resulting from higher unemployment and policy changes made in this period suggest that both were important causes of growth of expenditure on unemployment compensation. Although the sample of countries examined is small, the simulations also suggest that most of the additional costs came from policy changes in the early 1970s. Second, unemployment compensation schemes have been characterised by decreasing effectiveness in that they have not reached high risk groups such as first-time job seekers (e.g. youths), those re-entering the labour force (mainly females), the long-term unemployed and workers who have had multiple spells of unemployment and who are no longer entitled to benefit (the former) or have lost coverage (the latter). Also, unemployment compensation has severe limits in dealing with structural adjustment problems, disadvantaged groups (e.g. certain social groups and racial minorities) and economically depressed regional areas.

Inequities between covered and non-covered unemployed have thus been aggravated, effectiveness reduced and economic efficiency problems exacerbated as disposable income differentials between those at work and out of work have narrowed, and the reservation wage possibly affected.(7)

The economic and labour market situation since 1973-1974 has constituted a severe test for unemployment compensation programmes. It is likely that, because of

79

the automatic responsiveness of unemployment compensation programmes to the number of jobless, Member countries have been able to withstand the high levels of unemployment of the 1970s without serious social unrest. In itself, this is a clear measure of success and confirmation of the necessity of a public system of insurance against the hazards of unemployment in free-market economies. Nevertheless, the arguments mentioned above, coupled with shrinking public sector resources, rising programme costs and increasing deficits, suggest that this situation should not lead to complacency. Present and expected levels of unemployment also leave little room for optimism: increases in unemployment now expected for 1983 and 1984 will make the cost of unemployment compensation grow to levels (in real terms as well as in per cent of GDP) in many Member countries never reached before in the past 20 years,(8) thus compounding public sector budget difficulties and making it even more difficult to restrain public expenditure growth.

II. OBJECTIVES AND FUNCTIONS OF UNEMPLOYMENT COMPENSATION

The purpose of unemployment compensation systems in the majority of OECD Member countries is to alleviate the distress consequent on unemployment which is unpredictable, not to prevent unemployment nor to provide a minimum income welfare programme. This intention is clearly emphasized, for instance, in a 1937 pamphlet published by the United States Social Security Board:

"Unemployment compensation is a method of safeguarding individuals against distress for a short period of time after they become unemployed. It is designed to compensate only employable persons who are able and willing to work and who are unemployed through no fault of their own ... Unemployment compensation sets aside contributions during periods of employment and provides the individual with benefits as a legal right when he becomes unemployed. During the periods of prosperity a fund is built up, to be available for the payment of benefits in the periods when industry fails to maintain employment.

Unemployment compensation is not a system under which every unemployed person is assured of benefits for any and all unemployed time. It provides protection primarily for the persons who normally are steadily employed."(9)

Since the first oil crisis, measures have been taken to extend insurance coverage and periods of payment of benefits. Additionally, benefits have been inflation-

proofed and linked to average earnings. To the extent
that coverage has been extended to groups who have not
paid contributions to qualify for benefits (e.g. in
November 1975 in France, to young people who had completed their national service), or benefits have been
granted in excess or even without payment of contributions (e.g. the period of payment of benefits has been
extended from a short to a long or indefinite period,
such as in the case of older unemployed workers), unemployment compensation systems have clearly been
stretched beyond their original objectives.

Whether or not these additional tasks have over-
burdened existing systems and deflected them from their
original aims depends upon the answers to the following
two questions:

. Has the insurance principle, wherever it existed,
  and the financial soundness of programmes suffered because of recent policy changes?
. Which functions are proper to unemployment insurance programmes and should be safeguarded?
  Which, if any, should be transferred to other
  areas of government responsibility?

III. CURRENT CONCERN WITH UNEMPLOYMENT COMPENSATION
       SCHEMES: SOME OF THE ELEMENTS

The elements of the current concern with unemployment compensation are many and varied. Some of them are,
to some degree, impressionistic and reflect a revival
of the long-standing ideological debate on individual
and collective responsibility, benefit abuse, and work
incentives. To a certain extent they stem from a number
of empirical studies which have concluded that:

   i) it can be cheaper to provide jobs rather than
      pay income support;
  ii) replacement ratios are in various instances too
      high;
 iii) unemployment insurance influences the behaviour
      of the unemployed and the unemployment rate;
  iv) financing of unemployment insurance can affect
      the behaviour of firms in influencing an indi-
      vidual's probability of entering unemployment;
   v) unemployment insurance has consequences for
      the achievement of macro-economic policy
      objectives.

On balance, however, this empirical evidence is
often weak and much less decisive than some authors have
suggested. For example, a number of studies have recently been faulted on methodological grounds. This,

however, cannot be taken to mean that the true effect of unemployment benefit on economic performance has been overstated. Indeed, a recent study(10) has suggested that the use of appropriate estimating techniques and more suitable data may well lead to the conclusion that this effect is understated.

Additional factors which are perhaps more immediate causes of concern are concrete policy questions which are increasingly being asked as the current economic situation remains unsatisfactory. These include: are governments doing as much as they can to help the unemployed, particularly the long-term and structurally unemployed? Should money be spent differently (e.g. more on labour market services and less on cash payments)? Should manpower and income support measures be better integrated and tailored than at present to the varied needs of different groups of unemployed (e.g. those with employable skills, those with no recognised formal skill, the long-term unemployed, etc.)? Are equity criteria respected (e.g. taxation of benefits)? Can a new wave of ad hoc measures be taken (as at the time of the first oil crisis) to deal with the problems posed by the more recent substantial increases in unemployment and the persistence of high levels of unemployment, without putting in jeopardy the financial foundations of unemployment insurance systems?

There appears then to be a real and widespread, though clearly ill-defined, malaise caused by a multiplicity of factors all intermingled to such an extent that it is impossible to say what is causing what. The detailed examination of some current systems also suggests that this malaise is more vividly felt in some Member countries (e.g. Canada. the United Kingdom, the United States)(11) than in others.

IV. POLICY ISSUES

Any review of unemployment compensation systems involves examining political choices as well as functional or operational issues. Political choices (e.g. the level of benefits) pertain to national governments and are mostly amenable to solutions which seldom apply to different socio-economic and cultural contexts (e.g. benefits which are acceptable in one country may be too high or low in another). Functional and operational issues, on the other hand, transcend national boundaries and are common to countries whenever problems are common and institutional arrangements similar. As such, it is on these latter that comparisons of international experience can be most profitable.

Two broad groups of questions seem to embrace most
of today's policy issues in unemployment compensation
programmes:

a) issues arising because of dramatic changes in
labour markets since the mid-70s;
b) operational and design issues concerning equity
questions, minimisation of negative economic
effects and administration.

a) Policy issues arising because of dramatic changes in
labour markets

Economic, labour market and social changes since the
early 1970s and the anticipated characteristics of the
labour market in the 1980s have brought increased concern
with the targeting and cost-effectiveness of unemployment
compensation programmes. Three sets of questions seem
relevant in this respect:

i) Do changed labour market conditions require
changed policies towards unemployment compensation?
ii) Is the financing of job search as efficient for
structural unemployment as it is for cyclical
and frictional unemployment?
iii) Are unemployment compensation systems properly
tailored to the unemployed person's changing
needs?

i) Do changed labour market conditions require
changed policies towards unemployment
compensation?

Since most unemployment compensation systems were
implemented, profound changes have occurred in Member
countries, labour markets and socio-economic structures.
These include: faster growth in insured rather than
non-insured activities (e.g. manufacturing and services;
and, in general, wage and salary earners); higher female
activity rates and, linked but not fully accounted for
by this, proportion of multi-earner families; the unemployed no longer come from blue collar workers only, but
also from the educated and skilled labour force, etc.
In general, comparisons of the unemployed show an increasingly heterogeneous pool of unemployed.

The continuation of policies based on a vision of
a homogeneous group can rest only on the premise that
the group has remained homogeneous or that all unemployed
workers can get back into a job, independently of their
circumstances, if financially assisted. The unemployed
of the 1980s are, however, a more heterogeneous group
than the unemployed of the 1960s or of earlier periods:
the difficulties of first-time job seekers (mainly youths)

and labour market re-entrants (mainly females) are enhanced; the position of disadvantaged groups, racial minorities, aged workers and workers living in depressed areas has worsened; more stay unemployed for longer periods; and the problems of the long-term unemployed are growing in severity with more persons in this category. The question raised by these changes is:

. Can the premise of an homogeneous pool of unemployment still be maintained in the 1980s?

Additional issues include:

. Can the employment problems of young school leavers be equated with those of a worker who has lost his job in an expanding sector? Or should the problems of the latter be equated with those of a worker who has lost his job in a declining sector (e.g. textiles)?
. To what extent are needs of these different groups similar?
. Should an array of policies linking unemployment compensation and other labour market programmes be established so that the needs of different groups can be treated differently?
. Is the provision of labour market services more expensive than income transfers? What is known about the cost-effectiveness of transfers and services for specific groups?
. Additionally, to what extent can unemployment insurance schemes be used to provide labour market services (e.g. community work and training) as an alternative to cash payments? Can current systems accommodate this change and at what net cost for public sector budgets(12)?

ii) Is the financing of job search as efficient for structural unemployment as it is for cyclical and frictional unemployment?

The purpose of unemployment compensation is to provide protection primarily for the persons who normally are steadily employed. When, however, employment problems are due to major employment dislocations which create severe difficulties within particular labour markets or among particular skills, income support policies are not only powerless in getting people back into jobs but can act, by maintaining income, as a buffer which can inhibit and postpone industrial redeployment.

Adjustment is always easier when growth is buoyant, when it tends to have a "natural" solution. When unemployment rates are high, problems become particularly acute and policies to increase adaptability command priority.

Changes in taste, technology, relative prices or
increased international trade and related employment
consequences have assumed particular importance together
with the need for policy to smooth change and maximise
its benefits in the late 1970s and 1980s. The fundamental policy issue which arises is:

. If, in the case of displaced workers, income
   transfers are an ineffective policy tool, what
   alternative policies, given costs to governments,
   can be devised? e.g. should unemployment compensation insurances be used to pay for an internal
   mobility premium; temporary reduction in working
   hours; early retirement; voluntary quits premiums;
   lending and transferring of workers; retraining,
   redeployment of workers, etc., rather than paying
   people an income simply to search for a job for
   which they may be suitable but for which vacancies
   are extremely limited?

iii) <u>Are unemployment compensation systems properly
tailored to the unemployed person's changing
needs?</u>

In the previous section the problems of different
needs and demands of different unemployed were considered.
However, not only do needs differ among workers but they
tend to change as the duration of unemployment lengthens.
There are two reasons for this. First, the psychological
attitudes of an unemployed person change, with ups and
downs in morale and self-confidence. Second, economic
circumstances vary from a peak figure when unemployment
starts (e.g. redundancy pay money, payment in lieu of
notice, tax refund, holiday pay, etc., becomes payable
and savings are highest) to a fixed amount (or to amounts
which decline at given periods) which reaches a minimum
when unemployment insurance benefits are exhausted.

The current role of unemployment benefits is to
avoid any abrupt short-term decline in living standards.
In most Member countries, benefits are highest when unemployment begins and then tend to decline as the spell
lengthens (e.g. the earnings-related supplement is exhausted; eligibility to generally higher insurance
benefits ends and gradually lower unemployment assistance
benefits become payable). This practice comes from the
time unemployment compensation systems were first established for blue collar workers whose standards of living
were close to subsistence and wholly determined by the
wage which was earned. Three facts have, however, modified this situation. First, unemployment systems have
become generalised to most in the labour force: blue
collars as well as white collars, low and high income
earners. Second, unemployment compensation is no longer
the only means of income support over and above personal
savings.

Other forms of income maintenance are available to many workers who are made redundant, mainly in the form of substantial lump-sum payments. Third, standards of living are much higher than 30 or 40 years ago and there may be little justification now to pay benefits which are inversely related to the duration of unemployment.

The basic policy issue which needs consideration is whether paying flat-rate or declining benefits is the most effective policy to help unemployed workers throughout their spell of unemployment. What is hinted here is that at different stages in an individual's spell of unemployment he should perhaps qualify for more than just money or normal placement services. Issues which arise include:

. what is the appropriate short-, medium- and long-term benefit level and structure? (e.g. is the short-term level of benefit too high?).
. what integration or co-ordination of income-maintenance programmes (such as unemployment compensation, disability pension and early retirement schemes) and labour market services (e.g. guidance, placement, training and provision of temporary jobs) can be established to better tailor policy to the unemployed person's changing needs?

b) Operational and design issues

Since the mid-1970s, the design features of unemployment compensation systems have changed in various Member countries almost continuously: sometimes to strengthen one objective (e.g. income protection), sometimes another (e.g. labour market objectives). Some of those changes were taken under the pressure of events since the first oil shock. They have often resulted in a changed balance among various programmes aspects, especially the important balance between the income protection and labour market roles of unemployment compensation programmes.

In seeking the best direction for programme changes in the years ahead, three questions need consideration: what changes are required to

i) strengthen equity aspects;
ii) improve the contribution of unemployment compensation systems to labour market objectives;
iii) reduce complexity and improve administration.

i) Strengthening equity

Many policy discussions about adequacy of unemployment benefits and their potential work disincentives effects are based on simplified notions of replacement

ratios, most often defined as the ratio of average benefits to average earnings. Chapter IV shows a broad range
of estimated replacement ratios and argues the importance
of basing policy on appropriate replacement calculations.
One reason for this is because of the interactions of
tax/benefit schemes. In particular, it shows that "tax
savings" realised because of changes in average tax rates
due to income tax progressivity can constitute important
"additional" unemployment benefits especially at higher
earnings levels. Some of the issues which arise from an
integrated approach are:

. To what extent should unemployment benefit levels
  and durations take into account interactions
  between unemployment compensation schemes, other
  income maintenance schemes and taxes? Should not
  tax "savings" and refunds be treated as "negative"
  unemployment benefits? Can tax systems accommodate
  this possibility?
. Non-taxation of unemployment benefits can distort
  tax burdens of people in similar positions. On
  what equity grounds can this be justified?
. To ignore interactions between unemployment insurance and other income-support programmes may
  have significant work disincentive effects. First,
  net disposable income differentials between those
  at work and those out of work can be affected to
  such an extent that they become very small or
  even negative (i.e. income out of work is higher
  than at work)(13). Second, additional potential
  earners can be discouraged from entering the
  labour market if income-maintenance money is reduced or lost as a result (e.g. in the United
  Kingdom supplementary benefits paid to a family
  where the head is unemployed are reduced or lost
  if the wife becomes employed). This, in turn,
  raises the questions:
. Should the family or the individual be the relevant unit for the payment of unemployment benefits?
. Which systems do not discourage, or discourage
  loss, individual and family responsibility (i.e.
  self-support) when unemployment occurs?

ii) Improving the contribution of unemployment com-
    pensation systems to labour market objectives

    Two dilemmas have always beset policy-makers in the
determination of the level(s) of benefits. On the one
hand, there have been equity considerations, i.e. the
notions of "fair benefit" given contributions paid for
insurance schemes; and of "minimum adequate benefit"
for assistance programmes. On the other hand, there
have been well-known economic efficiency considerations,
i.e. the problems arising out of methods of financing and
benefit structures of unemployment insurance schemes
on labour markets.

Since the early 1970s the problem of the role of unemployment compensation in the recent rise in unemployment has been the subject of renewed research. The wealth of assertions about the labour market effects of unemployment compensation is substantial. A study prepared by B. Walsh for the OECD comes, however, to the following conclusions: "Whatever conclusions emerge in the longer run from the continuing academic debate about the importance of insurance-induced unemployment, the evidence so far suggests that this phenomenon does exist and should be taken into account in policy evaluations of the rise in officially measured unemployment during the 1970s. However, the evidence lends no support to the more lurid views of the importance of this phenomenon that have gained some popular credence."

Whatever the conclusions emerging from the debate recalled above there is, however, another and more important reason to increase the capacity of unemployment compensation systems to enhance labour market adjustments (in spite of the fact that encouraging search activity may well appear very unreal in today's slack labour markets). This is the employment dislocations anticipated in the years ahead and the need for significant labour market adjustments to take advantage of emerging opportunities. In this context it will be important to encourage human resources redeployment by strengthening work incentives and mobility. The relevant policy issue which arises is:

. what changes in compensation programmes can best contribute to labour market objectives without undermining their income protection functions? Implied in this is a reconsideration of a number of aspects, such as entrance requirements and benefit levels and durations, penalties for the work-shy and the voluntary unemployed, and impediments to labour mobility; as well as (an aspect discussed earlier on under a, ii), use of unemployment insurance funds for developmental or adjustment purposes.

iii) Reducing complexity and improving administration

Administration of unemployment compensation systems is cumbersome, complex and expensive compared to other forms of income maintenance. In some countries claimants have to deal with more than one office, which creates a flow of paper work and information which is not always essential. Payments are sometimes subject to considerable delays. Important errors can occur and appeal procedures are handled with difficulty. Systems are open to fraud.

These and other considerations have led some Member governments to examine thoroughly present administrative arrangements so as to identify any changes in procedure which would reduce administrative costs and/or improve the service to unemployed people. Relevant policy issues include:

. Are current methods of determining whether unemployed people are available for work satisfactory or, indeed, as indicated by at least one
country, are they really necessary under today's
conditions?

. What should be the relationship of unemployment
compensation systems to the Employment Service
operations of a country? Countries are divided
on the issue - some adhere to an integrated relationship, others favour separation as far as
possible(14).

. What improvements and developments are possible
in procedures for detection of fraud and error?

. Unless paid promptly, benefits do not serve the
purpose of helping people cope with unemployment
when they most need the money. Are promptness
standards in making payments and hearing appeals
satisfactory? What improvements are possible?

FOOTNOTES

1. See: OECD, The Challenge of Unemployment, Paris, 1982, and OECD Employment Outlook, Paris, September 1983.

2. For a more detailed discussion see Chapters I and II.

3. e.g. employment stabilization measures, subsidies paid to employers to maintain the work force of firms at unchanged levels or to hire new workers; early retire-ment practices. For a description of these policies in Member countries, see the OECD Inventory of Employment and Manpower Measures, Paris, various years.

4. The resource implications of public policies for the unemployed are discussed in detail in Chapters I and VII.

5. OECD, _Unemployment Compensation and Related Policy Measures_, Paris, 1979, and OECD, _Manpower and Employment Measures for Positive Adjustment_, mimeo, Paris, 1981.

6. See Chapter VII.

7. See Chapter IV.

8. Simulations carried out by the OECD using the equations estimated in Chapter VII suggest that the ratio of expenditure on unemployment compensation to GDP may rise to 2.2, 2.1, 0.8, 0.5 and 0.6 per cent in Canada, Germany, Italy, Japan and the United States respectively.

9. United States, Social Security Board, _Unemployment Compensation, What and Why_? Publication No. 14 (1937), p. 7.

10. V. Halberstadt, K.H. Haveman, B.L. Wolfe and K.P. Coudswaard, _Inefficiencies in Public Transfer Policies in Western Industrialised Democracies_, paper presented at the 38th Congress of the International Institute of Public Finance, Copenhagen, 23-26 August 1982, p. 26.

11. See the reviews completed by the Canadian Task Force on Unemployment Insurance (published in July 1981), the United States National Commission on Unemployment Compensation (published in July 1980) and, in the United Kingdom, by the Rayner scrutiny team (published in 1980).

12. See A.W. Dilnot and C.M. Morkis, "The Exchequer Costs of Unemployment", _Fiscal Studies_, 3 November 1981, pp. 10-19.

13. This point is especially debated in the United Kingdom (see R. Klein, _Inflation and Priorities_, Centre for Studies in Social Policies, London, 1975) and the United States (see U.S. General Accounting Office, _Report to the Congress_ of the U.S. by the Controller General, August 1974.

14. OECD, _The Public Employment Service in a changing Labour Market_, forthcoming.

MAJOR POLICY ISSUES IN UNEMPLOYMENT COMPENSATION

A comment
by
Arlene Holen*

Expenditures for unemployment compensation have risen sharply since 1970, inspiring a re-examination of existing schemes. In this re-examination, central issues should be considered in the light of empirical evidence.

Equity: Unemployment does not carry the hardship it did during the Great Depression, when the unemployed were largely male heads of households who had lost their jobs. The characteristics of the unemployed, including income and family structure, as well as reasons for un- employment should be taken into account in setting benefit levels and durations. The circumstances of tax- payers as well as the circumstances of recipients of compensation are relevant in determining overall benefit liberality.

Labour Market Effects: Research evidence indicates that income maintenance tends to retard labour market adjustment. Higher net replacement rates lead to longer spells of unemployment, and longer entitlement periods lead to longer durations of unemployment. Higher levels of compensation, however, may not necessarily lead to better jobs. Unemployment compensation has also been shown to reduce wages below the level that would have existed in its absence. This effect occurs because higher wages would otherwise be needed to attract workers to jobs with less stable employment patterns. The dis- incentive effects of unemployment compensation can be mitigated through more stringent screening for eligi- bility and careful application of the work test.

---

* These comments do not necessarily represent the views of the U.S. Department of Labor, or any official agency.

United States evidence shows that experience-rated UI
tax structures reduce layoffs, improve financial solvency
and provide an incentive for employers to help improve
UI administration.

   Income Support vs. Adjustment Assistance: Although
individuals increase their earnings by investing in
education and training, evidence on the effectiveness
of government-provided training is not conclusive.
Similarly, the effectiveness of other types of adjustment
programmes, such as relocation and job search, has not
been established.

LABOUR MARKET CONDITIONS: PAST TRENDS AND OUTLOOK;
POLICY ISSUES FOR UNEMPLOYMENT INSURANCE PROGRAMMES

A comment
by
Bertil Rehnberg

Economic developments in the industrialised world
during the past decade have been a great disappointment.
The rapid pace of post-war growth has decelerated, oil
crises and other factors have led to very extensive
problems of economic balance, and this in turn has restricted the scope available for policies of expansion
and job creation. The immediate outlook is a gloomy one.
One of the gravest features, of course, is rising youth
unemployment, which during 1983 is expected to reach
about 18 per cent in the OECD area. Another very grave
feature is the rise in long-term unemployment, which means
that more and more people are in danger of social
rejection. In some countries, more than a quarter of unemployed persons have been out of work for over a year.
Employment is not merely a source of livelihood. Mass
unemployment creates a breeding ground for despair and
criminality. Active measures for the prevention of unemployment are not only desirable but absolutely necessary. Acceptance of mass unemployment implies a social
attitude which I do not endorse.

It is hard at present to discern any clear signs of
developments in the OECD labour markets which can appre-
ciably reduce the level of unemployment. One vital
question concerns the future development of labour demand,
particularly in view of the likelihood of labour supply
continuing to increase as it has done hitherto. Although
the demand situation today is very much cyclically condi-
tioned, there are several factors pointing to slacker
demand even in the longer term. One such factor is the
low growth rate anticipated in large parts of the industrialised world. Another is technological development,
which will probably result in economic growth generating
less employment than before.

New techniques will provide opportunities to improve productivity by changing from labour-intensive to capital-intensive methods. Data techniques and micro-electronics can be expected to gain an entry in many sectors. In manufacturing industry, industrial robots, computerised design, numerically controlled machines, etc. are expected to become increasingly common. Computerisation can also be expected to spread in the service sector where a number of different functions and activities of a more or less routine nature are carried out. It is reasonable to suppose that changes will not be made as rapidly in the service sector as in competitive industry.

From the viewpoint of labour market policy, we can expect technical progress to result in lower levels of labour demand and at the same time in a growing need for mobility and adaptability within the labour force. The volume of labour demand is, of course, a question of general economic policy. On the other hand, one of the main tasks of labour market policy must be to respond to the demands for adjustment and adaptability entailed by structural changes. New production techniques are bound to increase the need for skilled labour and hence to require an increasing amount of retraining and further training.

In contrast to demands for greater mobility and adjustment, we have observed trends during the past decade towards greater inertia and a growing imbalance between job applicants and vacancies. There are several reasons for supposing that these tendencies will be accentuated. The workforce has gradually become a more fixed factor of production. Recruitment, induction and training costs connected with the hiring of new workers have risen, and companies therefore have an interest in persuading established labour to stay put.

Consequently the links between employers and employees are tending to become more durable. This adds to the importance of the internal labour markets. Mobility within undertakings is also facilitated by the fact that units of enterprise have become progressively larger. If more vacancies are filled through the internal market, fewer vacancies will come on to the external market, and those which do will tend to be for jobs which established employees are unwilling or unable to take. Vacancies will then become harder to fill and correspondingly prolonged. It is also conceivable that, if hiring decisions become more and more like investment decisions, this could result in more careful grading of job applicants in connection with recruitment, dividing up the workforce into competitive and non-competitive sections. This kind of segmentation of the labour market would mean less flexibility. The problem of unemployment would be shifted more and more on to disadvantaged groups, whose unemployment would then be made more persistent.

I have now pointed to a number of factors which seem likely to influence labour markets in the future. Very great demands will be made on labour market policy, and these demands will have to be met by means of various selective measures, focusing on special groups within the workforce on particular branches, localities or regions. Measures to facilitate adjustment within the labour market will be critically important. The really crucial question, of course, will be how to stimulate labour demand enough to bring it into balance with labour supply. One-sided concentration on unemployment compensation, of course, cannot provide the solution to unemployment problems which are not of a temporary nature.

As we in Sweden see it, active measures can save the unemployed individual and the community great economic and social expense. Heavy resources are therefore devoted to placement services with the aim of shortening vacancy and job-seeking periods. Computer techniques make it possible for vacancies and job seekers to be matched more rapidly. From the viewpoint of government finance, intensified placement activities are a cheaper alternative than unemployment compensation, training and job creation measures. Experimental schemes of intensified placement have shown that many of the people occupied by means of some measure of labour market policy could probably have found employment immediately if sufficient placement resources had been available.

Placement measures, however, are only appropriate for part of the job-seeking population. The remainder require work preparation measures of some kind. Often a job seeker needs to acquire vocational skills which are in demand. Together with education authorities, we have built up a comprehensive programme of education and re-training aimed among other things at enhancing the vocational mobility of the workforce. In September 1982 there were 34 700 persons undergoing labour market training, which is 0.8 per cent of the workforce. The financial benefits for trainees are normally on the same scale as unemployment insurance benefits.

Adjustment in the labour market depends partly on whether the job seeker is prepared to migrate to localities where suitable job opportunities are available. Migration generally imposes considerable strains on the individual household, while from the viewpoint of the community it implies considerable gains through the better utilisation of resources. This is the justification for tax-free relocation grants to migrants.

Job creation measures, usually in the form of what are known as relief work projects, are organised in order to counteract cyclical and seasonal fluctuations in labour demand and also to offset structural unemployment among individual groups. Relief work projects for young

persons have the dual purpose of providing employment
and of enabling the job seeker to acquire practical
experience which can facilitate placement in the open
market, as well as providing a foundation for vocational
decision and an incentive for training and education.
At present there are 35 400 persons employed on relief
work projects, and two-thirds of them are young persons.
These projects account for roughly a quarter of the
total budget for labour market policy.

Unemployment assistance also has an important part
to play primarily for what is expected to be short-term
unemployment or as financial support until more active
measures can be arranged for the applicant. It accounts
for about 20 per cent of the labour market policy budget.
In September 1982 there were some 110 000 persons receiving this assistance. By comparison, some 133 600 persons
were involved in the various policy programmes at the
same time. Excessive concentration on unemployment assistance during prolonged unemployment is more likely to
perpetuate than to counteract unemployment. In our
opinion periods of unemployment ought instead to be used
for meaningful vocational education, further training
and retraining or for temporary jobs where there is a
great need for active measures.

Our interpretation of unemployment assistance as
being a supplement to other active measures is also reflected in the fairly strict rules which apply concerning the suspension of benefits. Unemployed persons
declining an offer of employment, vocational education
or vocational rehabilitation can, if reported by the
employment office, be deprived of compensation for at
least six weeks.

This, of course, involves the difficult question
of striking a proper balance between the right of the
individual to a free choice of work and, on the other
hand, the duty of society to assume responsibility for
the individual. We have taken the view, however, that
society's view of what is a suitable measure ought in
some cases to override the opinions of the individual.
I believe that we can retain these rules as long as
there are alternatives to offer job seekers. Referral
to training and vocational rehabilitation is based on
the conviction that the individual concerned cannot obtain lasting employment unless measures of vocational
preparation are taken.

One of the points in the international debate concerns the risk of social security being abused and of
excessively high unemployment benefits themselves being
conducive to rising unemployment because job seekers
prefer to be out of work as long as they enjoy financial
security. In Sweden, questions of this kind have played
a very limited part in the debate on labour market policy.

This is because job seekers involved in active measures exceed those receiving passive financial assistance, and also because of the control measures built into our rules of compensation. Abuse can be restrained because employment offices regularly consider the possibility of active placement measures for the individual or else, for example, offer him or her vocational education. This makes it difficult for people to obtain compensation for any length of time if they are not genuinely available for employment or if they already have jobs, provided of course that the Employment Service has sensible alternatives to offer.

There are also economic arguments in favour of active measures rather than passive disbursements. In Sweden a person who is unemployed and belongs to an unemployment benefit fund receives financial assistance which falls short of regular earnings, but the differences are often very slight. Here is an example. A worker earning 6 500 Swedish kronor a month will incur a reduction of his annual available income by something between 3 and 10 per cent depending on whether he is unemployed for one or six months. In terms of government finance, the cost of an unemployed person is almost as great as his gross earnings, owing partly to the cost of unemployment benefit, most of which is financed by the State, and also due to the loss of income tax, consumer tax and employers' social security contributions.

Thus a long period of adjustment involving heavy unemployment affects national government finance both directly and indirectly, entailing expenditure which, without substantially impairing the budgetary balance, could instead have been devoted to measures aimed at finding him productive employment. In other words, unemployment assistance is not a cheap alternative. This must be all the more true in countries where unemployment benefits are more generous than in Sweden.

The budgetary consequences to the State of having a person employed on relief work in the service sector are also very small compared with the cost of unemployment assistance. A socio-economic estimate in which allowance was made for all revenues and expenditures for the community as a whole would, of course, provide further argument in favour of measures such as relief work projects.

Summing up, my aim here has been to indicate a number of central problems of labour market policy and the measures which are needed to deal with them. Above all I have been at pains to demonstrate and plead for various alternatives to the excessively one-sided use of unemployment assistance, which even in Sweden has its appointed but still very limited place.

IV

UNEMPLOYMENT COMPENSATION REPLACEMENT RATES*

by
P. Roberti

I. INTRODUCTION

Information on the weekly or monthly benefits of unemployment insurance beneficiaries and their weekly or monthly earnings when they are employed are important for judgements as to the adequacy of unemployment insurance benefits and their potential work disincentive effects.

The ratio between benefits received and earnings when employed is known as the replacement ratio or rate (RR). Most commonly RR has been measured by the ratio of average weekly benefits to average weekly wages. However, surveys of replacement-rate research reveal a broad range of estimated RRs. Thus, in the United States RR can be very high (above 60 per cent) or very low (20 per cent or below)(1). Much of this variance, though by no means all of it, is due to the different RR concepts used in the various studies.

Given the wide range of estimates which different RR concepts can generate, an obvious observation is that policy analyses and, perforce, recommendations need to be based on appropriate RR notion(s).

This chapter has three main objectives. The first (in Section II) is to examine RR definitions which can be established and have been used. The second (in Section III) is to examine issues of variability in actual RR distributions and their implications for policy purposes. The third (in Section IV) is to discuss the

* To calculate internationally comparable replacement rates, assistance is acknowledged from G. Busch (Austria and Germany), J. Byrne (United States), J. Lion (France), D. Pichaud (United Kingdom) and L. Vitali (Italy).

many problems encountered in making international RR comparisons and present (in Section V) a methodology to derive internationally comparable RR statistics.

II. REPLACEMENT RATE CONCEPT

A number of RR definitions are possible. First a distinction can be made between:

i) macro replacement ratios which are estimates of economy-wide RRs and most appropriate in analyses of the automatic stabilizing properties of unemployment insurance programmes(2);

ii) micro replacement ratios which provide a central tendency measure of the RR distribution and are relevant for discussion about adequacy and work disincentive issues as well as for inter-group and intra-group comparisons.(3)

Secondly, various (macro or micro) distinct but related RRs can be established. W. Vroman, in a comprehensive study for the U.S. National Commission on Unemployment Compensation, has identified the following:

a) gross statutory RR, i.e. benefits as determined by unemployment compensation norms as a percentage of base-period earnings;

b) gross narrow RR, i.e. the ratio of weekly benefits to average weekly wages;

c) net narrow RR, as (b) above but adjusted for income tax and social security contribution payments, loss of non-wage labour compensation and savings on work-related expenditure made by unemployed workers;

d) gross broad RR, i.e. the ratio between benefits received and the gross wage loss. Unlike (b) above, this ratio reflects the fraction of time the unemployed person does not collect benefits, e.g. because of the waiting period, payment lags, etc.;

e) net broad RR as (d) above but with the adjustments mentioned under (c);

f) gross total transfer RR which measures the part of total wage loss replaced by all income transfer payments (public and private) combined. Unemployment benefits in various countries constitute only one of a number of payments jobless workers can receive (for instance, unemployed persons can qualify for food stamps and AFDC in the United States; and for supplementary benefit and rates and rent rebates in the United Kingdom). This ratio catches the effects of programme overlapping making it possible to examine

tax/benefit systems interactions(4);
g) <u>net total transfer RR</u>, as above, but adjusted
as under (c).

In general, RR gross statutory is greater or equal
to RR gross narrow, which in turn is greater than RR
gross broad. Equally, RR net narrow is greater than RR
net broad. Also, net RRs are typically greater than
gross RRs and total transfer RRs, gross or net, tend to
show the highest values of all RRs.(5)

In the United States, 1980 macro and micro estimates
for various RR definitions prepared for the National
Commission on Unemployment Compensation have yielded the
results shown in Table 1. These show much lower RR
estimates than those suggested by earlier research, notably by M. Feldstein(6) which range from 0.60 to 0.70.
The explanation for this is that the <u>net wage loss</u> used
in previous RR studies provides an under-estimate of the
<u>net loss</u> which also includes work expenses, fringe bene-
fit losses and money wage growth.(7) The use of net wage
loss has, therefore, the effect of over-estimating RR
ratios.

Another interesting feature of the information displayed in Table 1 is the suggested wide variability in
individual RR experiences. This is the subject of the
next section.

III. REPLACEMENT RATIOS VARIANCE

The usefulness of measures of central tendency such
as RR is, is negatively correlated with dispersion in the
underlying distribution. The wider the dispersion of the
RR distribution, the less representative are mean or
average RR values of the diverse experiences of workers
under employment compensation programmes. Table 1
suggests a variability between 0.37 and 0.55 amongst
United States unemployed workers.(8) Comparable statistics are not available in other Member countries, but
somewhat similar information for the United Kingdom,(2)
France(3) and Canada(4) also suggest a wide dispersion
in jobless persons experiences. The source of this variability are manifold and vary in different Member
countries. Thus, in the United States, inter-state differences are marked. In the United Kingdom an important
source of variability is eligibility for supplementary
and other related benefits and for the earnings-related
supplement. In France, programmes eligibility and age
are main causes of variability. Other factors which affect RR variance include differences in eligibility provisions under public and private schemes, employment
history, weekly wage, tax treatment of benefits, duration
of unemployment and numbers of dependents.(12)

Table 1

ESTIMATED MACRO AND MICRO REPLACEMENT RATES
UNITED STATES, 1980

A. Macro RR			
	Experienced unemployed workers	State UI beneficiaries	Non-beneficiaries of State UI
Gross narrow	-	0.332	-
Gross broad	0.171	0.269	-
Net narrow	-	0.346	-
Net broad	0.177	0.280	-
Gross total	0.194	0.290	0.027
Net total	0.201	0.302	0.028

B. Micro RR				
	Replacement rate definition			
	Gross narrow	Gross broad	Net narrow	Net broad
Mean	0.408	0.347	0.457	0.391
Standard deviation	0.151	0.156	0.224	0.216
Coefficient of variation	0.370	0.450	0.490	0.552

Source: W. Vroman, State Replacement Rates in 1980, op.cit. pp. 174 and 176.

RR variability cannot, necessarily, be taken as an indicator of a negative feature of unemployment compensation programmes. Indeed, the opposite may be true and RR variability may just be a reflection of deliberate policy decisions, i.e. the political will to differentiate income support according to some notion of fairness (e.g. by income level, type of occupation, family circumstances, etc.). If this were so, variability would then be the product of the fact that unemployment has different effects on people in different circumstances, rather than of different treatment of "similar" workers. Knowledge of a statistic of dispersion and inequality does not, therefore, permit any judgement on the efficiency or effectiveness of UI systems. This can only depend upon:

   i) horizontal-type comparisons of UI beneficiaries,
       i.e. do workers with similar earnings end up
       with different RR ratios depending on, say,

occupation, sex, age, regularity of employment, etc.?

  ii) vertical-type of comparisons, i.e. are RR ratios for workers with similar circumstances but different earnings consistent with accepted equity principles?

iii) adequacy of benefit assessments (e.g. UI cover of essential expenditures),

  iv) a judgement of the overall effect of UI programmes upon income distribution curves and poverty counts (e.g. how many workers would be in poverty without UI schemes?).

IV. INTERNATIONAL COMPARISONS OF REPLACEMENT RATIOS: CONCEPTUAL PROBLEMS AND OPTIONS

The multiplicity of RR concepts and the variations of unemployment benefits for "typical" workers make international comparisons of unemployment benefits extremely difficult.

Comparative analyses of unemployment benefits can be found in a number of studies(13). Methodologies, however, tend to lack consistency and comparisons are limited. The most extensive comparative study so far carried out is the 1979 OECD study on Unemployment Compensation and Related Employment Policy Measures which presented gross and net narrow RR for six OECD Member countries at the average earnings level for (i) a single person and (ii) a married couple with two dependent children with wife not in paid employment. More recently, the Commission of the European Communities has produced similar figures for its ten Member countries.(14)

It is obvious from existing international comparisons that the problem of how best to compare ways in which the unemployed fare under different systems and in different countries has been tackled but not solved. It is also obvious that:

   i) the conceptual and methodological problems encountered in calculating internally comparable RR statistics, as well as the options which are possible, are numerous. This makes it clear that no matter which route is followed some massive simplifications always have to be made, or the scale of the task becomes altogether impractical;

  ii) the way ahead lies in the direction of developing past work so as to give a fuller representation of the impact of a wider range of policies on a wider range of personal circumstances.

The OECD has recently extended its earlier work. Comparable RR statistics for six countries (i.e. Austria, France, Germany, Italy, the United Kingdom and the United States) are shown in Section V. Warnings, however, are necessary as to the degree of comparability of the figures which have to be understood as being limited for the reasons which are explained in the rest of this Section.

A. Problems in Replacement Ratio Comparisons

There are many different ways, or dimensions, in which unemployment benefits differ between and within Member countries. These include:

A.1 Differences between countries

a) Regimes: most studies of unemployment benefits have, not surprisingly, concentrated on that part of social security known as "Unemployment Benefits". But in many countries there are other social security and income maintenance arrangements of relevance to unemployed people. In Britain, for example, means-tested social assistance in the form of Supplementary Benefits is a determining factor in net incomes of many of the unemployed - not the level of National Insurance Unemployment Benefit. Thus, to exclude social assistance schemes and concentrate only on schemes called unemployment benefits may seriously distort the position of certain Member countries.

Income tax and social security contributions clearly affect disposable incomes, and have been included in recent RR comparisons. Other income-related schemes (cash transfer as well as in-kind programmes) may also influence replacement ratios. Means-tested housing, education, health or other benefits may boost the command over resources of those with low gross incomes and thereby boost replacement ratios. Additionally, unemployed workers may qualify for special benefits and cash payments under a number of occupational or contractual arrangements. To ignore such benefits will, again, distort the true position.

Special occupational and contractual schemes aside, the relevant regimes may include:

    i) insurance-type unemployment benefits;
   ii) assistance-type benefits for which the unemployed may be eligible;
  iii) income tax and social security taxes;
   iv) means-tested benefits for which those in work and the unemployed may be eligible;
    v) compulsory and publicly financed lump-sum payment programmes such as redundancy pay.

b) <u>General rules</u>: existing studies have identified a number of key dimensions of variation in unemployment benefits. To those may be added a number that can be important. The relevant dimensions need little explanation and include:

   i) Coverage (e.g. by age and by occupation).
  ii) Duration (e.g. waiting days before benefit received, duration of benefit and "linking" rates for recurrent spells of unemployment).
 iii) Levels of benefits (benefit formula, method of calculation - e.g. if benefits are percentage of earnings, how are earnings defined? - and additions for spouse and children).
  iv) Taxability of benefits (e.g. differences arising from stage in tax year).
   v) Effects of earnings or other income during unemployment on benefits.

In addition, other general aspects, such as the frequency and method of payment, may be relevant, depending on the purpose of the comparisons.

c) <u>Special groups</u>: certain groups of people are in many countries treated for unemployment benefit purposes in a manner substantially different from the general system. In most instances, these would include (i) school-leavers, (ii) married women, (iii) older workers (usually aged 55 or over), and (iv) seasonal workers.

A.2. <u>Differences within countries</u>

Having characterised some of the dimensions by which unemployment benefits vary <u>between</u> countries, the dimensions on which benefits vary <u>within</u> countries are now reviewed. Five main types of variation may be distinguished:

   i) Variations by sex, marital status and age.
  ii) Variations by occupation due to differences in coverage or benefit formula.
 iii) Variations by earnings level. These may be linked to occupational variations but may be quite separate. Not only differences in the last, most recent, earnings may be relevant, but also differences over the entire employment history.
  iv) Regional and local variations. Most insurance-type unemployment benefits are part of national schemes; in some countries national schemes provide different rates for particular regions. Assistance-type schemes and means-tested benefits such as housing allowances are commonly administered on a regional basis with rules

and benefit rates unique to that region.

   v) Variations in take-up of benefits. Some social
      security benefits are not claimed by many of
      those eligible because of ignorance, because
      the benefit is not felt to be needed, because
      the cost of claiming in time, travel or stigma
      is too high, or for other reasons.

B. Factors Making it Difficult to Select a Common
   Comparative Basis

   In purely descriptive terms, unemployment benefits
can be compared in terms of numbers of beneficiaries,
total expenditure and other aggregate statistics. But
such comparisons are of little value if the purpose is
to compare the manner in which benefits affect people in
like circumstances in different countries. For this
purpose any comparison must, in essence, consist of an
analysis of how each country's policies would affect a
person with a defined set of characteristics. The
question then arises of what is the appropriate set of
characteristics. If the unemployed in all countries had
broadly similar characteristics - in terms of age,
marital status, family size, employment history and
previous earnings - then no problem would arise. This
is clearly not the case.(15)

   To illustrate the problem, imagine two countries, A
and B: in A, virtually all the unemployed are young
school-leavers whereas in B they are very largely elderly.
To make the comparison between A and B based on how
policies affect either the young or the elderly or (as a
compromise) the middle-aged would, in every case, be to
conceal the most relevant aspects of countries.

   The incidence of unemployment in, for example, Great
Britain, differs greatly between age groups, family sizes,
occupations and earnings levels. For Great Britain it is
possible to construct a number of reasonably typical
"model" unemployed individuals and families; the effect
of British policies on such typical unemployed people can
then be assessed. The problem is that the characteristics
that describe typical British unemployed people are not
necessarily typical of unemployed people from other
countries.

   A different problem arises in relation to earnings
levels. Two approaches might be adopted:

    i) To compare those at the same absolute level, in
       terms of real purchasing power.
   ii) To compare those at the same relative level -
       e.g. at average earnings in each country.

Since discussions on comparative replacement ratios focus on comparable earnings levels, (ii) is probably to be preferred. But it must be borne in mind that the same relative level in different countries represents very different real living standards.

C. Possibilities

It is obvious from the above that the task of calculating internationally comparable replacement ratios is extremely complex. If, for example, the impact of policies were analysed for 3 different age groups, 3 family sizes, 3 earnings levels, 3 occupational histories, and 3 unemployment patterns, this would involve, for any given country, assessing the impact of policies on 243 model families. Adding regional variations and regime differences, the scale of the task becomes altogether impractical for OECD countries. There is then no alternative but to make some massive simplification, as indeed was the case with the 1979 OECD Study(16) which was confined to two family sizes and one earnings level.

The most important question then is what simplifications result in the least distortion of a complex picture. An answer to this question may be attempted by specifying what seem to be the most serious limitations of highly simplified models. These would seem to be:

a) The concentration on insurance-type systems in countries where assistance-type systems may be of greater importance.
b) The exclusion of major income support systems, such as housing rebates.
c) The exclusion from analysis of school-leavers and married women, even though both these groups have seen rapid increases in unemployment.
d) The exclusion of long-term unemployed (who in many countries lose eligibility for insurance-type benefits).
e) Lack of information on what were the actual past earnings of the unemployed. This may mean that the model earnings chosen for comparison (e.g. average earnings) are far from typical of the unemployed.
f) Lack of information on actual receipt of benefits by the unemployed. This may mean 100 per cent take-up is being assumed when this may not be the case.

To remedy these limitations means in many cases either vast complexity or some very broad assumptions. For example, social assistance may vary locally, and within a locality, with housing or other personal circumstances; to allow for even a few "typical" cases multiplies the number of model families. For this reason such complex systems tend to be excluded from comparative studies. This may, however, introduce an important bias in intra-country comparison.

V. INTERNATIONAL COMPARISONS OF REPLACEMENT RATIOS: PRESENT DEVELOPMENTS IN OECD WORK

A. Methodology

The 1979 OECD Study on Unemployment Compensation and Related Employment Policy Measures covered six countries - Canada, France, Germany, Sweden, United Kingdom, and the United States - and data related to 1976 or earlier. The basic information collected and analysed concerned (a) the nature, date of application and date of the last fundamental reform of the basic legislation; (b) coverage of schemes; (c) eligibility conditions (e.g., period of insured employment prior to unemployment; obligations incumbent on the unemployed during the period of unemployment); (d) information about benefits (e.g., amount of benefit in current money or as a percentage of the previous wage; minimum and maximum benefits; supplements for dependants; duration of payment of benefits; waiting period for the payment of unemployment insurance; tax treatment); and (e) financing arrangements.

To compare benefits, gross and net replacement ratios were calculated at the average earnings level for (i) a single person and (ii) a married couple with two dependent children with wife not in paid employment. The calculation was based on the following steps:

1. Former gross average earnings.
2. Plus: family supplements in cash.
3. Former gross average income (= 1+2).
4. Less compulsory insurance contributions paid by the worker (as a percentage of gross wage).
5. Income tax (as a percentage of gross wage).
6. Former average disposable income $/3-(4+5)x1/$.
7. Unemployment benefits (as a percentage of former gross wage).
8. Plus family supplements or family allowances.
9. New gross average income (= 7+8).
10. Less taxes on unemployment benefits (as a percentage of these benefits).
11. New average disposable income (= 9-10).
12. Rate of gross income replacement (= 9/3).
13. Rate of disposable income replacement (= 11/6).

The earlier OECD work is extended in this study in three important dimensions. First, different earnings levels are considered: average, two-thirds average, and twice average earnings. Second, different durations of unemployment are considered: three months and six months. Third, the importance of fiscal factors (i.e. changes in income tax and social security contributions) as well as unemployment and other income-maintenance programmes is more explicitly examined (i.e. changes in income taxes and social security contributions) as replacement factors are examined.

Similar to the previous OECD study and recent work by the Commission of the European Communities, the basic data and methodology used - only modified to take into account spells of unemployment - are those developed by the Committee on Fiscal Affairs of the OECD to derive "reasonably comparable data for OECD countries to illustrate the impact of payments of direct taxes and social security contributions and receipt of certain cash transfers upon the disposable income of typical family units at different income levels".(17)

The statistics presented here have the same advantages and disadvantages as those of the "average production worker" who experiences no unemployment. To the extent, however, that certain means-tested and discretionary benefits available to the unemployed cannot be included in the calculations in any satisfactory way (for instance, rates and rent rebates), an additional limitation is introduced in the data. This kind of limitation is, however, inherent in all existing calculations and can only be overcome through extending the scope of this study to cover a wider spectrum of social policies implemented in Member countries.

With these limitations in mind, this study aims at comparing annual ex-post earnings profiles(18) and how these may be modified by unemployment. This will permit identification of the "net income loss" due to unemployment taking into account the interplay between tax/benefit schemes. Reference to ex-post net earnings profiles allows a number of the problems to be overcome, e.g. existence of waiting periods; the possible non-taxation at source of unemployment benefits; the concentration of tax refunds in a given week or month of the year; and delayed payment of benefits. It does not, however, overcome the problems relating to fringe benefits, money wage growth and work expenses.

The following assumptions are made to calculate "typical" unemployment insurance coverage:

a) The period referred to is the same as that used by the OECD Committee on Fiscal Affairs.
b) The spell of unemployment occurs during the last three months (e.g. during the last quarter) or half way through the fiscal year (e.g. during the third and fourth quarters of the fiscal year).

c) The worker remains unemployed for the rest of the tax year.
d) There is only one active member in each household and the family has no other source of income (to avoid complications arising from otherwise arbitrary earnings splittings or incomes combinations).
e) The worker has full eligibility to unemployment benefit.

The disposable resources calculations are based on the following steps (all data refer to annual figures):

1. Gross income for tax purposes (i.e. gross average earnings plus unemployment compensation money if applicable).
2. Income tax allowances (only standard tax reliefs are taken into account, expenditure-related reliefs are excluded).
3. Tax credits or cash transfers included in taxable income.
4. Taxable income (1-2+3).
5. Income tax liability.
6. Tax credits.
7. Income tax finally paid (5-6).
8. Employees' social security contributions (defined as compulsory levies paid to governments or their agencies).
9. Additional income tax paid to political sub-divisions.
10. Taxable payments by employee to governments (7+8+9).
11. Cash transfers from government.
12. Disposable resources (1-10+11).

Calling:

Y_g = gross earnings

IT = income tax

SSC = social security contributions

CT = any cash transfer from government not included in earnings

DY = disposable income

$\left.\begin{array}{l}\\\\\\\\\\\\\\\end{array}\right\}$ for workers with no unemployment experience

and

$UY_{g_i}^i$ = gross earnings
UIT^i = income tax
$USSC^i$ = social security contributions
UB^i = unemployment benefits
UCT^i = any cash transfer from government not included in earnings or UB
UDY^i = disposable income

} for workers suffering 3 or 6 months' unemployment

where $\underline{i}$ can be equal to 3 or 6.

The following statistics are shown in Tables 2 and 3 contained in this chapter:

Table 2:
$$\frac{UDY^i}{DY} = \frac{UY^i - UIT^i - USSC^i + UB + UCT^i}{Y_g - IT - SSC + CT}$$

which provides a measure of the difference in the disposable income of workers suffering unemployment or no unemployment.

Table 3: $UB^i/(Y_g - UY_g^i)$ which shows unemployment benefit as a percent of the gross wage loss;

$(IT-UIT^i)/(Y_g - UY_g^i)$ which shows the change in income tax due to unemployment as a percentage of the gross wage loss;

$(SSC-USSC)/(Y_g - UY_g^i)$ which shows the change in social security contributions due to unemployment as a percentage of the gross wage loss.

B. Results

The tables which follow use net disposable income figures for workers with no unemployment experience prepared by the Committee on Fiscal Affairs of the OECD. The methodology outlined in the earlier section has been employed to calculate net disposable income statistics for workers experiencing 3 or 6 months' unemployment. In all instances, the basic earnings data used are from the same source and are only modified to take into account the gross earnings loss.

The following statistics have been calculated:

a) Ratios between annual disposable incomes of "average production workers" (APW)(19) suffering 3 to 6 months' unemployment and no unemployment. These are shown in Table 2. These figures are close to a "net narrow transfer RR" concept and depict differences in disposable incomes for APWs with some unemployment and without unemployment. The higher the value of the ratio the smaller are differences in annual disposable incomes.

b) Unemployment and related benefits, and changes in income tax and social security contributions as a percentage of the total gross wage loss. These ratios are shown in Table 3. They portray the relative importance of different elements in covering income losses.

The following are some of the conclusions suggested by the statistics in Tables 2 and 3:

i) In the six countries examined, ratios between annual disposable incomes of APWs suffering some unemployment and APWs with no break in employment averaged between 98-78 per cent and 92-56 per cent in 1978, for 3 and 6 months' unemployment respectively(20). France and Germany generally appear as the countries with highest ratios. The loss of disposable income caused by 3 and 6 months' unemployment is generally limited and, with the exception of Italy and the United States, never exceeds one quarter of the gross income loss. Indeed, in France, APWs with two thirds of the average earnings who are made unemployed for economic reasons show, on an annual basis, no loss at all in disposable income. Rather, they end up somewhat better off because they do not pay social security contributions while unemployed.

ii) The proportion of income replaced tends to decline with the earnings level - at 200 per cent average earnings, the proportion of the wage loss covered is, on average, substantially below that at lower earnings levels. There are cases, however, where income tax "savings" affect this pattern and highest replacement occurs at the average earnings levels (e.g. in Austria, Germany and Italy).

iii) In spite of the higher unemployment benefits for larger family units, the proportion of total disposable income replaced is not always larger for single persons than for married couples with two children. The pattern is clear in the United Kingdom and Austria where the income loss of married couples with children is more fully covered than for single

111

Table 2

RATIOS OF ANNUAL DISPOSABLE INCOMES OF PRODUCTION WORKERS
EXPERIENCING 3 OR 6 MONTHS UNEMPLOYMENT (UDY_i) AND NO
UNEMPLOYMENT (DY), SELECTED OECD COUNTRIES, 1978

Single and married workers, earnings equal to 66,
100 and 200 per cent of average production worker earnings.

Unemployment (months)	Earnings level (% of average)	Replacement ratio(a) UDY_i/DY	
		single person	married 2 children
AUSTRIA, 1978			
3	66	91.3	95.6
3	100	91.5	95.1
3	200	85.4	88.1
6	66	79.8	87.9
6	100	82.1	88.8
6	200	69.8	75.3
GERMANY, 1978			
3	66	93.0	94.2
3	100	96.3	94.0
3	200	92.7	92.2
6	66	86.7	88.8
6	100	88.5	88.3
6	200	84.0	81.2
ITALY, 1978 (Unemployment benefit only)(b)			
3	66	77.8	77.2
3	100	77.9	85.0
3	200	78.4	79.2
6	66	55.2	59.4
6	100	54.7	61.8
6	200	55.4	57.1
UNITED KINGDOM, 1978/1979			
3	66	92.8	99.1
3	100	88.7	94.8
3	200	82.9	86.8
6	66	85.1	96.0
6	100	78.1	90.3
6	200	66.4	74.5
UNITED KINGDOM, 1980/81			
3	66	90.2	96.5
3	100	86.7	91.8
3	200	81.7	84.8
6	66	81.2	93.9
6	100	73.8	85.3
6	200	60.1	67.4

Unemployment (months)	Earnings level (% of average)	Replacement ratio(a) UDY_i/DY single person	married 2 children
UNITED STATES, 1978			
3	66	95.41	n.a.
3	100	89.60	94.74
3	200	87.42	87.66
6	66	92.12	n.a.
6	100	79.87	87.48
6	200	72.04	73.52

Unemployment (months)	Income level (% of average)	Replacement ratio(a) UDY_i/DY single person economic reasons (c)	non-economic reasons	married, 2 children economic reasons (c)	non-economic reasons
FRANCE, 1978					
3	66	100.9	93.7	100.1	95.3
3	100	101.9	92.0	96.4	93.1
3	200	100.1	90.0	99.7	90.2
6	66	101.8	85.1	100.2	88.9
6	100	101.8	81.9	98.8	83.9
6	200	100.1	78.5	99.4	78.5
FRANCE, 1980					
3	66	100.7	95.8	100.2	96.2
3	100	98.9	93.0	98.9	92.9
3	200	96.6	90.8	96.6	90.4
6	66	101.4	91.7	101.4	92.3
6	100	96.6	86.0	96.6	85.9
6	200	92.1	81.7	91.7	80.7

a) Figures are close to a "net narrow transfer RR". See Section II.

b) Higher benefits are payable to construction workers (80 per cent of their earnings) and to workers in industry and commerce covered by the "cassa integrazione salari" scheme.

c) Unemployed workers have to fulfil a number of conditions to receive the "allocation supplémentaire d'attente" introduced on 31st December 1974. This is paid to workers who lose their job for reasons which are recognised as "economic" (i.e. conjunctural and structural) by competent administrative authority.

Table 3

PER CENT OF GROSS INCOME LOSS COVERED BY UNEMPLOYMENT BENEFIT AND BY CHANGES
IN INCOME TAX AND SOCIAL SECURITY CONTRIBUTION DUES

	Earnings level (% of average earnings)	Single worker		Married worker with 2 children	
		unemployment		unemployment	
		3 months	6 months	3 months	6 months
GERMANY, 1978					
1. Unemployment benefit	66	47.6	47.6	51.6	51.6
	100	43.2	43.2	48.9	48.9
	200	28.9	28.9	35.7	35.7
2. Income tax "savings"	66	16.8	17.6	12.7	13.5
	100	31.7	26.0	17.0	17.2
	200	42.7	41.1	30.4	25.7
3. "Saved" social security contributions	66	15.4	15.5	15.7	15.7
	100	15.2	15.6	15.5	15.6
	200	11.1	11.1	11.1	11.1
AUSTRIA, 1978					
1. Unemployment benefit	66	41.1	41.1	53.8	53.8
	100	40.3	40.3	48.7	48.7
	200	21.5	21.5	25.7	25.7
2. Income tax "savings"	66	17.7	13.2	14.5	7.3
	100	20.5	19.4	19.7	17.2
	200	27.9	25.7	27.1	24.9
3. "Saved" social security contributions	66	13.3	13.3	13.3	13.3
	100	13.2	13.2	13.2	13.2
	200	8.8	9.5	8.8	9.5
ITALY, 1978					
1. Unemployment benefit	66	7.4	7.6	16.5	17.1
	100	4.9	5.0	10.9	11.3
	200	2.4	2.5	5.4	5.6
2. Income tax "savings"	66	8.5	7.5	6.0	4.9
	100	14.0	11.9	12.3	10.2
	200	23.5	21.5	22.6	20.7
3. "Saved" social security contributions	66	7.8	7.8	7.8	7.8
	100	7.8	7.8	7.8	7.8
	200	7.8	7.8	7.8	7.8
FRANCE, 1980					
(a) Non-economic reasons					
1. Unemployment benefit	66	71.7	71.7	71.7	71.7
	100	60.1	60.1	60.1	60.1
	200	51.0	51.0	51.0	51.0
2. Income tax "savings"	66	1.7	1.7	-	-
	100	4.9	4.8	-	-
	200	10.9	10.9	4.4	4.3
3. "Saved" social security contributions	66	12.8	12.8	12.8	12.8
	100	12.8	12.8	12.8	12.8
	200	11.1	12.8	11.1	12.8
(b) Economic reasons					
1. Unemployment benefit	66	90.0	90.0	90.0	90.0
	100	81.2	80.6	81.2	80.6
	200	75.0	72.5	75.0	72.5
2. Income tax "savings"	66	-	-	-	-
	100	0.7	1.2	-	-
	200	4.0	4.7	1.9	1.9
3. "Saved" social security contributions	66	12.8	12.8	12.8	12.8
	100	12.8	12.8	12.8	12.8
	200	11.1	11.1	11.1	11.1

	Earnings level (% of average earnings)	Single worker		Married worker with 2 children	
		unemployment		unemployment	
		3 months	6 months	3 months	6 months
UNITED KINGDOM, 1980					
1. Unemployment benefit	66	34.6	35.1	50.5	54.4
	100	25.9	26.6	36.4	39.3
	200	14.9	15.4	20.2	21.8
2. Income tax "savings"	66	30.0	30.0	30.0	27.8
	100	30.0	30.0	30.0	30.0
	200	30.0	30.0	30.0	30.0
3. "Saved" social security contributions	66	6.7	6.7	6.7	6.7
	100	6.7	6.7	6.7	6.7
	200	4.8	4.8	4.8	4.8
UNITED STATES, 1978					
1. Unemployment benefit	66	-	-	-	-
	100	39.0	39.0	51.4	51.4
	200	19.5	19.5	25.7	25.7
2. Income tax "savings"	66	-	-	-	-
	100	17.3	18.3	18.7	15.5
	200	36.7	35.0	26.7	24.0
3. "Saved" social security contributions	66	-	-	-	-
	100	6.0	6.0	6.0	6.0
	200	4.1	4.1	4.1	4.1

workers. France also fits with this pattern,
especially in the case of unemployment due to
"economic reasons", but differences are less
marked. Small differences between single persons and married couples with two children are
also observed in the United States. In Germany,
the income losses of single workers appear to
be more fully replaced than those of married
couples with children.

iv) Unemployment benefits, on average, constitute
the most important element of income losses
replacement. "Savings" in income taxes and
social security contributions, however, are
also very important, especially for higher
income groups and single workers. Thus, as
shown by statistics in Table 3, at 200 per cent
average earnings, unemployment benefits in
Germany represent about 29 per cent of the
income loss while "saved" taxes constitute
43 per cent of it. Comparable figures for the
other countries are, respectively, 22 and
28 per cent in Austria; 3 and 24 per cent in
Italy; 15 and 30 per cent in the United Kingdom;
20 and 37 per cent in the United States. Only
in France do "tax savings" replace a low proportion of the wage loss.

VI. CONCLUSIONS

Replacement ratios have been established in recent
research on a number of different notions which have
yielded a broad range of results. Most often, crude
average RR statistics (the ratio of average benefit to
average earnings) have been established and then applied
to derive efficiency or equity judgements, as well as to
propose policy changes in current systems of compensating
unemployment.

This approach has, however, shown two main shortcomings. The first is that average RRs such as these
hide important variance in the diverse experience of
workers under unemployment compensation programmes (see
the discussion in Section III). The second is that not
all changes in the net disposable income equation of
unemployed workers are equally well depicted; notably,
regarding income tax and social security contributions,
where important "savings" can occur, especially at higher
income levels. If figures are to have any relevance for
policy discussions, it is therefore necessary that more
diversified situations are considered and that a more
integrated approach is used to take into account tax/
benefits interrelationships and multiplicity of income
support schemes. This is especially so when international

comparisons are made, because of different reliance in different Member countries upon different policy instruments (see the discussion in Section IV).

The RR statistics calculated in Section V have confirmed the need for this more diversified and broader approach. When this is done four general conclusions seem to stand out:

- statutory replacement ratios do not provide a good proxy for actual replacement ratios;
- differences between replacement ratios taking or not taking into account tax/benefit relationships are important;
- given income tax progressivity, tax "savings" can be as important if not more important than unemployment benefits, especially at higher earnings levels;
- commonly applied equity criteria may be violated once the interplay between taxes and benefits is considered, e.g. RR for married couples with children may be below those for single people.

The methodology developed in this report, while representing a move in the direction of more comprehensive and diversified RRs, is not without limitations (see Section IV). Its critical examination should permit refinement and thus make a further move towards developing RR which is more equitable for policy purposes.

FOOTNOTES

1. W. Vroman, "State Replacement Rates in 1980", in Unemployment Compensation: Studies and Research, National Commission on Unemployment Compensation, US Government Printing Office, Washington, July 1981, Vol. 1, pp. 170-172.

2. This is equal to the ratio of the sum of all benefits ($\sum_i B_i$) received by unemployed workers and the sum of all economic losses ($\sum_i L_i$) suffered by them, i.e.

$$\text{RR Macro} = \sum_i B_i / \sum_i L_i$$

3. This is equal to the average of individual replacement ratios (rm_i). If B_i is the benefit paid to the ith unemployed worker, and L_i are his losses then:

$$RR\ Micro = \frac{1}{n}\ rm_i = \frac{1}{n} \sum B_i/L_i$$

4. The importance of forms of income support other than unemployment compensation is recognised in a number of studies. See, among others, W.W. Daniels, The Unemployed Flow, Stage 1, Interim Report, Policy Studies Institute, London, 1981, Chapter III.21, and Survey of Unemployment Insurance Claimants, Canada Employment and Immigration Commission, Ottawa, 1976.

5. The inequality between RR gross narrow and RR gross broad is mainly a function of the times when job-less workers collect benefits - the gap between the two measures tending to widen the shorter the duration of spells. The relationship between gross and net RRs is explained by the importance of taxes; the generally higher values of total transfer RRs by that of income transfer programmes. For a more detailed discussion of these relationships, see. W. Vroman, op.cit. pp. 169-170.

6. M. Feldstein, "Unemployment Compensation: Adverse Incentives and Distributional Anomalies". National Tax Journal, June 1974, pp. 231-44

7. The latter is especially important for workers whose age-earnings profiles slope upward very steeply, e.g. youths. High inflation also affects it. On the definition of "wage" for RR calculation purposes, see J.M. Becker, Unemployment Benefits. Should there be a Compulsory Federal Standard?, American Enterprise Institute in Public Policy Research, Washington D.C., 1980.

8. See also, for the United States, U.S. Department of Labor, The Adequacy of Unemployment Insurance Benefits: An Analysis of Weekly Benefits Relative to Pre-unemployment Expenditure Levels, Washington, 1978; and J.M. Becker, Unemployment Benefits. Should there be a Compulsory Federal Standard? op.cit.

9. See Working Mates No. 2, 3, 4 and 8 reporting research results of work on unemployment carried out by A.B. Atkinson, J. Gomulka, J. Micklewright and M. Rau at the London School of Economics and Political Science.

10. See CERC, Les revenus des Français, 3e rapport, Albatros, Paris, 1981, p. 30; and Liaisons sociales, No. 5167, 13 April 1982.

11. See Taxation Statistics, 1974-1977 Editions, Table 2, Revenue Canada Taxation.

12. Interactions between all these factors are complex and can result in important differences amongst unemployed persons in "horizontally comparable" situations (i.e. with similar earnings levels but different circumstances). A number of studies have increasingly been devoted to exploring RR differences for a multiplicity of representative households. See CERC, Les revenus des Français, op.cit., pp. 382-383; "Einkommenseinbussen bei Arbeitslosigkeit", Deutsches Institut für Wirtschaftsforschung Wochenbericht 45/81; and the Columbia University School of Social Work Cross-National Studies directed by A.J. Kahn and S.B. Kamerman.

13. These include the great deal of descriptive information, though no comparative analysis, brought together by the United States Social Security Administration (see Social Security Program throughout the World, Washington, D.C., periodical); P.R. Kaim-Caudle, Comparative Social Policy and Social Security, Martin Robertson, London, 1973; S.J. Blaustein and I. Craig, An International Review of Unemployment Insurance Schemes, W.E. Upjohn Institute, Kalamazoo, 1977; A. Mittelstädt, "Unemployment Benefits and Related Payments in Seven Major Countries" Occasional Studies, OECD Economic Outlook, July 1975; and OECD, Unemployment Compensation and Related Employment Policy Measures, Paris, 1979.

14. See also the very interesting report recently published in France by CERC on "L'indemnisation du chômage en France et à l'étranger", document n° 62, Paris, 1982.

15. See OECD, The Challenge of Unemployment. A Report to Labour Ministers, Paris, 1982, Chapter II

16. OECD, Unemployment Compensation and Related Policy Measures, op.cit.

17. See OECD, The Tax/Benefit Position of Selected Income Groups 1974-79, Paris, 1981 and OECD, The 1980 Tax Benefit Position of a Typical Worker in OECD Member Countries, Paris, 1981.

18. The annual cash flow position of a worker may differ from his ex-post position because the timing of the receipt of benefits and the payment of taxes will vary over the year and as between years. The study is intended to compare the ex-post position of a worker initially in employment who becomes unemployed for a certain period.

19. Defined as "male full-time manual worker in the manufacturing industry whose earnings are equal to the average earnings of such workers". See OECD, The Tax/ Benefit Position of Selected Income Groups in OECD Member Countries, Paris, 1980, p. 13.

20. In interpreting these figures, it should be borne in mind that lower bound values for these ratios cannot fall below 75 and 50 per cent for 3 and 6 months' unemployment respectively. This is because, assuming a constant monthly wage, a three month wage loss amounts to 25 per cent of the annual wage figure and a six month loss to 50 per cent of that figure.

UNEMPLOYMENT COMPENSATION REPLACEMENT
RATES - A UNITED KINGDOM VIEW

A comment
by
C.H. Smee*

The increase in unemployment in the United Kingdom in the last decade has been accompanied by a growth of interest in the relationship between the incomes of unemployed people when in work and when out of work. The interest has been fuelled by concerns about both benefit adequacy and work incentives, though the latter issue has tended to receive more public attention.

Until recently serious discussion, particularly of work incentives, has been hindered by the lack of hard facts. Arguments about replacement ratios have had to rely either on comparisons of the positions of hypothetical family types or on the actual ratios derived from small or biased samples. To provide a firmer basis for policy development, in 1978 the Department of Health and Social Security (DHSS) launched a Cohort Study of unemployed men. A nationally representative sample of just over 2000 men who registered as unemployed in autumn 1978 were interviewed three times in the following year. Data on their incomes prior to unemployment, while unemployed and in most cases on return to work, were collected from the men themselves and from DHSS benefit records. This note draws on the experience gained from that research(1) and from the wider United Kingdom discussions of replacement ratios.

The replacement rate concept

As Chapter IV states, there are a large number of possible definitions of replacement rates. Indeed, in Britain the number of different definitions in use has itself been a major cause of confusion. Conclusions drawn

---

* The views expressed are those of the author alone and in no way commit his Department or the British Government.

from one set of definitions can frequently be rebutted by resort to a different concept. Five particular issues are worth mentioning.

First there has been controversy about the value of hypothetical replacement rates for "typical" family types. These have been heavily used in time-series analysis. Prior to the generation of information on actual incomes in and out of work there was no effective alternative. But now that there is hard information on the income and family characteristics of the unemployed, it can be seen that the "typical" family types used were often in no sense typical of the unemployed; for example, the frequently quoted "unemployed married man with two children" represents only 9 per cent of unemployed men. Moreover, some of the assumptions used in calculating the hypothetical ratios for each family type have also been called into question. The earnings of the unemployed have turned out to be lower than expected and the take-up of some income-tested in-work benefits appears to be closer to 0 per cent than to the 100 per cent optimistically assumed. The conclusion to be drawn is not that there is no role for theoretical replacement ratios, but that their contribution is limited and they need to be handled with great care.

Second, in judging the adequacy of benefits and in considering work incentives there is the question of what income unit to use. When unemployment insurance was the predominant form of unemployment compensation and most of the unemployed lived in families (or households) with no other important sources of income, the simple benefit/ earnings ratio for the individual appeared the appropriate concept. But with the growth in reliance on income-tested unemployment benefits - a development that does not appear to be unique to the United Kingdom - and the growth of two- and three-earner households, there are strong arguments for using the family or the household as the income unit. Official British analyses tend to be based on the family unit (defined as the unemployed person and, where applicable, the spouse and dependent children) though because of the growth of unemployment among young people and married women, a household-unit analysis can give a very different picture. The choice between the various income units is hindered by the lack of information on the extent to which decisions about labour supply are made on an individual, family, or household basis and on the extent of income sharing within households.

Thirdly, there are a number of particular problems in choosing the appropriate replacement rate for examining work incentive questions. The standard theoretical approach based on long-run optimisation would point to something close to Vroman's "net total transfer replacement ratio". But implicit in this approach is the assumption that most unemployed people enjoy a degree of certainty (e.g. about the wage offers they will receive), knowledge (e.g. about benefit eligibility and tax repercussions) and computational skills, that in practice is probably found among very few of the population. We clearly need to know more about how unemployed people perceive the choices open to them. There is limited British evidence that many may think primarily in terms of the relationship between unemployment benefits and net earnings (i.e. Vroman's "net narrow replacement ratio"). There is certainly good evidence that when unemployment benefits were tax-free many people failed to claim the tax rebates due to them; and that currently the take-up of some income-tested in-work benefits is low. It is not therefore self-evident that the development of more sophisticated and complex replacement rates will necessarily increase understanding of work disincentive effects, particularly if these concepts bear little relation to how the unemployed perceive the world.

A fourth but related question is whether previous usual earnings should form the main element in the denominator of the replacement ratio. In periods of deep recession and large structural unemployment, as at present, it is arguable that replacement ratios based on previous wages will be systematically biased downwards. But if previous wages are not a good guide to the wage offers open to many of the unemployed, what should we put in their place?

Finally, there is a school of thought in Britain that believes replacement ratios for the unemployed should be complemented by the estimation of similar (hypothetical) ratios for people in employment. Applied to household survey data, these provide an indication of work incentives for the whole working population that may be relevant for modelling the inflow into unemployment or for monitoring the motivation of those remaining in work. Have other countries developed such wider measures?

Variations in replacement ratios

In Britain there have been a number of attempts to represent replacement ratios by averages or means (Figure 1 shows one of the more defensible exercises) but because of the dispersion in the underlying distribution, such exercises have limited value. The variation in replacement rates in Britain is very large. Analyses from the DHSS Cohort Study illustrate some of the main sources of variability. Replacement ratios(2) vary by:

a) Family type (Figure 2)
   Because unemployment insurance benefits and, more markedly, social assistance benefits are related to family responsibilities, replacement ratios rise steeply with size of family;

123

b) <u>Earnings level</u> (Figure 3)
   The earnings-related element in insurance benefits
   was relatively small in 1978 (it has since been
   abolished) and social assistance benefits are not
   related to earnings levels. As a consequence
   replacement rates fall rapidly as earnings rise;

c) <u>Benefit type</u> (Figure 4)
   The main feature of replacement ratios by benefit
   type is not the differences but the similarity of
   the patterns. Recipients of supplementary allowance, the main social assistance benefit for the
   unemployed, experience family income replacement
   rates very close to those of men receiving unemployment insurance benefits only. Is this a
   feature unique to the United Kingdom?

d) <u>Presence of working wives</u> (Figure 5)
   On a family income unit basis, presence of other
   sources of family income, such as working wives,
   will tend to raise replacement rates. Interest-
   ingly, while the two-earner married couple is now
   the norm for the working population as a whole,
   this is still far from true for the unemployed.
   Only about one-third of the wives of unemployed
   married men report any earnings. Is this
   phenomenon found elsewhere?

Replacement ratios do not only vary markedly between
unemployed people: they can also vary significantly for
the same person through time. One cause of such variation
is the movement between benefit regimes as unemployment
spells lengthen. Because of the similarity in the levels
of assistance benefits and insurance benefits and the
relatively small proportion of unemployed people with
other major source of income, for most people in Britain
benefit levels probably do not vary greatly with unemployment durations. (Again one wonders whether this
feature is widely found.) A more important source of
variation over time is the difference between earnings
levels prior to unemployment and post-unemployment.
Figure 6 shows that in Britain pre-spell replacement
ratios are a relatively poor guide to post-spell replacement rates. Just over a third of our sample of men had
ratios that fell within the same 25 per cent band under
both definitions.

Political and policy interest in Britain has tended
to concentrate on the unemployed people at the extremes
of the replacement ratio distribution. Averages are no
guide to the numbers of the unemployed with limited
financial incentives to work - commonly equated with
weekly replacement rates of 80 per cent or more - or to
the numbers experiencing very substantial falls in their
income (for example replacement rates of 50 per cent <u>or</u>
<u>less</u>). As the figures previously referred to show, in

124

Britain rather large numbers of the unemployed fall at
both extremes. One of the main values of collecting
information on actual family incomes in and out of work
is the light shed on the proximate causes of the extreme
ratios. The evidence of the DHSS Cohort Study is that
the main reasons for the high replacement ratios are
unemployment benefits that are high in relation to previous earnings, increases in other sources of family
income after unemployment begins, and low take-up of the
main in-work income-tested benefits.

Interpretation of replacement rates

Chapter IV has little to say about the interpretation
of replacement ratios. But the policy implications of
any particular level or distribution of ratios are not
self-evident.

If the concern is with benefit adequacy, the dis-
covery of significant numbers of high replacement rates
might be interpreted as implying that benefit levels are
more than adequate. An alternative interpretation would
be that incomes in work are inadequate either because of
low wages or because of a failure to claim in-work benefits. It requires judgement and detailed information on
actual cases to distinguish between these interpretations.

Again, if the interest is in potential work disincentives, the significance attached to high replacement
ratios will (or should) depend on the evidence linking
replacement ratios with labour market behaviour. Unemployment durations are dependent on many other factors
apart from replacement ratios. Indeed there is some
recent and highly tentative evidence(3) from British
research that there is a smaller association between
benefit levels and unemployment durations among those
types of men most likely to have high replacement rates -
middle-aged men with dependent children - than among the
men most likely to experience low replacement ratios -
young single men. Thus, it is by no means certain that
reducing benefits across the board would be the most
effective way of speeding up job search. A further consideration is that the importance of replacement ratios
will probably vary with the state of the labour market.
The latest research evidence from Britain is consistent
with the assumption that as unemployment rises there is
a decline in the responsiveness of unemployment durations
to benefit levels.

The OECD replacement ratios

The OECD is to be commended for the progress it has
made in placing replacement ratios on an internationally
comparable basis. Compared with the earlier OECD work

the use of a wider range of earnings levels and of unemployment durations and the incorporation of fiscal effects
are all obvious advances. The use of an annual accounting
period does have the presentational disadvantage of making
the replacement ratios appear extraordinarily high - certainly higher than as perceived by the unemployed who are
more likely to think in terms of weekly or monthly
accounting periods - but this is probably an unavoidable
cost of incorporating fiscal effects.

   With some effort it would presumably be possible
further to refine the replacement ratios, for example by
incorporating housing benefits (which are important in
Britain and in some other OECD countries). But given the
emphasis in this note on the variability of replacement
ratios, a potentially more useful development might be to
collect information that would place the current ratios in
context and provide some indication of their representativeness. The kinds of questions that come to mind are:

   i) What proportion of the unemployed in country X
      actually receive the unemployment benefits
      used in calculating the illustrative replace-
      ment ratios?
  ii) For the unemployed receiving different kinds of
      benefits (or no benefits) how do replacement
      ratios compare?
 iii) What are the family characteristics of the
      unemployed in country X? What proportions are
      single people or married with two children and
      without working spouses?
  iv) What are the earnings levels of people experi-
      encing unemployment?

   With unemployment at post-war record levels and
large proportions of the unemployed exhausting unemployment insurance benefits, the first two of these questions
may be the most important. In Britain more than half of
unemployed benefit-claimants now receive social assistance, with or without unemployment insurance benefits.
Even among those unemployed for less than six months,
40 per cent are receiving social assistance. Some other
reports suggest that while the British position may be
extreme, it is certainly not different in kind from that
in many other OECD countries: unemployment insurance
benefits are rarely being received by more than two-thirds
of the unemployed, however defined, and the figure is
often closer to half.

   Figure 7 shows (for one particular family type and
earnings level) how the replacement ratio for a supplementary assistance recipient in Britain compares with the
ratio for an unemployment insurance benefit recipient,
in both cases using the OECD methodology. It also shows
how the position has changed since 1980-81 for the two
benefit types. There has been a significant reduction

126

in the ratios for both types of recipients, reflecting
the bringing of unemployment benefits into tax, but the
decline has been much more dramatic for insurance benefit
recipients, mainly due to the abolition of "earnings-
related supplement". (For comparison we also show
replacement ratios on a wider DHSS definition of "total
income support", which incorporates the other income-
tested benefits available both in and out of work.)
The main point is that, for Britain, OECD replacement
ratios based only on insurance benefits give a very partial view of recent developments in replacement rates
for the unemployed as a whole.

One final thought: the representativeness of hypothetical replacement ratios of the kind the OECD has
developed can only be fully tested by collecting information on the actual replacement ratios of a sample of
the unemployed. Do other Members have comparable data
to those collected in the DHSS Cohort Study, or plans to
collect such data?

FOOTNOTES

1. The findings of this research have been reported
in a series of survey articles - five to date - in the
Department of Employment's Employment Gazette. A series
of more substantial "Working Papers" is also being
published.

2. The concept used here is called the "family income
replacement ratio". The family unit was defined as the
unemployed man and, where applicable, his wife and
dependent children. The total of all forms of regular
family income while out of work is expressed as a proportion of total income prior to unemployment. In
addition to benefits paid in respect of unemployment,
account is taken of other state benefits actually received
and of other sources of income such as wives' earnings
and occupational pensions. Tax refunds are not included.
Apart from this major difference, the concept is similar
to the "net total transfer replacement ratio".

3. W. Narendranathan, S. Nickell and J. Stern:
Unemployment Benefits Revisited, Centre for Labour
Economics, London School of Economics, Discussion paper
No. 153, March 1983.

Figure 1 **TOTAL BENEFIT PAID TO UNEMPLOYED PEOPLE AS A PROPORTION OF THEIR ESTIMATED TOTAL NET EARNINGS IN WORK GREAT BRITAIN 1950-1982**

Source : DHSS.

Total benefit paid is total expenditure on unemployment
benefit, supplementary benefit and child benefit/family
allowances for the unemployed divided by the average
number of registered unemployed people.

Total net earnings is a weighted average of the estimated
net earnings of the various age, sex and family groups
represented on the unemployment register. The net
earnings of the groups have been adjusted in the light
of the findings of the 1978 DHSS Cohort Study on the
actual earnings of men experiencing unemployment.

Figure 2

FAMILY INCOME REPLACEMENT RATIOS(a) FOR MEN BECOMING
UNEMPLOYED IN 1978 - EARLY PART OF SPELL(b)

| | % of male unemployed stock (Nov. 81) | Income replacement ratios | | | | |
		Up to 50%	50% - 80%	80% - 100%	100%+	Total
Single men	53	67	28	3	2	100
Married couple no children	23	30	43	16	11	100
Married couple 1 child	8	18	48	21	11	100
Married couple 2 children	9	22	46	22	9	100
Married couple 3 children	4	13	47	25	14	100
Married couple 4 + children	3	12	32	33	24	100
Total	100	45	36	12	7	100

a) All sources of regular family income while out of work, including unemployment benefits, housing benefits, free school meals, wives' earnings and occupational pensions expressed as a proportion of total weekly family income prior to unemployment.
b) Ratios relate to the first three months of unemployment.

Source: DHSS Cohort Study

129

Figure 3

FAMILY INCOME REPLACEMENT RATIOS BY NET EARNINGS
LEVELS - MEN BECOMING UNEMPLOYED IN 1978(a)

Income replacement ratios	Net earnings(b)					
	up to 20	20-40	40-60	60-80	80-100	100+
(%)						
0	6.4	0.7	1.3	0.0	0	2.1
up to 25	0	4.2	3.5	11.5	17.2	33.2
25 to 50	6.4	20.8	28.2	27.9	37.9	59.4
50 to 75	31.9	38.8	32.0	42.3	34.5	2.6
75 to 80	0	7.6	8.2	3.8	0	.5
80 to 100	26.5	14.9	20.6	11.5	3.4	.5
100 plus	28.8	13.2	6.3	3.8	6.9	1.6
	100.0	100.0	100.0	100.0	100.0	100.0
(Distribution by earnings level)	(4.0)	(34.9)	(38.2)	(12.6)	(3.5)	(6.7)

a) Ratios relate to average benefits between the
fifth and thirteenth week of unemployment for men who
remained unemployed for at least three months.
b) Total gross earnings less deductions (such as
income tax and NI contributions) and travel to work
costs.

Source: DHSS Cohort Study

Figure 4

FAMILY INCOME REPLACEMENT RATIOS(a)
BY TYPE OF UNEMPLOYMENT BENEFIT RECEIVED –
MEN BECOMING UNEMPLOYED IN 1978(b)

Replacement rates	Benefit received			
	Unemployment insurance benefit (UB)	UB + supplementary allowance	supplementary allowance	None
(%)	(%)	(%)	(%)	(%)
0	0	0	0	37
up to 25	6	4	14	16
25 to 50	26	23	33	44
50 to 75	36	35	29	3
75 to 80	7	6	5	0
80 to 100	16	21	9	0
100 plus	8	11	10	0
	100.0	100.0	100.0	100.0
(Distribution by benefit type) =	(51.7)	(28)	(17)	(3)

a) As defined in Figure 2
b) As for Figure 3

Source: DHSS Cohort Study

Figure 5

FAMILY INCOME REPLACEMENT RATIOS BY WHETHER OR NOT WIFE
WORKING – MARRIED MEN BECOMING UNEMPLOYED IN 1978(a)

Replacement rates	Wife working	Wife not working
(%)	(%)	(%)
0	0	1.4
up to 25	1.4	8.5
25 to 50	22.4	27.8
50 to 75	38.1	32.6
75 to 80	9.5	5.6
80 to 100	23.8	14.2
100 plus	4.8	9.9
	100.0	100.0

a) As for Figure 3

Source: DHSS Cohort Study

Figure 6

PRE-SPELL FAMILY INCOME REPLACEMENT RATIO(a)
BY POST-SPELL REPLACEMENT RATIO(b):   FOR ALL MEN WHO
HAD BOTH MEASURES AND WERE UNEMPLOYED FOR
MORE THAN 13 WEEKS (360 WEIGHTED CASES) -
MEN BECOMING UNEMPLOYED IN 1978

Post-spell replacement ratio	Pre-spell replacement ratio					
(%)	Less than 25%	25-50%	50-75%	75-100%	100%	Total
Less than 25	7.0	6.0	3.7	1.2	0.6	19
25 - 50	1.2	12.4	16.1	3.6	0.9	34
50 - 75	0.9	6.9	11.4	8.8	3.4	32
75 - 100	0.7	0.8	3.1	3.0	1.7	9
100 plus	0.2	0.2	1.6	2.2	2.2	7
All	10	26	36	19	9	

a) Pre-spell replacement ratios are all sources of
regular family income between the fifth and thirteenth
week of unemployment (for men who remained unemployed
for at least three months), expressed as a proportion of
total weekly family income when the man was in his last
full-time job prior to unemployment.
b) Post-spell replacement ratios are all sources of
regular family income in the last eight weeks of unemployment (for men who returned to work within a year of
registering), expressed as a proportion of total weekly
family income when the man was in his first full-time
job after unemployment.

Source: DHSS Cohort Study

132

Figure 7

RATIOS OF ANNUAL DISPOSABLE INCOMES OF
PRODUCTION WORKERS EXPERIENCING SIX MONTHS UNEMPLOYMENT
AND NO UNEMPLOYMENT – MARRIED MAN WITH 2 CHILDREN
ON TWO-THIRDS OF AVERAGE EARNINGS

Year and definitions	Benefit	Replacement ratios
1980-81		
OECD Disposable Resources	Unemployment Benefit	93.9
OECD Disposable Resources	Supplementary Allowance	99.9
DHSS Total Income Support	Supplementary Allowance	99.5
1982-83		
OECD Disposable Resources	Unemployment Benefit only	76.7
OECD Disposable Resources	Supplementary Allowance	93.1
DHSS Total Income Support	Supplementary Allowance	87.8

UNEMPLOYMENT COMPENSATION REPLACEMENT RATES

A comment
by
Johs Due

One of the reasons for producing a report on unemployment insurance benefit schemes and replacement rates is of course the Secretariat's wish to provide comparable figures between Member countries. This is of course a natural desire for an international body such as the OECD.

But it seems to me that the OECD has focused too much on technical matters in its efforts to make comparisons. In doing so some crucial points are neglected or insufficiently touched upon. This is most apparent when you study the material concerning replacement rates at the micro level. Even when you use the measures put forward, and even if these measures show similar figures for different countries, there seem to be some serious shortcomings. The report mentions the problem of the variations behind the calculated figures. If these variations followed a known and well-defined statistical distribution - such as the normal distribution for example, this variability would only be a small statistical problem. But I <u>think</u> that most of the variations behind the figures reflect the fact that unemployment insurance benefit schemes differ significantly between different Member states.

Let us take an example. If the unemployment compensation replacement rate is 60 per cent in two countries this could hide a vast difference between these countries. The first country could have a scheme which guaranteed 60 per cent to all unemployed, no matter what their labour market history had been. The other country could have a dual system in which you could perhaps meet two groups of unemployed, one group with a compensation replacement rate of 90 per cent and one group of equal size with a replacement rate of only 30 per cent. The average replacement rate of 60 per cent in this country would in my opinion not be comparable with that in the first country.

The fact that the figures are not sufficiently comparable implies that you cannot deduce political or
administrative conclusions from the facts, that replacement rates differ or, on the contrary, do not differ from
one country to another.

The lack of knowledge of variations is of course a
well known fact in evaluating one-dimensional figures.
Whether this makes the figures of no use at all has yet
to be discussed.

In the report it is also argued that an ex-post
measure is the most relevant approach, due to the fact
that not all benefits are paid immediately at the start
of an unemployment spell. Some of the contributions
from the social security system are not available until
the end of the year or perhaps later. I do not agree in
valuing ex-post measures that high. Ex-post measures are
only suitable for calculating long-run levels of living
and studies of life-incomes.

But I think that the most crucial question concerning replacement rates relates to the eventual interdepen-
dence of rates and labour supply. Will high replacement
rates have a disincentive effect upon labour supply? The
disincentive effect in itself is not the item for discussion here, although international comparisons would
be very interesting. But I think that the discussion of
the willingness of the unemployed to take a new job or
not (granted that he is free to choose between these
alternatives) is more dependent on the actual unemployment benefit compared to the future wage and not to some
synthetic ex-post measure.

This last criticism has focused on the lack of
relevance of the ex-post measure. Now I would like to
return to the shortcomings of using a one-dimensional
measure at all. Instead of comparing figures, I think
it is more appropriate to compare systems. To illustrate
that point of view, I would introduce you to some
elements of the Danish unemployment insurance system.

These are as follows:

1. There are 50 UIB-funds (related to trade unions)
2. They cover almost all relevant groups on the
   labour market (including self-employed and job-
   seekers without work experience).
3. Apart from some minor exceptions, all benefits
   are calculated solely on the basis of former
   wage income.
4. The rule of calculation is 90 per cent of the
   former income with a ceiling corresponding to
   90 per cent of the average national wage during
   the previous year.

5. More than 80 per cent of the women and about 45 per cent of the men do not reach the ceiling. In other words they have a gross replacement rate of 90 per cent.
6. Benefits are taxable without exemption. Net replacement including saved taxation will at least be 95 per cent for the above-mentioned groups. Taking transport and other work-related expenses into consideration, some might have a replacement rate near 100 per cent.

But the Danish system is not fairly described simply by mentioning these replacement rates without further comment. In order to maintain these high replacement rates without having severe disincentive problems, we have some rather tough rules concerning the behaviour of the unemployed when they are offered a new job at the public employment service. If they wrongly refuse, they lose two weeks' benefits. If they refuse twice in a year, they are excluded from the benefit scheme until they have established a certain record of regular work. There are also rules which "punish" people who leave their jobs voluntarily.

I think that these dimensions are also very relevant when you compare systems. But why compare at all?

I think that the OECD has focused too much on creating a rating-scale. Indeed the Report itself recognises that certain factors could distort the true position of Member countries. I do not find that creating such a (more or less fair) rating scale is as important as mentioned in the report.

It must be more relevant to make comparisons of the different UIB systems in the Member countries.

V

A REVIEW OF MEMBER COUNTRIES' EXPERIENCES
WITH ALTERNATIVE USES OF UNEMPLOYMENT INSURANCE MONEY

by
Donald McBain

The purpose of most unemployment benefit systems in OECD countries is to provide income support during periods of involuntary unemployment to persons with established work records who are capable of employment and actively seeking it. Not everybody actively seeking work is automatically covered by the unemployment insurance system. This can be illustrated by the following table comparing average beneficiaries of unemployment insurance schemes in some of the major OECD countries with average unemployment.

Date	Country	Beneficiaries	Unemployment
		(figures in thousands)	
1982	Canada	1 138	1 305
June 1983	France	971	1 878
June 1983	Germany	902	2 127
1980	Italy	652	1 698
1980	United Kingdom	709	1 660
Nov. 1982	United States	4 635	11 906

The idea behind alternative uses of unemployment benefit monies is to provide income support for employment-related activities other than the job search. Sometimes the terms "positive", "more positive" or "productive use" of unemployment benefit are given to such alternative uses. But the more neutral term of "alternative uses" seems to be (a) less pejorative by implication and (b) more accurate for many members of the labour force. After all, the whole point of measures to combat

137

unemployment is to help ensure that "all those who are able and want to work"(1) can do so. Fortunately, even in recession a sizeable proportion of the persons becoming unemployed in any given period find employment after a relatively short time. For example, of the 789 000 persons becoming unemployed in France in the three months January, February and March 1983, 57.2 per cent had left unemployment three months later. In Great Britain in the same 3-month period up to 13 January 1983, 948 000 became unemployed and 47.8 per cent had left unemployment three months later; and in the United States only 28.2 per cent of those recorded in July 1983 as having 5 weeks' unemployment or less were still unemployed one month later. For many persons whose unemployment does not exceed, say, six months, an income maintenance system to support them during their job search plus the best possible labour market information system are probably the most productive or positive ways of assisting them.

However, many persons who become unemployed are unable to re-enter employment merely by dint of searching for it, however diligently. They need to adapt themselves to new employment requirements, or the demand for labour needs to be tilted in their favour. Can unemployment benefit systems be used to provide some of the funds and/ or the institutional machinery needed to enable this process of adaptation to take place? This chapter seeks to answer this question by listing some possible alternative uses of unemployment benefit and reviewing the experience countries have had with such use(2).

One point needs to be brought out before considering alternative uses of UB actually practised in the various countries: how much scope is there in the system for developing alternative uses of benefit money? There would seem to be three types of constraint here, on which general comments may be made:

The first comes from the legal basis of schemes. Do they enable benefit money to be used to finance activities other than a straightforward job search during a period of involuntary unemployment? If not, can they be altered to allow for this possibility?
The second arises from the method of financing Unemployment Benefit. There are some countries where UB is funded exclusively by general government revenues whether it be from taxation or borrowing. In such countries (e.g. Australia) there would seem to be no advantage in developing alternative uses for UB money unless this enabled the government to have access to a new revenue source in politically attractive circumstances (for example, as part of a "national solidarity" package). Other countries may finance their UB systems exclusively through a fund built up from earmarked contributions of employers and employees. In such countries, when substantial

funds have accrued or when earmarked contributions can be increased without politically or economically damaging consequences, the development of alternative uses of UB would seem to be attractive. But probably most countries have a mixed source of finance, partly earmarked contributions topped up by general government revenues. For these countries the question whether alternative uses of UB would enable increased total expenditure on employment measures to be financed (3) is uncertain.

The third constraint derives from the administrative complexity of the UB system where entitlement to benefits varies considerably both between individuals and over time. This means that it may be difficult both to estimate how much allocated UB funds could be diverted to alternative uses and to make payments to individuals taking part in an alternative use scheme.

A list of possible alternative uses of unemployment benefit funds is given in the communiqué issued after the March 1982 meeting of the Manpower and Social Affairs Committee of the OECD at ministerial level. The Ministers "agreed that it was worthwhile to discuss the merits of partly using these funds for training schemes to help the unemployed to get into new jobs; short-time work combined with partial unemployment compensation; temporary public jobs with a strong training element; subsidies for net additions to employment; and financial support for unemployed people who wish to create their own enterprise."(4)

In addition to this list one could add using unemployment benefit funds to help promote geographical mobility, part-time employment, early retirement, voluntary unpaid work or to provide a wage supplement to workers accepting lower-paid employment than they had previously held or a starting allowance.

Even with these additions the list of possible alternative uses is still not exhaustive, but most of the other possibilities seem more debatable. For example, is the payment of benefits during vacations an acceptable alternative use of the funds intended to support a period of active job search? Some countries seem to adopt a pragmatic attitude: at a time when the unemployed are no longer required to attend in person once or twice a week to prove they meet the "availability for employment" conditions for the receipt of benefit, the practice is tolerated. But in at least one country, the argument seems to have been accepted that after a vacation morale will be boosted and the job search renewed with greater vigour and perseverance.

The alternative uses with which we are concerned are financing various activities as follows:

a) training
b) short-time working
c) temporary employment
d) net additions to employment
e) assistance in running own business
f) voluntary unpaid work
g) early retirement
h) wage supplement
i) starting allowance
j) geographical mobility
k) part-time employment

Each of these will now be considered in turn. It will be apparent that there is a degree of overlap between some of these alternatives. For example, a scheme to support short-time working may well be combined with training support.

a) Training

The use of UB to help finance training activities of the unemployed is quite widespread. Eleven OECD countries appear(5) to have recourse to it in one form or another. These countries are: Australia, Belgium, Canada, Finland, Germany, Japan, Luxembourg, Netherlands, Spain, Switzerland, United States. Most often these countries allow unemployed persons taking training courses to continue receiving UB. Canada, for example, allows trainees to continue receiving UB for the duration of the training course even if entitlement would normally lapse in this time and then provides a further short extension (up to six weeks) to cover a period of active job search on completion of the course. However, there can be other uses. Thus the Netherlands allows unemployed persons being given on-the-job training by a firm to continue receiving benefits.

As regards the use of UB to help promote training, two questions seem to arise:

i) Are there grounds for paying training allowances to unemployed workers on approved training which are higher than the UB levels they would be entitled to? In the case of Canada and Spain, which pay UB to eligible workers on approved training, this question could be rephrased as: Are there grounds for paying an increment to UB to unemployed workers on approved training? On this question it will be recalled that in the past it was sometimes argued that income support during training needed to be sufficiently attractive to encourage ambitious and able workers to abstain from immediate employment whilst they acquired new skills. As this required a high level of support it was felt in some countries that part of this support could be in the form of

140

refundable loans. But have present conditions of slack in the labour market made the unemployed more or less willing to make the commitment involved in taking a training course? It would seem there could be two contrary tendencies, some optimistic workers being more prepared to invest the time and effort involved in taking training in the hope this will pay off in the future, while others less sanguine are less willing to miss the earliest possible job opportunities.

ii) Are there possibilities and advantages in using UB funds to pay for the costs of instruction rather than merely provide income maintenance for trainees whilst they receive instruction? On this question, there might be advantages in using UB funds to finance on- or off-the-job training for workers in the context of short-time working arrangements. This is referred to below.

b) <u>Short-time working</u>

This, too, is frequently used, being found in eleven OECD countries (Belgium, Canada, France, Germany, Ireland, Italy, Japan, Luxembourg, Portugal, Switzerland and the United Kingdom). The idea is a very simple one. Rather than providing a stark choice between full-time employment on wages or salary and unemployment on UB, enterprises are enabled to reduce hours worked when business is slack without severing their employment contracts with their workers and so without the costs involved in hiring new workers when demand recovers; and workers are given more security of tenure and a higher level of income than if they were simply paid for hours actually worked. In a sense, therefore, short-time working arrangements can be likened to a form of wage subsidy for employment maintenance.

A major risk with employment maintenance subsidies is that they might hamper positive adjustment by enabling inefficient firms to survive. To diminish this risk, countries paying UB in cases of short-time working often impose restrictions on the sectors eligible for this aid. Japan's employment stabilization fund pays grants to employers in approved industries who provide extra rest days to their workers or training without reducing wages or numbers employed at times of reduced demand. Germany restricts the period for which short-time work allowances can be paid to a maximum of six months, although the Federal Minister of Labour and Social Affairs can extend this to up to 2 years. Frequently use has been made of this extension during periods of economic slack.

Such arrangements may, however, carry another risk - that if, at the expiration of the period of support, an enterprise is still not profitable and competitive, it might then be forced to discharge workers at a time when the possibilities of alternative employment are even fewer than when the enterprise first resorted to short-time working. Can the public administrations concerned with a request for the introduction of short-time working recognise that they are dealing with an enterprise which will be viable without having to adapt and shed labour? Governments have been criticised for not having a good record at "picking the winners" and investing in them. Are they better at picking and not helping the losers?

c) Temporary employment

Australia, Belgium, Canada, Luxembourg and the Netherlands have schemes under this heading. The Australian scheme (the Volunteer Youth Programme) enables unemployed persons to be engaged on works of value to the local community whilst continuing to receive UB plus an increment to cover the extra costs involved in working.

Canadian experience is summarised in a speech which the Minister of Employment and Immigration made to the Canadian Construction Association annual meeting in Halifax on 23 July 1982:

> "To respond to short-term problems we have increased our commitment to direct job creation and have used the unemployment insurance system in new ways to preserve the skills base and provide economic and community benefits.......... We have also signed major agreements in the forestry, fishing and mining sectors to create work which will add to the long-term productivity of Canada's resource base. This year, over 21 000 workers will be employed in reforestation work, fisheries enhancement projects and environmental improvements in mining communities -- work which means that unemployment insurance expenditures become an investment to some degree in future production and future jobs."

Luxembourg's experience in this area is closely linked with the structural adjustment problems of the steel industry. To enable surplus labour to undertake productive work outside the steel industry, the "Anti-Crisis division" has been set up. This division is responsible for paying the wages of surplus steel industry workers engaged on work not connected with the steel industry. The division in turn receives finance from the unemployment insurance fund.

The Netherlands envisaged the possibility of UB funds being used to enable young unemployed persons to work on a temporary basis in the Employment Plan introduced in Spring 1982. The intention was that in this way local initiatives could be exploited to the benefit of young long-term unemployed in particular.

Two of the schemes mentioned here are directed at young people. Whilst youth is an obvious group requiring special support to promote integration into the labour market, it might be considered whether such schemes could not be opened more generally to all unemployed likely to benefit from this form of work experience (e.g. those unemployed for more than, say, six months). Some of the questions which might arise in this context are whether trade unions or society in general would feel that cheap labour was being encouraged; whether sufficient work could be provided together with necessary managerial support and whether such schemes would appear attractive to the unemployed.

A general question which is often asked in connection with such schemes is: What happens to an unemployed worker given temporary employment if, at the end of this period, he or she is unable to find more permanent unsubsidised work? The answer to this question needs to bring out:

    i) whilst temporary work is being undertaken, the registration for employment is maintained and as a general rule the temporary employment can be terminated at short notice to enable a worker to move into more permanent employment;

    ii) the work experience gained during temporary employment increases the worker's employability perhaps sufficiently to enable him to return to normal employment, perhaps in other cases enough to enable him to benefit from training;

    iii) the employment results (or should result) in the production of socially useful goods or services.

d) Net additions to employment

Here the idea is that the employer engaging an unemployed worker who had been in receipt of benefit receives an employment subsidy from UB sources in recognition of the fact that such a worker is likely to be less productive at the outset and that the engagement results in a decrease in the charges on the UB fund. This approach can be distinguished from those envisaged in (h) and (i) below, both of which are directed more towards different aspects of the needs of workers restarting to work after a period of unemployment. It is not a widely used approach, although it must be pointed out that it is very much akin to reduced social security contributions in respect of new engagements. This latter has been a quite widely employed measure (although one which falls out of the scope of the present chapter).

Japan has measures to provide a subsidy either for elderly unemployed workers or for workers unemployed in depressed regions or industries. These subsidies are financed solely by employers' contributions to the Japanese Employment Insurance System, the same system under which unemployment benefits are financed, although UB is financed by joint employer and employee contributions. The subsidies vary according to circumstances. For example, a small or medium-sized enterprise gets a subsidy of 80 per cent of wages for up to 1 year and 66 per cent for six months when it engages an older worker (between 55 and 65) as a regular worker (i.e. under the lifetime employment system). Subsidies at lower rates are paid for engagements by large enterprises and for shorter periods for middle-aged workers (between 45 and 55). A large enterprise could receive a subsidy of 60 per cent of wages for 6 months and 50 per cent for a further 6 months for engaging a middle-aged worker. This scheme helped create employment for 100 000 workers in the 12 months July 1979- June 1980. The scheme is not permanent but is introduced when the employment situation of this group of workers justifies it.

In similar fashion, the Japanese Employment Insurance System provides subsidies to employers engaging and training workers from selected depressed industries or areas.

A number of questions could be discussed on the basis of this experience:

i) does financing a range of employment-promotion measures by means of employer contributions raise problems by favouring capital-intensive production and raising indirect labour costs?
ii) do large conglomerates straddling a number of industries and with less flexible recruitment procedures derive benefits from the schemes or do they merely contribute to financing schemes of benefit to smaller enterprises?
iii) do problems of thresholds occur, for example at ages such as 44 and 54, at the frontiers between small and large enterprises? (In some countries such problems are said to detract from the operational efficiency of schemes.)

e) Incentives to found and run own business

In France the Council of Ministers has adopted the principle of financial support for unemployed persons or groups of unemployed persons who establish a new enterprise or take over an existing industrial, commercial, agricultural or craft enterprise, or enter a profession on their own account. The details of this scheme will be made public in the near future. An earlier experimental scheme had given encouraging results (9 200 unemployed helped to found a business in 1979 and 6 600 in the first half of 1980).

The United Kingdom is also running an experimental scheme under which unemployed people setting up a new business in the three pilot areas receive a weekly allowance during the first year of operation.

This sort of scheme seems likely to appeal mainly to persons with fairly precise qualifications or experience who might be expected to have above-average chances of re-entering employment. That does not mean, of course, that such schemes are not performing a useful function if they encourage an expansion of total employment. But would they still be performing a useful function if they led to subsidised enterprises driving out the unsubsidised? Can the risks of that happening be avoided? A further issue is how to balance the amount and duration of funding needed to establish a viable business with the needs to avoid excessive subsidisation and to preserve the elements of equity on which the UB system is based?

f) Voluntary unpaid work

This is used by two countries, Australia and the United Kingdom. The Australian Community Youth Support Scheme is intended to help young unemployed persons maintain a positive orientation to work and job-finding by participating in community-based activities. Participation is voluntary. During their participation, young people remain eligible for UB and receive reimbursement of incidental expenses. Community groups, including recognised youth organisations, are given financial assistance to enable them to provide supportive programmes and services to the young people. This programme was expected to help over 48 000 young people in 1979/80.

The United Kingdom scheme for voluntary unpaid employment allows participation in approved schemes of benefit to the community at the same time as receipt of UB. Participants can also be paid a small allowance to cover necessary expenses.

These schemes raise a number of issues:

i) Would or could the work performed by unpaid volunteers have been undertaken by persons in normal employment? If this is the case, how can trade unions' fears of unfair competition from cheap labour be allayed?
ii) If the unpaid worker is not competing with workers in normal employment, a risk arises that he/she simply becomes accustomed to working in a very protected environment. Is this risk greater in the case of young people with less experience of paid employment?
iii) The existence of voluntary unpaid work schemes may mean that the unemployed will gradually be

145

put under pressure to "earn their UB". This
could be a socially divisive and undesirable
development. Can it be averted?

g) Early retirement

Although a great number of countries have introduced
early retirement schemes, it appears that UB provides finance for this purpose in only six countries - Belgium,
Denmark, Finland, Luxembourg, Netherlands and Portugal.
The Danish and Luxembourg systems can apply in the case of
employed or unemployed workers reaching the age for early
retirement and satisfying the eligibility conditions. The
schemes in the other countries apply only to unemployed
workers. In the Danish scheme, for example, eligibility
is restricted to persons between the ages of 60 and 66 who
have been members of recognised unemployment insurance
funds for 5 out of the preceding 10 years and who have
been employed for 26 weeks in the preceding 3 years.
They receive an early retirement pension equal to 100 per
cent of their entitlement to UB for $2\frac{1}{2}$ years, decreasing
for the next 2 years to 80 per cent and thereafter 60 per
cent until retirement age is reached. Take-up under this
scheme has been at the rate of roughly half the eligible
population.

A question which might be discussed under this heading is whether such schemes constitute an alternative use
of UB any more than the example quoted in the opening
paragraphs of this chapter concerning payment of holidays
whilst unemployed. In the case of schemes applying only
to the unemployed, the reasoning behind the scheme seems
to be an acknowledgement that unemployed older workers
have practically no chance of getting back into employment. In the case of schemes open also to older employed
workers, the hope is that their places will be taken by
younger unemployed workers. But there will be no increase in total employment, maybe merely a decrease in
recorded unemployment combined with an increase in public
sector outlays as an older worker with greater entitlements to public support leaves the labour force and a
younger person with lower entitlements leaves recorded
unemployment.

The foregoing puts the case against early retirement
on general grounds. It needs to be related to at least
two other aspects. The first of these concerns the social welfare gains when older workers voluntarily withdraw from employment with the assurance of a reasonable
level of income support. The other concerns the possible
advantage to an individual firm in replacing an older
worker by a possibly better-trained or more adaptable
younger worker.

h) Wage supplement

Luxembourg and the Netherlands use UB as a source of funding for wage supplements paid to unemployed persons accepting employment at wages/salary lower than in their previous employment. In both cases the supplement declines over a period of time. The idea behind these schemes is that they will help diminish workers' reluctance to accept lower wages than they previously had. This should lead to a shorter job search time and so to lower levels of unemployment.

In inflationary periods such schemes may not be sufficiently attractive. However, they could perhaps be of use when wage and price levels are more or less stationary. Such schemes may be introduced with a view to reducing unemployment among groups of redundant workers from industries where wage levels are above average (steel, for example). However, where the terms of the redundancy procedure are financially attractive, the redundant workers may not be interested in wage supplement offers.

i) Starting allowance

The idea behind a starting allowance is that after a period of unemployment a worker may find himself in financial difficulties when he first starts work, partly because his initial earnings are likely to be below average for the job (lower output, small bonuses, starting at bottom of pay scale, etc.) and partly because outgoings are above average at the outset (re-equipping himself with appropriate tools and clothes, costs of transport, etc.). Japan seems to be the only country paying something akin to a starting allowance from UB sources. It is known as the Outfit allowance and is reserved for older or handicapped workers placed in full-time employment by the Employment Service.

It seems at least superficially attractive to pay this form of incentive to overcome any reluctance on the part of the unemployed to return to employment. It might be thought that the reason this approach has not been adopted more often is the fear that it would encourage undesirable labour turnover, with periods of employment long enough to qualify for the allowance being followed by spells of unemployment. Preventing abuses of this sort could create administrative problems.

j) Geographical mobility

With the exception again of Japan, none of the countries seems to fund geographical mobility payments from UB sources. A number of countries limit such payments to persons who are unemployed and in receipt of UB and some special groups. On the whole, the scale of geographical mobility schemes is very small both in terms of different types of aid given, amounts of aid and numbers of persons affected.

k) Part-time employment

It is suggested that there might be scope here for devising schemes to be funded from UB under which employers could be paid incentives to split full-time jobs into a greater number of part-time jobs. As far as the Secretariat is aware, no country yet finances such operations from this source.

FOOTNOTES

1. OECD Council, "Recommendation on a General Employment and Manpower Policy".

2. The source for this latter information is primarily the information supplied in the OECD inventory of employment and manpower policy measures. No specific enquiries have been addressed to countries to ascertain whether experience has been gained in alternative uses of UB. The information contained in the chapter should be regarded as illustrative rather than exhaustive.

3. If alternative uses could be found which would lead to reductions in the total outlays on measures to cope with unemployment it would seem reasonable to consider a move away from income maintenance on efficiency as well as cost-effectiveness grounds.

4. Press/A(82)12, para.12.

5. A deliberately vague turn of phrase has been used because (a) it is not always clear that UB funds are put to these alternative uses and (b) the fact that a country has not specifically mentioned putting UB funds to alternative uses does not preclude that it does in fact do it.

VI

ALTERNATIVE UTILISATION OF UNEMPLOYMENT COMPENSATION FUNDS: A COMPARISON OF OVERALL FISCAL COSTS

by
Lutz Reyher and Eugen Spitznagel

This chapter seeks to examine how part of the money spent by governments to finance unemployment compensation could be used in ways which would be more rational and more productive not only for the unemployed but for society as a whole. This view is based on a comparison of real costs of unemployment and, more generally, under-employment (which would provide a picture of the resource side of the balance sheet), and the costs of improved labour market measures (which would provide a picture of the expenditure side of the balance sheet). The study is based on German experience and practice which, however, should not be untypical of other OECD countries.

The first section seeks to give a comprehensive view of the various costs of unemployment and/or underemployment, as well as their institutional distribution, i.e. how the budgets of different levels of government are affected.

The section which follows looks at the costs implied by a number of employment policy alternatives to unemployment compensation, with the aim to go well beyond the superficial concept of costs limited to "expenditure appearing in the budget of the Federal Employment Institute" to arrive at an overall dynamic fiscal costs concept. The cost comparisons carried out are restricted to three measures, which can be regarded as representative of the different categories of measures to reduce unemployment, i.e.:

- Vocational training and re-training which is the main labour market policy instrument to reduce shortages through improving qualifications - and at the same time lead to greater equality of opportunities.

149

- <u>Job creation measures</u> which fulfil the double
  function of enhancing the supply of jobs, on the
  demand side, and of contributing to the maintenance and improvement of the qualifications of
  the potential labour force.
- <u>Short-time work</u> which aims at preventing cyclical
  unemployment and at maintaining employment in a
  quantitative and qualitative sense.

For these three instruments, aims, conditions, take-
up, labour market effectiveness and finally overall fiscal costs are described. Consideration is given not only
to direct costs, but to those costs which, while not
directly measurable, are nevertheless relevant to the
individual and to the economy as a whole, e.g. the costs
of the erosion of skills during unemployment. Additional
long-term revenue implications as well as positive influences (gains in qualification by vocational training
and retraining) are considered.

The final section contains a summary of results and
draws some conclusions with respect to budgetary, institutional and labour market policy aspects.

THE COSTS OF UNEMPLOYMENT

One argument against measures to provide alternatives to unemployment is that their cost would be too
high. This brings the question of what concept of "costs"
is used. Does it cover real, as distinct from money and
budget, costs? And is the fiscal connection between unemployment and labour market measures perceived realis-
tically? These questions are explored below on the basis
of the German experience.

First let us consider visible budget costs and differentiate between those who receive unemployment benefits, unemployment assistance or neither of these. The
Federal Employment Institute at present pays DM.19 600
per recipient of unemployment benefits (on a man/year
basis). The unemployed person himself receives 60 per
cent - this is somewhat less than DM.12 000, the remaining 40 per cent cover payments by the Institute to pension
and sickness insurance for the unemployed. In addition
to these payments, unemployment causes losses of tax
revenue. First the State loses the direct income taxes
which could be expected in the case of employment.
Second, there are losses from indirect taxes due to the
lower income and consumption expenditures of the unemployed. Both these kinds of tax losses can be estimated
to add up to about DM.6 000 (on a yearly basis) per person receiving unemployment insurance benefits. Finally,
there are reductions in the revenues of the various

institutions of social security (unemployment, pensions and sickness insurance) amounting to a further sum of about DM.1 700 altogether. All this brings total costs per recipient of unemployment benefit up to about DM.27 000.

Roughly 20 per cent of the registered unemployed receive, however, employment assistance which is somewhat lower than unemployment benefit (58 per cent of the previous net income compared to 68 per cent paid by unemployment insurance). Their overall fiscal costs can be estimated to be about DM.25 000 per person per year. Unemployed persons who do not receive any benefits from unemployment insurance or employment assistance are not costless either but can cause expenditures (if they receive social aid) and, especially, losses of revenues by social security and the tax budgets of DM.18 000.

On average, present unemployment costs the public sector as a whole something like DM.24 000 per person per year. Multiplied by more than 1.8 million unemployed, this equals annual reductions in revenues and additional expenditures of about DM.45 billion. This sum can be compared to the actual yearly net borrowing requirement of the federal government (DM.40 billion).

More than a quarter of this sum consists of lost tax revenues; more than 10 per cent of it is borne by the social security system and more than 46 per cent (DM.21 billion) is borne by the Federal Employment Institute. Differences in the shares of tax revenues by the three levels of government (federal government, regional states and local authorities) mean that these losses are distributed as follows: about 50 per cent (DM.6 billion) are lost by the federal level, about 40 per cent (DM.4½ billion) by the regional states and some 10 per cent (DM.1.3 billion) by local authorities. For each of these three levels of government these amounts constitute roughly 3 per cent of tax revenue. Including the obligatory contributions of the federal budget to the Federal Employment Institute the share of the federal government amounts to over 7 per cent relative to federal tax revenues. These are only the overall fiscal costs of registered unemployment. If one considers also the costs of hidden unemployment, the overall fiscal burden could well be about DM.54 billion in 1982.

The economic losses to society, however, exceed these estimates by a substantial amount. These economic losses can be conceived of as gains which would have resulted from an alternative use of unutilised factors of production, arithmetically expressed in units of gross domestic product ("opportunity costs"). Even with rather conservative assumptions with respect to the possibility of a fast re-integration of the unemployed and also their average productivity, the volume of production lost by underemployment can be estimated at about DM.100 billion in 1982. This equals about 7 per cent of gross national product at current prices.

However, this is not yet the complete extent of the costs of unemployment. In addition to these statistically estimated costs, longer-term effects occur. Unemployment tends to undermine work incentives and disrupt social harmony, all the more so the longer it lasts for the individual. Unemployment also entails loss of qualifications, for vocational qualifications cannot be stored and brought back and returned to use without significant deterioration.

THE COSTS OF LABOUR MARKET POLICY MEASURES

The question arises whether these enormous fiscal "expenditures" (including losses of revenues) are inevitable. Would it be possible to change the allocation of resources in ways that would make more sense fiscally and socially in the future?

A cardinal problem of labour market and economic policy, particularly for the future, is the deficit of vocational qualifications. The cause of labour market slack during recent years stems mainly from slow economic growth, but even during the present period of slack the demand for skilled workers has continued in some industries, and there are widespread complaints about the inadequate adaptation of vocational qualifications to rapidly changing technologies. These kinds of shortage will become much more pronounced however, when - after about a decade - the potential labour force will decrease substantially for demographic reasons and continued economic development will heavily depend on the full use of highly qualified manpower.

It is therefore an important aim of labour market policy to make use of all possibilities during the phase of labour market slack to reduce existing qualification deficits and to avoid the generation of new ones. The Employment Promotion Act provides the means to do this. It includes not only the promotion of vocational training and retraining and vocational rehabilitation, but also general measures of work creation or temporary short-time work.

ADVANCED VOCATIONAL TRAINING AND RE-TRAINING MEASURES

The Employment Promotion Act requires the Federal Institute to promote participation in vocational

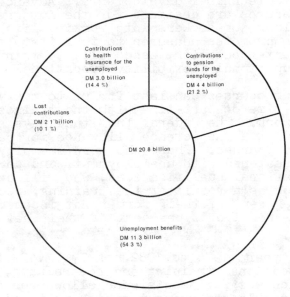

Diagram 1 COSTS OF UNEMPLOYMENT FOR THE *FEDERAL EMPLOYMENT INSTITUTE*
(Estimates for 1982)

Contributions to health insurance for the unemployed
DM 3.0 billion
(14.4 %)

Contributions to pension funds for the unemployed
DM 4.4 billion
(21.2 %)

Lost contributions
DM 2.1 billion
(10.1 %)

DM 20.8 billion

Unemployment benefits
DM 11.3 billion
(54.3 %)

Source : Institute of Employment Research *(IAB)* of the Federal Employment Institute *(BA)*.

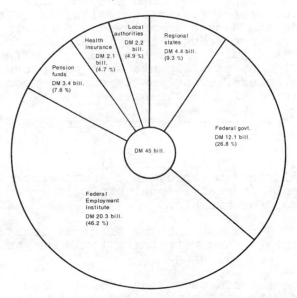

Diagram 2 INSTITUTIONAL DISTRIBUTION OF *OVERALL* COSTS OF UNEMPLOYMENT
(Estimates for 1982)

Health insurance
DM 2.1 bill.
(4.7 %)

Local authorities
DM 2.2 bill.
(4.9 %)

Regional states
DM 4.4 bill.
(9.3 %)

Pension funds
DM 3.4 bill.
(7.6 %)

Federal govt.
DM 12.1 bill.
(26.8 %)

DM 45 bill.

Federal Employment Institute
DM 20.3 bill.
(46.2 %)

Source : Institute of Employment Research *(IAB)* of the Federal Employment Institute *(BA)*.

training measures designed to maintain and extend the vocational knowledge and skills of workers and/or to adjust these to technical developments. Advanced vocational training measures are designed for the integration of women and older job-seekers into working life. The Institute also promotes measures to facilitate transfers to a different occupation, especially to maintain or improve occupational flexibility (vocational re-training).

Training courses can last for up to two years. They may be full-time or part-time with the trainee continuing his normal work. The Federal Institute pays some of the costs including a subsistence allowance for participants in full-time courses. Those who were unemployed or directly threatened with unemployment, and participants without vocational qualifications, who will acquire a qualification as a result of the training, receive between 68 and 75 per cent of their former net income. Other participants receive 58 per cent of their net income as a loan.

In the years 1974 to 1982 nearly DM.19 billion was spent on vocational training and re-training, three quarters of which was for subsistence allowances alone. This very considerable sum shows the high value attached to training measures within the framework of the Federal Institute's range of manpower policy instruments.

Both the quantitative and qualitative effects of training need to be taken into account in an analysis of the impact of training. The quantitative effects are reflected in the number unemployed. Participation in full-time training reduces individual working life and hence reduces supply. This has a direct effect on unemployment if the participants were unemployed prior to joining the scheme. That is the case at present for about one-third of participants.

There is an indirect effect on employment in the form of lower inflows to unemployment if participants were employed but threatened with redundancy. Here we may assume that only two thirds of this effect will be felt in registered unemployment. Furthermore, indirect effects result from additional expenditure on courses and teachers, for example.

Table 2 shows the numbers of participants in vocational training and retraining (on a man/year basis). It suggests the following:

- Since the mid-seventies training has not kept in step with either the growth of the potential labour force or with unemployment. On the contrary, the number of participants in all these years was lower than in 1975, sometimes substantially lower.

Table 1

EXPENDITURES OF THE FEDERAL EMPLOYMENT INSTITUTE FOR
LABOUR MARKET POLICY MEASURES(a)

Year	Advanced vocational training & retraining	General work creation schemes	Short-time working
1974	334.6 (1 494.2)	31.8	677.7
1975	491.9 (1 991.4)	125.9	2 207.1
1976	405.2 (1 426.7)	169.2	989.5
1977	334.3 (770.9)	570.6	594.5
1970	449.1 (743.9)	706.2	596.4
1979	575.0 (1 179.8)	1 004.2	334.0
1980	752.2 (1 497.8)	947.1	471.2
1981	988.6 (2 120.5)	901.2	1 284.6
1982*	1 021.3 (2 250.0)	920.5	1 090.0

  * Planned
  a) Expenditure for courses, etc. (in million DM.)
and (in brackets) expenditure per participant

Source: Institute for Employment Research (IAB) of
the Federal Employment Institute (BA).

- Take-up of training is highly dependent on the
  conditions attached to the courses. These conditions were tightened leading to a drastic decline in participation to less than half the former level. The more stringent conditions agreed
  upon for 1982 have not yet affected the annual
  figures. However, the decreasing number of applicants and new entrants already indicates that the
  number of participants may fall again with only
  a short lag.

The effects on productivity and growth potential in
the medium and long-term are more important than the
immediate quantitative effects of reducing unemployment.

This entails looking at the development of manpower
potentials during the nineties and thereafter: investment in education and training increases the stock of
human capital and thus increases the potential future
performance of the economy.

GENERAL JOB CREATION SCHEMES (ABM) AND THEIR DIRECT AND INDIRECT EFFECTS ON EMPLOYMENT AND UNEMPLOYMENT

General job creation schemes provide financial incentives (from funds of the Federal Employment Institute, the federal government and the regional states) to increase demand for goods and services and hence the demand for labour and employment. In contrast to measures aimed at reducing supply or slowing down the advance in productivity, job creation schemes are part of the range of active employment policy strategies. Unemployed persons are referred to schemes through the employment offices. Job creation schemes have an anti-cyclical and a regional character. In principle any kind of work can be supported. The aims of work creation schemes are both quantitative and qualitative. Projects can be initiated by legal entities under public law and by companies and institutions under private law. Generally, projects should be carried out by a business enterprise.

Projects can attract a subsidy of between 60 and 100 per cent of the workers' wage, and supplementary loans are possible. Workers who were registered as unemployed and who were receiving unemployment benefits should be engaged for one year. In special cases this period may be lengthened to three years.

In addition to the unemployed referred by the employment offices, "core workers" can be employed in job creation schemes and their wages can be subsidised.

The contractual relations between the employer and newly engaged workers are governed by the labour legislation and wage agreements which apply to the rest of the staff. The new member of staff is not subject to a statutory period of notice if he takes up other work which he has found himself or if he is placed elsewhere by the employment office.

Job creation schemes have acquired increasing importance in past years with continued underemployment. This is suggested both by the strong increase in the Federal Institute's funds for them and by the increase (especially between 1974 and 1978) in the number of participants in the schemes (see Tables 1 and 2).

In 1982 total funds used for these projects amounted to nearly DM.1 billion in subsidies and loans. Calculated on a yearly basis about 30 000 people were in job creation schemes in 1982. As each person worked on average for about 6 months, the number of participants is approximately twice this average figure.

The focus of job creation has shifted from the secondary sector, where mainly building projects are

Table 2

DIRECT AND INDIRECT EFFECTS OF LABOUR MARKET POLICY MEASURES
ON EMPLOYMENT AND UNEMPLOYMENT 1975 - 1982
(annual basis)

	Participants in 1 000								Total employment effect(a) in 1 000								Unemployment effect(a) (avoided unemployment) in 1 000							
	1975	1976	1977	1978	1979	1980	1981	1982(a)	1975	1976	1977	1978	1979	1980	1981	1982	1975	1976	1977	1978	1979	1980	1981	1982
Short-time working	773	277	231	191	88	137	347	570	223	96	55	50	29	46	122	193	147	63	36	33	19	30	82	129
Job creation schemes	16	29	38	51	51	41	30	30	41	75	72	90	86	60	63	49	30	38	61	77	75	59	55	43
Vocational training and retraining	127	37	65	63	73	90	111	122	127	97	65	63	73	90	111	122	93	76	54	52	60	73	92	103
	916	403	334	305	212	260	496	722	391	260	192	203	108	204	296	364	278	197	151	162	151	162	229	275

a) Estimated

Source: Institute of Employment Research (IAB) of the Federal Employment Institute (BA).

carried out, to the tertiary or services sector. This
is clearly shown by the figures below:

	1974	1978	1982 (June)
Total participants	3 208	51 236	28 594
of which (in per cent)			
Agriculture, forestry and fisheries	26.7	31.4	30.8
Transport, civil engineering and utilities	31.7	17.9	12.2
Administration and social services	26.9	45.6	49.7
Others	14.7	5.1	7.3

Since 1980 the number of participants in job
creation schemes has diminished partly as a result of
more restrictive conditions. However, the share of projects carried out in the tertiary sector has continued
to rise.

The direct employment effect of job creation schemes
is the number of participants in the various schemes,
i.e. unemployed referred by the employment offices and
"core workers". Job creation schemes, however, may also
have indirect effects on employment, through the inter-
dependence of the various sectors of the economy and the
income multiplier. An input-output analysis has been
used to quantify these effects (see Table 2). The results suggest that the net employment effects of job
creation schemes have helped to prevent unemployment
from rising higher. This is because:

- when unemployed persons are engaged there is an
  immediate corresponding reduction of unemployment;
  and
- the employment of "core" workers and workers employed as a result of indirect or secondary effects helps to reduce the decline in employment.
  On balance, it can be estimated that two-thirds
  of these numbers would otherwise have been trans-
  lated into registered unemployment and one-third
  into non-registered unemployment and in higher
  outflows abroad.

For 1982 the additional reduction in registered unemployment through job creation schemes can be estimated
at 43 000 persons.

Although these achievements may appear quantitatively modest in comparison with the unemployment total, the fact remains that every year tens of thousands of unemployed persons are, at least temporarily, employed through job creation schemes when they would otherwise have remained unemployed.

In public discussions a number of doubts are expressed about job creation schemes, e.g.:

- To what extent does the subsidising of job creation schemes result in a displacement of the financial burden, for example from local authorities who carry out projects to the Federal Employment Institute? In other words, is there a substantial amount of fiscal substitution?
- To what extent do job creation schemes induce additional employment opportunities and to what extent do they induce fewer hires and/or more dismissals? To what extent is regular employment "crowded out" by subsidised employment in work creation schemes?
- To what extent does participation in job creation schemes create new claims on unemployment insurance, thereby increasing its costs?
- To what extent are earnings expectations generated which cannot be fulfilled later in the regular labour market?

With respect to fiscal substitution, a careful examination is made to determine whether projects represent "additional" employment in the legal sense or not. More restrictive conditions have been formulated to prevent fiscal substitution. However, in spite of this the possibility of its occurrence cannot be excluded. How important this is cannot be estimated. It often seems that single cases are over-generalised in public discussion. The increasing share of job creation activities in social services leads to the conclusion that in future fiscal substitution will become less important because new activities are characteristic of social services.

The question of fiscal substitution should also be related to the twofold character of job creation schemes: on the one hand they help maintain a higher level of employment; on the other hand they help to avoid or reduce the loss of vocational skills. Among the nearly 2 million registered unemployed in Germany there are about 300 000 persons who are unemployed for more than one year. For another large group there are often individual spells of unemployment for relatively short periods.

It is an important task of job creation schemes to help preserve motivation for work. Schemes are increasingly directed to the supply side of the labour market in addition to the traditional demand-side orientation. As with vocational training and re-training there is a category of revenues which cannot be exactly quantified. Empirical research portrays the attitudes of workers who have taken part in schemes:

- 50 per cent of the surveyed participants consider the schemes have only advantages, explicitly excluding disadvantages;
- 44 per cent realise schemes have advantages as well as disadvantages;
- Only 3 per cent feel that schemes have only disadvantages.

Crowding-out effects, i.e. induced dismissals of regular employed persons in the case of unchanged overall demand, can be expected only where job creation functionally competes with under-utilised capacities in the competitive market. This hardly applies in the broad domain of social services and public administration. However, it is still necessary to examine as far as possible whether job creation schemes absorb demand which would otherwise have been satisfied by competing capacities in the market. In total, the small volume of employment in job creation schemes - at present 30 000 persons, i.e. 0.1 per cent of total employment - and its substantial regional and functional dispersion in a lot of small specific projects makes it difficult to believe that crowding-out could take place to a significant extent.

The argument that participation in job creation may generate new entitlements to unemployment insurance is less important from an overall fiscal point of view. As indicated above, there is only a small difference between overall fiscal costs of persons receiving unemployment benefits and those having no claims. After having exhausted their entitlement to unemployment insurance the burden generally shifts to other budgets. Moreover, many participants quickly re-enter the regular labour market.

Finally the possibility that untenable income expectations may result from participation in job creation schemes - for young academics for example - is hard to justify. In any event, only 3 per cent of the participants held a university degree, 2 per cent had other academic qualifications.

SHORT-TIME WORK

Short-time work is introduced when there is a temporary shortage of work to maintain jobs and this enables the company to keep its workforce intact. The loss of earnings is largely made up by the Federal Employment Institute, which provides short-time allowances amounting to 68 per cent of the loss in net earnings due to hours not worked.

a) The practical significance and frequence of short time

Short-time working increased strongly during the mid-seventies, as Table 2 shows. At the lowest point of the recession in 1975 there were almost 1 million workers on short time in more than 15 000 plants. Currently, short-time working is used intensively: the average number of short-time workers in 1982 was expected to amount to nearly 600 000, 2½ per cent of the employed. As one might expect, short-time working is most frequent in the production sector, in the manufacturing industry and crafts. These sectors account for more than 90 per cent of short-time workers but only 50 per cent of the total workforce.

b) The effects of short time on unemployment

On average over the last five years short-time workers lost about 25 to 30 per cent of their usual working time. The average length of individual short-time working is 3½ months. The "gross" (i.e. total) number of short-time workers is much greater than the average stock figure. It is at least three times higher. The actual number of hours lost for which allowances are paid is rather more than one month's working time per person distributed over three months. The volume of more than 250 million working hours lost in 1982 corresponds to about 190 000 persons on an annual basis. Theoretically, therefore, a decline in employment to this extent was prevented.

However, the actual effect on the number of unemployed is slightly less as experience has shown that only about 2/3 of a decline in employment is reflected in registered unemployment. So in 1982 short-time working is estimated to have prevented an increase in the number of registered unemployed of about 130 000 persons.

There is controversy over whether short-time working allowances fulfil their purpose as a manpower policy instrument and in fact stabilise employment in times of temporary slackness in demand. In other words, do all the effects on employment and the labour market assumed above really occur? The doubts, which spring mainly from a few notorious cases, are largely over whether (i) short-time working on balance really represents time lost or whether the time is not made up, either beforehand or afterwards, through overtime; and (ii) any

161

given loss in working time is really necessary and if the companies should not meet the costs either through loss of productivity or greater stockpiling.

The answers to these questions are of considerable importance, especially since short-time working has a number of very real advantages, such as being very flexible and, more than any other measure affecting working time, it can be adapted to any specific situation; it is reversible and can be suspended when the situation requires.

Empirical research results tend to suggest that short time working did on average fulfil its purpose, i.e.

- while it was not possible to prevent a reduction in the workforce altogether, a considerable brake was put on it;
- working time lost through short time was not made up either beforehand or afterwards through increased overtime. On the contrary, overtime was used as a regulator of output variations in the same way as short time.

For an assessment of the validity of this measure, it is worthwhile to look at the costs of short time work.

The firms working short time have to bear more than a quarter of the overall wage costs, plus the indirect wage costs which are relatively fixed in the short run. These are the costs of maintaining trained staff whilst avoiding the costs of dismissal, re-hiring and training. This cost sharing by firms as well as the definite pro-cyclical movements in take-up suggest that the measure is not widely misused.

GENERAL BUDGET COMPARISON

In this final assessment we make a comparison of costs and savings for the selected alternatives to unemployment compensation. It can be shown that the use of employment policy measures to reduce unemployment not only entails costs but also leads to savings and increased revenue in other parts of the public budget.

What matters is the balance for the budget as a whole and the question is: What would participants in manpower programmes cost if instead of participating they were unemployed and received unemployment benefits? Table 3 contains a comparison of the individual costs to the State. It reveals that:

- The costs of participation in full-time measures of advanced vocational training and re-training amount to DM.35 700 per person per year for the budget as a whole (including costs of courses). Thus the costs for the same person being a re- cipient of unemployment insurance benefits are exceeded by about DM.10 000.
- Employment of a person in a job creation scheme who otherwise would receive unemployment in- surance benefits or aid is not more expensive in an overall budgetary sense. The additional con- tributions to social security as well as the higher tax revenues caused by the wage of the participant balance the additional expenditures on wage subsidies for the participant and the supplementary loans.
- Short-time work calculated on a man/year basis is less expensive than unemployment and accom- panying compensation.

However, a comprehensive comparison of costs for the different measures has to take into account still other aspects of costs and revenues.

For a realistic assessment of the overall costs of measures to promote vocational training and re-training it is necessary to add to the immediate net costs those medium and long-term individual and economic additional revenues which have not been taken into account in our cost comparison. The results of evaluation research show that the great majority of participants in these measures make use of their increased qualifications on the labour market immediately after finishing training. On average they experience a considerable increase in income. This contributes to an upward shift in the qualification of the labour force and creates one pre- condition for a further increase in productivity and for the maintenance of the economy's international competi- tivity. Furthermore, about half the net costs of DM.10 000 (see Table 3) are contributions by the Federal Institute to the training institutions involved. From these contributions another positive employment effect results, which accrues to the Federal Institute's and other budgets. Despite the fact that these effects cannot be quantified easily, it is evident that these additional revenues will far exceed the net costs of training. This result still holds good, even if one takes into account that some participants in training are not entitled to unemployment insurance so that they represent net costs in the calculation.

In a dynamic comprehensive analysis of job creation measures one would also have to take into consideration the additional input by the institutions which implement projects. There are additional indirect employment ef- fects here (input/output relationships and multiplier

Table 3

FISCAL COSTS OF UNEMPLOYMENT AND OF LABOUR MARKET POLICY ALTERNATIVES -
A COMPARISON (DM. per head and year;
estimates for 1982)

	Advanced vocational training and retraining	General creation schemes	Short-time working	Unemployment
Federal Employment Institute (BA) expenditure (for persons or institutions respectively)	13 284(a)	26 058(a)	2 700(b) (9 000)(c)	11 297
Corresponding contributions to	8 460		1 068 (3 560)(c)	7 455
– pension funds	5 016		764 (2 547)(c)	4 405
– health insurance	3 444		304 (1 013)(c)	3 050
Other expenditures of the Federal Employment Institute (BA)	7 000(d)			
Total expenditures of the BA	28 744	26 058	3 768 (12 560)	18 752
Lost contributions to the BA budget	1 120		336 (1 120)	1 120
Lost direct and indirect taxes	5 847		1 754 (5 847)	5 855
Total fiscal costs	35 711	26 058	5 858 (19 527)	25 727

a) Subsidies and loans: without additional support.
b) Average hours lost 30 per cent of normal hours.
c) Annual basis (average hours lost 100 per cent).
d) Other costs (for example for courses, housing, fares).

Source: Institute of Employment Research (IAB) of the Federal Employment Institute (BA).

effects), which yield additional revenues to the budget as a whole. It can be proved in a dynamic simulation that the favourable result indicated above remains valid. Furthermore, it should not be overlooked that there are welfare gains from job creation measures in the form of the goods and services produced thereby.

There are some additional aspects of <u>short-time working</u>. The costs of unemployment compensation would be a bit less than indicated since the dismissals, which would happen without short-time working, would not result in an identical increase in registered unemployment, for some of the unemployed would leave the labour market. On the other hand, there are substantial gains for individuals, firms and for the society in avoiding the costs of losing skills, re-hiring and re-training.

CONCLUSIONS

There is no single panacea to solve the present intolerably high levels of unemployment. Instead, all available means have to be used, from the promotion of qualitative economic growth to a reduction of yearly working time and working life.

Unemployment is very expensive. For the unemployed themselves it means loss of income, psychological stress and the danger of loss of occupational skills. In public budgets it causes additional expenditures (unemployment insurance benefits and assistance and social aid), at the same time revenues decrease (direct and indirect taxes, social security contributions). In 1982, an unemployed person (an average covering both those who are entitled to unemployment insurance and those not entitled) costs about DM.24 000 per year to public budgets as a whole. The total overall budget losses resulting from unemployment was DM.45 billion, for example, greater than the net borrowing requirement of the Federal budget in 1982 (DM.40 billion). The economic losses of unemployment, calculated in terms of goods and services not produced far exceed this sum. In 1982, these losses amounted to about DM.100 billion at current prices, nearly 7 per cent of GDP.

The loss of these considerable resources (loss of revenues included) for consumption cannot be accepted as inevitable. Thorough cost comparisons show that measures to maintain or improve the qualifications of the unemployed do not exceed the costs of unemployment, if an adequate conception of costs is used.

Examples of overall fiscal cost comparisons have been provided for: "Promotion of vocational training and re-training", "job creation measures" and "short-time work". Although it is not possible to quantify all costs and revenues precisely, they can be estimated. In the case of short-time work moreover, the employment - and labour market - impact of working time reductions can be demonstrated.

In Germany these instruments have been used to a considerable degree during the recent years of recession. The average number of registered unemployed would have been higher by some 200 000-300 000 persons but for these activities. Consequently the expenditures on unemployment and the losses in revenues would have been much higher. From the point of view of the productive and future-oriented use of resources, more intensive recourse to these instruments would have been desirable to help the high and increasing number of unemployed. The allocation of resources and the conditions of participation in these schemes should not be reduced or tightened in the course of budgetary cutbacks. Nevertheless, an expansion of these measures would not solve the unemployment problem as a whole.

Beyond this, the Unemployment Insurance Fund could be used - directly or indirectly - to finance other employment or labour market policy measures, by which the number of unemployed and thus the expenditures on unemployment benefit could be reduced. The most recent example is a scheme to promote early retirement, jointly financed by employers, employees and the Federal Employment Institute.

Generally a higher degree of acknowledgement of these overall budget relationships in this context would be desirable, especially in the fields of policy planning and decision.

Finally, an examination should be made of how legal institutional and budgetary regulations could be better adapted to the requirements of a policy which takes into account the overall fiscal and dynamic aspects of the costs of unemployment.

ALTERNATE USES OF UNEMPLOYMENT
INSURANCE: THE CANADIAN EXPERIENCE

A comment
by
J.C.Y. Charlebois

Canada's experience with alternate uses of Unemployment Insurance (UI) funds is comparatively short, unlike
many other OECD countries. In 1977, the Canadian Par-
liament passed a bill to integrate the Unemployment Insurance Commission with the Department of Manpower and
Immigration, to form the Canada Employment and Immigration Commission/Department. Developmental uses of UI
funds formed part of this bill. The UI Act was amended
to allow for the use of UI funds in three areas:

- liberalisation of normal UI benefit entitlement
  provisions to allow for the payment of UI benefits in accredited work sharing schemes (section
  37 of the UI Act),
- the use of UI funds for unemployed people who
  become involved in developmental job creation
  projects (section 38 of the UI Act), and
- payment of UI benefits to qualified people on
  Commission-approved training courses (section 39
  of the UI Act).

TRAINING

History

Canadian government involvement in the training of
Canadians dates back to the early years of the century,
despite the fact that the provincial governments had
been accorded sole jurisdiction over education by the
British North America Act. From about 1913 to the passage of the Adult Occupational Training Act (AOTA) in
1967, federal involvement in this important area was
generally limited to the provision of ever-increasing
grants to the provinces. This direct federal funding
matched provincial outlays for technical and vocational

167

education. The AOT Act was, however, based on the as-
sertion that the training of adults according to national
economic priorities was well within the scope of federal
jurisdiction. The AOT Act abandoned the cost-sharing
approach and gave the federal government more control
over the training area.

The AOT Act was amended in 1972, changing the eligibility requirements and giving youth and women greater
access to training. Also, a basic training allowance
was introduced which could be topped-up by UI benefits,
for UI-eligible trainees.

An important step towards the present use of UI
funds in training was taken in 1975. A pilot project
was undertaken in which UI-eligible claimant/trainees
were paid only a very small share of their income maintenance in the form of training allowances. The larger
part was in the form of UI benefits. It was concluded
from this experiment that there was scope for increasing
the UI financial share of the claimant/trainee's income
maintenance during training.

In fact, two years later a new training arrangement
replaced the simple top-up formula. This new arrangement made UI the main source of income maintenance for
claimants on federally-sponsored training. This change
in financing would lead to a more effective resource allocation and free up resources for more training.

Experience

The UI Act allows the extension of the normal 52
weeks maximum benefit period to 104 weeks for claimant/
trainees. In this way, their UI benefits continue long
enough for them to finish their approved course when
their normal benefit period could have ended before the
course was finished.

These claimants are also allowed a six-week extension of their benefit period (within the 104-week maximum). This permits them to look for work after completion of the course while still receiving income
support.

Since 1975, UI funds have come to play an important
role in making training possible for many people. This
exceptional treatment of claimant/trainees under the UI
Act has been the most extensive and successful developmental use of UI funds.

In July 1982, a new National Training Act was passed
giving the federal government critical legislative authority to work with business, labour, community groups, in
addition to provincial governments, to change Canada's

training system so that it would better match the needs of a changing labour force. Although the AOT Act had accomplished much, it was found that it had not met some of the most critical skill needs and would not meet, in particular, the new high-skill training needs of the 1980s. The new Act enables the federal government to direct funds to training that is most essential for economic development. It will help train people for occupations in demand and eliminate training for labour surplus and redundant occupations by using limited public resources more effectively and ensuring that training pays off for people who take it. While taking courses in the classrooms of training institutions, trainees can collect UI benefits if they are eligible or training allowances if they are not.

Unemployment insurance and training programmes are, in fact, complementary. Developing new skills or upgrading existing skills reinforces UI's objective of helping claimants return to productive work and reduces the chance of unemployment.

UI PROGRAMME COSTS

1977 - 1981
($ millions)

	Total UI benefits paid	UI-funded training benefits
1977	3 928	34
1978	4 538	99
1979	4 009	138
1980	4 394	157
1981	4 828	165

WORK SHARING

History

The history of work sharing is short in Canada, when compared to many OECD countries. In essence, the aim of the Canadian work-sharing programme is similar to programmes in other countries - to keep trained workers on the job in periods of short-term adverse economic conditions. The goal is to help keep a stable work force and avoid the erosion of worker skills, habits and patterns of work which could follow from periods of unemployment. By obtaining agreement from all employees to work a shorter work week and receive UI benefits for the rest of the week, work sharing can reduce the costs of unemployment to workers, employers and the economy in general.

The Canadian experience began with a pilot project phase in the period 1977 to 1979. (An amendment to the present UI Act was passed in 1977 giving the Canada Employment and Immigration Commission the authority to use UI funds for work sharing.)

Although generally based on the normal benefit structure, work sharing departed from it in several ways, virtually all involving a liberalisation of standard benefit entitlement provisions. Specifically, work-sharing benefits are available without the normal waiting period of two weeks. And receipt of these benefits does not reduce the normal UI entitlement of work-sharing participants.

Evaluations from the early pilot project stage were ambivalent. The reports stated that while the theoretical aims may have been justified, other factors such as cost mitigated against viewing the programme as anything but a qualified success.

Even though the work-sharing programme was costly when measured in short-term cost/benefits terms, the short- and longer-term social, psychological and economic benefits (which are often difficult to quantify) appeared to justify these costs, particularly in times of a serious economic recession.

Experience

In the last half of 1981, with economic conditions worsening not only in Canada but in all Western industrialised countries, and unemployment continuing to climb in Canada, the government decided to go ahead and put to the test the use of UI funds for work sharing. It was encouraged to do this by the support of the employee/employer sectors for work sharing, particularly at the firm level. National media coverage of projects showed the private sector generally to be in favour of the programme, based on the feeling that "anything is better than a mass layoff".

The government repeatedly raised the limit on spending for work sharing, to a maximum of $200 million for 1982. Near the end of the third quarter of 1982, we had committed over $175 million on funding work sharing agreements with about 4 500 businesses, large and small. Over 150 000 workers "shared" the burden of a temporary downturn in production to save the jobs of some 65 000 workers. It showed what could be done through the co-operation of government, labour and business. For 1983, $150 million has been allocated to fund work-sharing projects.

History

Section 38 of the present UI Act came into effect
in 1977, along with the previously mentioned Sections 39
(training) and 37 (work sharing). At the time, the purpose of UI-funded job creation was to experiment with an
approach that would help claimants use their time on claim
more productively by working in community-oriented projects which might otherwise not be carried out because
of lack of money.

As in the case of work sharing, pilot projects were
set up and evaluated before national implementation of
the UI job creation programme. Again, several provisions
of the UI Act had to be changed to accommodate this new
use of UI funds. The most important was to allow payments well above the worker's normal entitlement and, in
some cases, considerably above the maximum benefit usually
payable.

Experience

Under the original pilot programme in 1979, just
over $1 million was paid out in benefits to UI claimants
participating in the three pilot projects. In 1982, the
federal government announced that it was allocating
$170 million in UI funds and $50 million in project support funds to a considerably expanded UI job creation
programme in 1982 and 1983. Towards the end of the third
quarter of 1982, around $108 million had been approved
for job creation proposals with a potential of creating
some 25 000 jobs.

The original rationale for the use of UI funds for
job creation still applies. UI-funded job creation
enables unemployment insurance claimants with little
chance of finding temporary jobs and every chance of
being reliant solely on income support, to use and maintain their skills by taking part in productive activities.

In overall terms, it is presently part of a national
employment strategy that responds to the labour market
needs of the 1980s. Because the current labour market
circumstances are considerably different from those prevailing when the original pilot programme was launched,
certain changes have been made to the programme to enable
a more appropriate response to current labour market conditions. The application of the programme is now possible in a larger range of circumstances than before.
(Such circumstances include re-construction in a community after a natural disaster and a temporary economic
crisis.)

The kinds of projects eligible for funding are those which provide unemployed workers with the opportunity to maintain their skills which contribute to the economic benefit of the community or the development of its economic potential. In 1982, the programme has been specifically directed to projects in resource sectors, such as forestry and fisheries. Through these projects, the programme has been successful in meeting both job creation objectives and resource management and enhancement objectives.

Again, it should be stressed that this developmental use of UI funds is particularly helpful in difficult economic times. It not only maintains income but also promotes productivity, helps blunt the social and economic costs of unemployment and helps industry and workers retain skills.

CONCLUSION

The Canadian experience with alternate uses of UI funds has been short and the results somewhat mixed. As mentioned earlier, basic inequities in the treatment of claimants, administrative complexity and higher costs have all raised questions among policy-makers. There is little doubt, on the other hand, that from a labour market perspective, using income maintenance only may not be the most effective way of addressing a UI claimant's employment difficulties, particularly during an extended economic downturn.

It is important to realise, however, that these limited uses of unemployment insurance funds for training, work sharing and job creation are effective within the broader context of labour market programmes. One of the major themes that runs through all of these programmes is that of preserving and developing needed skills. All of them, including those funded by UI, are aimed at preserving or producing skills needed either right now or in the coming decade.

The UI programme's main purpose is to provide unemployed workers with temporary income maintenance and to promote their return to stable and rewarding employment. Developmental uses of UI funds are an effective contribution to fulfilling this objective. However, in so far as they promote the preservation of valuable skills and the development of new ones, they also contribute to another broader objective of the programme: the facilitation of labour market adjustment.

The Canada Employment and Immigration Commission/ Department is evaluating the Canadian experience with work sharing and job creation, given their increased use in 1982. This further investigation will give the Commission/Department invaluable data at a time when the country's unemployment rate is higher than it has been for many years. This will provide a time-tested, more realistic basis for formulating recommendations to the government on the most effective labour market role for developmental uses of UI funds in the 1980s.

EXAMPLE OF ALTERNATE USES OF UI FUNDS IN CANADA

The Work-Sharing Programme

	As of 31 March, 1982	As of 7 September, 1982
Projects approved	489	4 868
Workers sharing work	26 708	153 355
Layoffs averted	11 610	65 794
Dollars committed	28 M	176 M

Industries involved:
. manufacturing   74 %
. retail and wholesale trades   14
. community, business and personal services   6
. transportation and communication   2
. construction   2
. miscellaneous   2

Company size (employees):
    10 and under   14 %
    11-49   41
    50-99   17
    100-199   12
    200 and over   15

Layoffs averted (workers):
    10 and under   36 %
    11-49   52
    50 and over   12

Workers involved:
. union   34 %
. non-union   66

PROBLEMS OF USING JOB CREATION SCHEMES
IN PLACE OF UNEMPLOYMENT COMPENSATION

A comment
by
Dr. R. Zeppernick

One alternative to the payment of unemployment compensation is to provide job creation schemes - JCSs for short. Views differ widely as to the employment policy efficiency of this instrument. But almost everyone agrees that its social policy effects are very worthwhile, since it makes it possible to get problem groups of the unemployed working again, if only on a temporary basis.

One of the reasons underlying the differing views as to the employment policy and hence economic policy effectiveness of attempting to replace unemployment compensation payment by JCSs is the fact that two basically different attitudes to economic policy are used to assess this instrument. The first is based on the assumption that the government is perfectly well able to create jobs; the second is doubtful as to the extent to which official intervention and government countercyclical and economic programmes can be used to create jobs that will be profitable in the long run. These doubts extend in particular to the use of JCSs. Irrespective of these differing basic approaches to economic policy, the following problems arise in considering the increased use of JCSs.

1. Supporters of the proposal argue that a person who is unemployed costs the state in any case almost DM.19 000 per year, whereas a JCS-employed person costs approx. DM.24 000 (1981 figures). So that the net cost of putting an unemployed person into employment is approx. DM.5 000.

This micro-economic view of the problem on the basis of ex-post figures ignores, or takes insufficient account of the following questions:

- how much money for JCSs is simply received as a bonus by enterprises which in any case planned to increase their workforces?

- how many other previously employed persons are possibly squeezed out into unemployment by JCSs?
- what happens to those employed under JCSs when their jobs cease to be subsidised by the Federal Employment Office?
- what are the possible macro-economic reactions - for example, how many jobs may be prevented from being offered because of increased interest rates or reduced private investment?

Only the net employment effects, which show how many persons in other jobs may also become unemployed, should be considered in assessing the employment policy success of JCSs.

2. To clarify the problem:

a) The bonus effect

If an employer takes on an unemployed person under a JCS, but had planned to create a new job in any case, the only effect is to provide him with a bonus. The total cost of this to the Federal Employment Office would in this case be DM.24 000, not simply DM.5 000. This DM.24 000 is precisely the amount the Federal Employment Office would have saved if the unemployed person had found a regular job without the JCS intervention.

b) The squeeze effect

It is much more difficult to judge the case in which the employer takes on someone under a JCS but at the same time dismisses one of the people he already employs. The employment policy effect is in this case zero, since the number employed is unaffected. The financial burden borne by the Federal Employment Office is approx. DM.24 000 for the person employed under the JCS, plus an additional approx. DM.19 000 on average for the newly unemployed person.

3. The government has attempted to prevent such bonus and squeeze effects by means of special regulations. Experience so far with this instrument has shown, however, that market forces are very difficult to influence by means of government regulations. The Expert Advisory Council (Sachverständigenrat) in its latest report seems resigned to this. It points out that bonus effects cannot be prevented and must simply be accepted. Since in everyday business life old jobs are continuously being abolished and new ones created, it is very difficult to prove how many additional jobs are actually being created by JCSs.

4. It is quite useless to limit the period of review for assessing the employment effects of job creation

schemes to one year. The important thing is to know how many JCS-employed are still in work in the period immediately following the expiry of the JCS and then at a later period. Previous aftermath analyses have shown, for example, that three months after expiry of a JCS only 40 per cent of those employed under it were still in employment. A study of such cases after two years had elapsed already made it clear that instead of providing employment relatively cheaply, JCSs simply postpone the cost of unemployment to a later date.

5. For the employment policy assessment of JCS jobs it is particularly important to realise that such jobs are highly subsidised. So long as the subsidy continues, the jobs can be kept in existence, but it has recently been shown that when the subsidy is discontinued these jobs can no longer be financed. A clear distinction must be made therefore as to whether the jobs created are highly subsidised ones which can only be financed for a limited period or whether JCSs are creating permanent profitable jobs capable of financing themselves.

6. It has often been argued that there is a big demand for public goods - particularly in the field of social services - which can be met by JCS jobs. Here it must be observed that the demand for public jobs can only be unlimited so long as they are provided free. But the question remains as to how big the demand for additional public goods would be if such goods had to be financed by additional taxes (or compulsory contributions). The numbers of those employed in the public services have risen steeply in recent years - by almost 8 per cent between 1975 and 1981. The resulting heavy additional burden on public spending on wages makes it clear that the possibilities of further increases in public service staffs are strictly limited (a 1 per cent increase in wages for the public services as a whole now costs well over DM.2 billion). Furthermore, the Federal Employment Office would be put in a difficult position if it had to decide on the usefulness and desirability of public goods - not to speak of the difficulties of the individual specialist in the Employment Offices, who is an adviser on labour questions, not on credit problems. One can well imagine the problems that could arise if the Federal Employment Office took over large-scale functions as a "public employment bank" and thus had in addition to wrestle with the risk of projects promoted by JCSs going bankrupt.

7. Further difficulties can arise because the unemployed taken on under JCSs receive incomes which they could not earn in normal employment on the market. In particular, with academics and persons with low professional qualifications there is a danger that through the relatively high rates of pay they receive under JCSs they come to expect levels of remuneration which the

market cannot afford. And that may mean that in many cases long-term unemployment is actually being programmed in advance. When this happens the process of widening differentials in earnings so urgently recommended by the Federal Government and the Expert Advisory Council could be rendered more difficult by the remuneration paid under JCSs.

8. JCSs are a relatively expensive instrument. Economic principle demands that it be asked how the maximum employment effect can be obtained with a given amount of resources. In practice this means investigating whether the employment effects of the amounts spent on JCSs would not be significantly larger if they were spent for example on further training and retraining. This question of the alternative use of resources is particularly important in periods of budgetary stringency. The approach generally should be to carry out a comprehensive analysis of the result of alternative employment policy instruments.

9. A clear distinction must be maintained between the employment policy significance of JCSs and their social policy significance. It is often quite rightly pointed out that unemployment involves problems for individual people whose personal destinies cannot be adequately taken account of in macro-economic accounting exercises. To the extent that severely affected groups on the labour market - e.g. long-term unemployed, or those handicapped by lengthy illnesses - can be given the opportunity of at least temporary employment, it seems perfectly reasonable and justifiable to use this relatively expensive instrument. Social suffering would be alleviated, and suitable arrangements could be made for individual cases. But this does not justify a decision to use JCSs on a large scale as an instrument to remedy unemployment. There is no doubt that highly subsidised jobs can always be provided for the unemployed. But from the employment policy point of view the decisive question is how many such people find permanent employment and what the total cost of such a scheme is. Judging by these criteria, it is extremely doubtful whether this instrument should be used on a large scale to combat unemployment.

A comment
by
L. Voogd

Last year the Dutch Government wanted to know whether unemployment benefits either directly, or indirectly through wage-cost subsidies, could be utilised to create structural employment. A positive answer would create a by-pass around the budgetary deadlock on employment plans. The cabinet decided to put the question to an ad hoc committee of civil servants and demanded an answer within three months. As Director for Social Assurances I chaired the interdepartmental committee that studied this question. The study took us to so many interrelated fields that the final report in a way represented the state of the art of last year's socio-economic policy-making.

The principal conclusions of our study were negative. But only in a superficial way: not to use unemployment benefits directly; not to introduce marginal employment subsidies on a large scale; not to abuse the budget mechanism.

The state of the socio-economic policy-making art contained actually some examples of positive and - in my undoubtedly biased view - even creative thinking. As good civil servants we of course kept this aspect of the report well hidden in clichés.

What the committee advised the Cabinet came down to the following: do not introduce a marginal employment subsidy unless the possible substitution effects are carefully studied and the possible outcome in terms of structural employment growth has been compared with the use of other instruments, like general wage subsidies or lower (corporate) taxes: do not make the mistake of using market-sector instruments in the budget sector: in the budget sector government should intervene directly by changing the rules. There is no advantage in using subsidies.

Our report in summary said:

a) Study marginal employment-subsidies, but

remember that many possible good economic effects can also be realised - and without expenditure - by moderating wage cost;

b) Direct the process of making budget decisions
towards what you want, through a clear outline
of priorities. If you want more employment,
create it by changing the budget towards that
end and pay for the extra cost (the net difference between wages and benefits plus overhead cost), preferably through salary and benefit cuts;

c) Do not create quasi-employment by paying wages
instead of benefits. Let unemployed people
keep their benefits while they train themselves,
receive schooling and do other useful things,
but do not pay them wages.

All members of the committee adhered to these main
conclusions. We differed in nuances. More or less so
in favour of creating jobs in the budget sector. Pre-
dictably, the division lines were drawn parallel to the
ministries involved. Since it was not our task to for-
mulate a Cabinet policy, we made no choices.

After the ICAU-Study was finished, I no longer worked
on the subject of employment schemes. What is written
here does not reflect the opinion of the department.
Nor are these thoughts up to the standards of thorough-
ness and detail that are expected from Dutch official
opinions. To be frank they are even somewhat speculative
to the civil servant's eye.

Adding today my personal opinion on the matter of
unemployment schemes, I think the state of the art has
shifted in two ways since last year. First it is no
longer possible to be content with studies. Something,
and on a large scale, has to be done about the frighten-
ing number of unemployed people, or anarchy - in the sense
that nobody will follow the unemployment benefit rules
any more - looms. And second, it is a terrible waste of
human productive potential to maintain a set of rules that
effectively ban the unemployed from productive labour.
I refuse to accept the notion that the artificial
reduction of the labour force, which is thus implied in
the unemployment laws, is the only - or even an adequate -
solution to the problems of false competition and maintaining proper budget techniques. What is an acceptable
technique in a period of full employment is clearly not
feasible at all when more than nearly 20 per cent of the
labour force is out of a job. Moreover, human nature is
against these "do nothing useful" rules. Everybody wants
to increase his psychological or physical income. So,
like everybody else, the unemployed person will direct
his behaviour towards greater personal satisfaction.
Since the rules and the economic situation prohibit him
from doing normal work he will look for a job in the

underground economy or if he is law-abiding, he will participate in the quasi-productive activities the employment programmes offer. In quasi-employment programmes people engage in meaningful activities that are not economically relevant and for which full wages, or supplements on the unemployment benefits are paid. Because the plans are costly (full wages and no production) only a few people benefit.

Based on this shifting emphasis are two further conclusions:

  i) The unemployment benefit laws will have to be
     changed insofar as they forbid productive
     labour, because that is socially and economi-
     cally counter-productive:
 ii) The quasi-employment programmes should be
     abolished, since their opportunity cost is
     high and their social and economic benefit
     is low.

Taking these points into account, other conclusions follow. Most work-programmes draw on volunteers, but, if the programmes are directed towards economically productive labour, it should not be left to the unemployed person to decide whether to participate or not. Benefits are given on the explicit condition that any suitable job should be taken. This condition could also be applied to participation in employment programmes. I am aware of the fact that work-programmes with an obligatory character (no allowance without work) from the 1930s and 1940s have a bad name and therefore have led to voluntary participation in present programmes. The older programmes got their bad name because they forced the jobless to accept work under inferior conditions for which they were not qualified socially, physically and mentally. I am certainly not in favour of a return to those stigmatised job programmes. There should not be any kind of discriminations of the unemployed.

But I am also convinced there should not be a "laissez-faire, laissez-aller" policy for the unemployed. Too much latitude is given in the present programmes to subjective considerations. If productive work is offered that corresponds with the capabilities of the unemployed, it should in principle not be refused, even if only the benefit is maintained. In this way the opposite situation of the quasi-employment programmes can be realised economically: productive work is done at the lowest possible wage cost. Unemployment benefits are not meant to freeze the status quo ante: social security has the functions to guard against poverty ("minimum" income guarantee), against sudden loss of income (wage loss compensation), and to facilitate the return to productive labour. Being unemployed therefore implies a willingness to maintain the capacity to work and the need

for labour market mobility. Therefore three more
conclusions:

    iii) employment programmes should have an obliga-
        tory character;
    iv) they should be directed at economically pro-
        ductive work; and
    v) should compensate the participant at the mini-
       mum (benefit) level, in order to accommodate
       the maximum number of participants.

Most wage loss compensations schemes are temporary.
How long "temporary" should be, I will not venture to
discuss. That is a political matter and depends in most
countries moreover on the social partners and on factors
like age and referral periods. So, without defining
"temporary", one may state that either directly or after
a certain period of time most unemployed persons enter
the minimum-benefit (welfare) stage.

My train of reasoning leads me to the conclusions
that to give welfare aid to people who are able and willing to work, is socially inadequate and economically
unattractive. It leads to social estrangement and deprivation and has a high opportunity cost. I would prefer instead a job guarantee scheme with compensation at
the minimum (welfare) income level. That would also be
in line with the employment goal of socio-economic
policy.

A recent experiment with an obligatory employment
programme in West Berlin appears to have been successful
in two ways. Two-thirds of the group of young people
called upon to do suitable work did their jobs to everybody's satisfaction: one-third did not show up and so
contributed significantly in widening social security
expenditure.

A job programme on the necessary scale could lead
to bureaucratic euphoria and to total disarray of the
market sector. Those are serious but not insurmountable
dangers. They can be controlled by good organisation
and decision-making. For the budget sector the answer
is to look at the first priorities: the activities that
would have been budgeted if the money to pay had been
available. Selection of priorities can be done generally
or selectively. Environment, housing and infrastructure,
education and development aid could be given preference.
While a national scheme does not yet exist, the municipal-
ities in the Netherlands who provide welfare are already
very active in this way by employing volunteers in a
variety of ways, though. In the budget memorandum 1984
a large-scale "third work circuit" is announced. The
scheme will provide quaternary sector employment on a
voluntary basis and with retention of benefits. And
the local schemes have a highly informal character,

probably because they border on the still forbidden "productive labour" line.

In the market sector, jobs can be created in different ways. Subsidising certain industries or professions is one way. (This would have to be done at least in an EEC context, in ways which prevent unwanted market disturbances.)

If it is true that economic growth and thus employment is derived from "God and the engineers", as some economists maintain, we could subsidise at least the engineers. If we need more entrepreneurs to create employment, as others believe, then let us encourage starting enterprises. Studies indicate that it is more efficient to use (selective, marginal) wage subsidies to create structural employment, than to lower corporate taxes or to moderate wage growth for the same objective.

Of course (wage) subsidies would change market conditions. So do taxes, social security premiums and benefits and governmental rules in general. That is what the mixed economy is all about. The only right question to ask is whether the conditions are being changed in such a way that more jobs are created than can be created with the same amount of money through another instrument. A pilot project can help to decide that question. If the answer is yes then let us not mourn the onslaught on the market mechanism. The mechanism seldom works properly anyway, and it would be like mourning the end of the nineteenth century.

Being a good Dutchman I should add a "guesstimate" on the budgetary and financial side. Obligatory employment programmes carry no extra wage cost if the unemployment benefit equals the job compensation. The existing bureaucracy can handle most of the schemes, so there is a limited overhead cost. There is a reduction of expenditure aspect because some jobless will prefer to lose their unemployment benefit rather than participate in a programme. Labour market conditions will improve because unemployed people will try hard to find a higher paid job and in the meantime are better trained.

Labour mobility and skill will also improve and thus labour productivity will go up while wages will tend to moderate. If the work-projects are chosen carefully, there is no disturbance in the market sector and thus no loss in employment. In the budget sector a reallocation between budgeted and fully paid jobs and employment-scheme jobs would be necessary. This "debudgeting" could be done with or without changing total paid employment.

Subsidies cost money and more so if they are ineffective. Together with the overhead and other costs of employment programmes the financial burden for a large-

scale scheme could be several per cent of GNP. To pay
this in the Netherlands either a 5 per cent ("guesstimate") withholding tax on all wages and benefits could
be contemplated, or, if one considers it essential not
to increase the budget, all collective sector incomes,
salaries and benefits, should be cut by 10 per cent.

LAST CONCLUSION

To pay for a large-scale employment scheme either
a plus-minus 5 per cent withholding tax or a plus-
minus 10 per cent collective sector salary cut
should be adequate.

Part Three

BACKGROUND DOCUMENTATION

VII

TRENDS IN EXPENDITURE ON
UNEMPLOYMENT INSURANCE AND FACTORS UNDERLYING THEM

by
P. Roberti

I. INTRODUCTION

This chapter presents an analysis of trends in expenditure on unemployment insurance benefits (EUB) and of the factors which underlie them. The time period covered is 1960 to date. The countries included are Canada, France, Germany, Italy, Japan, the United Kingdom and the United States.

The purpose of the following analysis is threefold. The first is to present an overview of the factors which can underlie changes in total unemployment insurance spending. This is done in Section II. The second is to identify among these factors those which are amenable to empirical economic analysis and discuss their relative importance by decomposing EUB into its constituent parts. This is the subject of Section III. The third and last is to develop a simplified EUB model and use it to present simulations as to possible trends in EUB under a number of different scenarios concerning unemployment, beneficiaries and level of benefit. This is dealt with in Section IV.

The analysis is limited to unemployment insurance spending only.(1) This is dictated by reasons of data availability, but also justified by the great heterogeneity of unemployment assistance data.

The conclusions suggested are:

. The behaviour of each factor has not been consistent throughout the period considered;

186

- Cyclical influences and long-term trends tend to interact(2) and the way they combine to affect expenditure changes over time.(3)
- The expenditure growth pattern changed dramatically with the first oil shock. Peak figures were reached in most Member countries around 1975-78. Since then, annual growth rates of real expenditure have slowed down and have even become negative. The new surge in unemployment since 1981 has, however, caused a substantial increase in expenditure.
- Changes in unemployment are clearly reflected in total spending and are thus a very important cause of trends in unemployment insurance expenditure. The role of political decisions is also of great importance. Policies to improve the real value of unemployment insurance benefits and towards adjustment of benefits for inflation had an important influence on the growth of expenditure on unemployment benefits in the 1960s and until about the second oil shock. Less stringent eligibility criteria have played a similar role since around the mid-1970s. Equally, in the late 1970s the need to place a check upon public expenditure growth has meant increased scrutiny of expenditure on unemployment benefits. The policy changes which have followed (e.g. little or no increase, if not actual cuts, in the real value of benefits or in the eligible population) have meant that some "control" has been established upon expenditure in unemployment benefits.

The second part of the study (i.e. Section IV) presents a three-equation model structured around the elements of the identity: (Total unemployment insurance expenditure) = (Average actual weekly benefits) x (Number of claimants per week) x (Average number of weeks of compensated unemployment) to explain expenditure on unemployment insurance. The regression results are encouraging, though improvements are possible and need to be pursued in future work. This model has three specific advantages. First, it is structured to be endogenous to most macroeconomic models, a feature which makes it possible to use it for the purpose of public expenditure forecasting. Second, it works well and appears to be easily applicable to data available for various Member countries. Third, it can be used to simulate the implications for expenditure of policy changes (such as variations in the level of benefits and duration of compensated unemployment) and of different unemployment rates.

The results of a number of simulations concerning various hypotheses about average benefits levels (see Table 11), unemployment rates (see Tables 13 and 14) and duration of compensated unemployment (see Table 12) are presented in Section IV(C). A summary picture of the simulated influence of different factors upon expenditure on unemployment benefits during 1970-78 in Canada, Germany, Italy, Japan and the United States is provided in the Summary Table hereafter. This table plus Tables 10 to 14 suggest the following conclusions, in addition to the obvious remark that unemployment insurance expenditure is sensitive (especially in Germany) to changes in unemployment:

- policy changes implemented after the first oil shock were the single most important factor in the growth of unemployment insurance spending during 1973-78 in Canada, Germany, Italy and Japan, though not in the United States.
- increasing duration of unemployment was probably the second most important cause of expenditure growth, with the exception of Germany and the United States.

II. FACTORS UNDERLYING CHANGES IN TOTAL UNEMPLOYMENT INSURANCE SPENDING: THE CONCEPTUAL FRAMEWORK

The relationship between total cash payments to unemployed workers and the unemployment rate is not at all straightforward, but complicated by a number of independent or interacting factors such as:

   i) inflow/outflow patterns and, a related element, duration of spells;
  ii) policy decisions concerning eligibility criteria and value of benefit;
 iii) family circumstances (e.g. single, married, number of dependents, etc.) and previous earnings of the unemployed;
  iv) general upward pressures from the growing labour force and share of covered dependent employment.

These two latter factors, in particular, may constitute a long-term cost-inflating force for expenditure on unemployment compensation. This is because the growth of total civilian and dependent employment may lead to more than proportionate increases in covered employment and, thus, for any given unemployment rate and unchanged beneficiaries to unemployed ratio, a greater number of beneficiaries (the factor determining expenditure once benefits are fixed).(4)

The relationship between expenditure on unemployment insurance benefit and the unemployment rate can therefore be expected to show some instability as the various factors influencing EUB combine in different fashion to produce total expenditure. On the whole, graphs 1a to 1g tend to support this hypothesis.(5)

188

Summary Table

EXPENDITURE ON UNEMPLOYMENT INSURANCE BENEFITS: FACTORS UNDERLYING CHANGES BETWEEN 1970-1978

	Canada	Italy	United States	Japan	Germany
1. Total expenditure					
total annual average growth rate	26.4	31.0	10.9	21.2	32.7
of which attributable to changes in:					
Prices(a)	7.6	13.0	6.7	9.8	5.2
Unemployment	2.8	2.8	3.9	1.6	22.3
Policy(b): real income adjustments	3.1	7.1	3.2	5.4	2.2
Other measures	11.2	7.1	-1.4	3.7	0.7
Unexplained(e)	1.7	1.1	+0.5	0.7	2.3
2. Average actual benefits					
total annual average growth rate	15.3	25.0	6.6	15.8	7.6
of which attributable to changes in:					
Prices(a)	7.6	13.0	6.7	9.8	5.2
Policy(b): total	7.7	12.0	-0.1	6.0	2.4
real income adjustments	3.1	7.0	-1.2	5.4	2.2
Other measures	4.6	5.0	-1.3	0.6	0.2
3. Number of claimants					
total annual average growth rate	2.7	2.1	2.8	-0.8	19.6
of which attributable to changes in:					
Unemployment	2.0	1.6	2.8	-2.8	18.6
Policy(c)	0.7	0.5	-	+2.0	1.0
4. Number of weeks of compensated unemployment					
total annual average growth rate	6.7	2.8	1.0	5.5	3.2
of which attributable to changes in:					
Unemployment	0.8	1.2	1.1	4.4	3.7
Policy(d)	5.9	1.6	-0.1	1.1	-0.5

a) Assumes that governments were committed to maintaining the real value of benefits, i.e. automatic adjustments for changes in the consumer price index only. This, however, may not be the case (e.g. in Italy).

b) It should be noted that the distinction of the effect of policy changes between real income adjustments and other measures is artificial. This stems from well-known difficulties of distinguishing discretionary and automatic policy changes. The distinction between changes due to real income adjustments and discretionary measures is thus illustrative in that it tries to disentangle what could be attributed to a policy allowing benefits to rise in line with real wages and earnings and to other policy changes (e.g. benefit adjustments above changes in wages and salaries).

c) e.g. eligibility changes.

d) e.g. longer duration of benefit.

e) i.e. attributable to interactions between the various components of the identity.

Unemployment benefit as a percentage of GDP

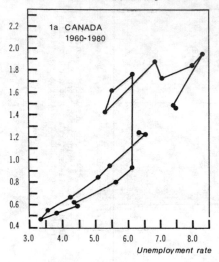

Unemployment benefit as a percentage of GDP

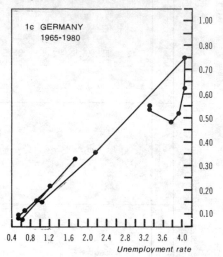

Unemployment benefit as a percentage of GDP

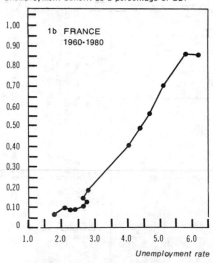

Unemployment benefit as a percentage of GDP

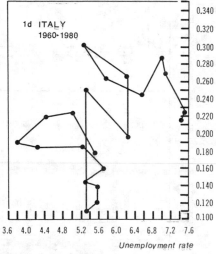

Unemployment benefit as a percentage of GDP

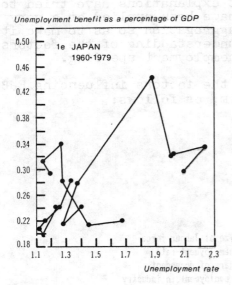

Unemployment benefit as a percentage of GDP

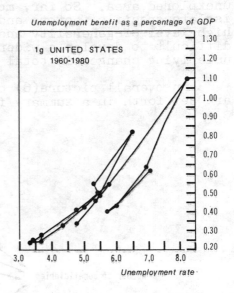

Unemployment benefit as a percentage of GDP

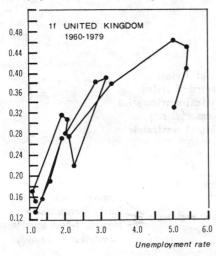

In most Member countries the identification, discussion and assessment of the relative importance of the causal factors which account for changes in spending on cash transfers to unemployed workers is still a relatively unexplored area. So far, most explanations have tried to isolate specific factors and have been applied at a very high level of generality and aggregation so as to make it difficult to develop a wider understanding of the factors underlying changes in total unemployment spending.

An overall picture(6) of the factors influencing EUB are set forth in a summary form, as follows:

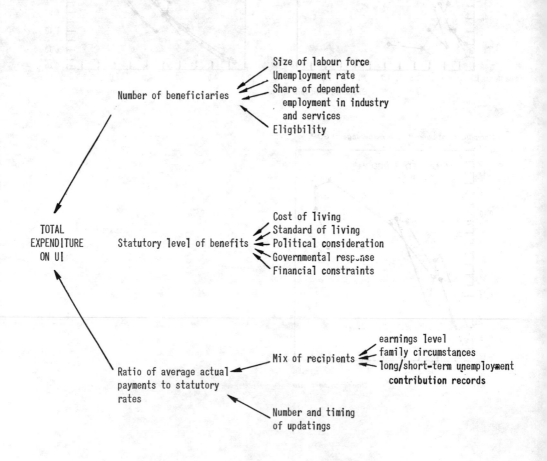

Not all factors are, however, equally important. Some are purely economic, others political and thus more amenable to control for policy purposes. Some are affected by cyclical change (e.g. the level of unemployment), others are mostly influenced by longer-term structural modifications (e.g. growing share of dependent employment in industry and services).

Once having identified the factors underlying unemployment insurance benefits, the most interesting questions to explore are:

  i) What accounts for the growth in unemployment insurance benefits? This can be appraised as an economic history question and thus investigated by means of descriptive analysis; and
  ii) What is the relative importance of different factors? This requires an investigation of behavioural relationships.

The former is the subject of the following section, and the latter of Section IV.

III. TRENDS IN UNEMPLOYMENT INSURANCE
SPENDING AND SELECTED CONTRIBUTING FACTORS, 1960-1980

A. Growth in unemployment insurance expenditure

No matter which indicator is taken, unemployment insurance spending has grown very rapidly: what was an upward drift in the 1960s has become a very steep uphill tendency in the 1970s and early 1980s. For the seven countries covered in this study, EUB in 1975 prices showed a tendency, on average(7), to almost double during the 1960s. In the 1970s it more than trebled. The picture is not less dramatic when EUB as a percentage of GDP (up from 0.3 to 0.6 per cent, on average, in the 1960s and 1970s respectively) or of total public expenditure (up from 1.0 to 1.5 per cent, on average, in the 1960s and 1970s respectively) or of total expenditure on income maintenance (up from 4.4 to 5.5 per cent in the 1960s and 1970s respectively), is considered. All these different ways of appraising EUB trends are illustrated in Table 1.

Naturally, the surge in unemployment is a major cause of EUB growth. Other factors also have been important. To understand the possible influence which a number of them may have had, EUB is decomposed into the following constituent parts:

  . average level of actual benefit per beneficiary and week of unemployment;
  . average length of time of unemployment for which benefits were paid;

Table 1

EXPENDITURE ON UNEMPLOYMENT INSURANCE BENEFITS(a), 1960-80

(Six-year averages)

	1960-1965	1965-1970	1970-1975	1975-1980
1. Total Spending(b,c) (national currencies and 1975 prices)				
Canada	733	667	2 111	3 167
France	214	778	2 491	104 111
Germany	n.a.	1 665(e)	3 075	7 927
Italy	136	129	281	354
Japan	202	282	504	673
United Kingdom	216	414	652	895
United States	5 189	3 780	8 356	11 747
2. Trend Growth Rate(d) (average annual growth rate)				
Canada	-9.6	+13.0	+25.9	-1.7
France	+21.4	+24.1	+40	+19.1
Germany	n.a.	-17.9(e)	+51.4	+21.0
Italy	+7.0	-3.8	+3.3	+0.3
Japan	+16.4	+6.2	+20.2	+3.9
United Kingdom	+2.6	+19.6	+11.4	+9.0
United States	-1.4	+7.3	+25.1	-9.5
3. Total Spending as a Percentage of GDP				
Canada	0.91	0.59	1.4	1.74
France	0.03	0.07	0.18	0.65
Germany	-	0.16(e)	0.27	0.58
Italy	0.2	0.14	0.23	0.25
Japan	0.33	0.29	0.31	0.41
United Kingdom	0.18	0.27	0.35	0.46
United States	0.54	0.29	0.56	0.68
4. Total Spending as a Percentage of Public Expenditure				
Canada	3.08	1.83	3.75	4.32
France	0.07	0.19	0.45	1.45
Germany	-	0.43(e)	0.65	1.3
Italy	0.62	1.41	1.6	1.59
Japan	-	-	1.18	1.24
United Kingdom	0.52	0.71	0.85	1.04
United States	1.84	0.94	1.65	1.95
5. Total Spending as a Percentage of Total Expenditure of Public Expenditure				
Canada	13.51	8.43	15.2	17.35
France	0.23	0.49	1.08	3.26
Germany	-	0.80(e)	1.85	4.16
Italy	1.81	1.11	1.63	1.75
Japan	-	5.28	4.75	3.83
United Kingdom	2.74	3.89	4.69	4.60
United States	9.92	4.81	6.30	6.53

a) Does not include expenditure on unemployment assistance programmes and special programmes.
b) Millions, except for Italy and Japan, which are billions.
c) The deflator used is the consumer price index.
d) Geometric mean of annual growth rates.
e) Refers to 1967-1970 only.

. EUB beneficiaries and proportion of insured
  unemployment;
. unemployment rate;
. size of the labour force;

each of which can subsume, as seen above in Section II,
influences of various other factors(8).

The rest of this section investigates the changes
that occur in these "constituent parts" during the period
1960-1980 and discusses how they might be associated
with changes in EUB.

B.   Average actual benefit

Under existing legislation, statutory benefits
can be flat-rate or a fixed or variable proportion of
previous earnings; be differentiated by family circumstances (e.g. single, married, etc.); be affected by
type of unemployment (e.g. seasonal unemployment), number of spells (e.g. spells may or may not be linked),
duration of spells (e.g. lower benefits may be paid as
the duration of spells lengthens), etc. Total EUB thus
is the sum of heterogeneous types of daily or weekly
benefits (t_j where j stands for the type of benefit)
weighted by the number of claimants receiving each of
them (b_j), and the number of days or weeks of each type
of compensated unemployment (d_j), i.e.:

$$EUB = \sum_j (t_j) \times (b_j) \times (d_j)$$

In practice, information on t_j, b_j and d_j is not
available in most Member countries. What is available
instead, or can be calculated from administrative
records(9), is the total number of EUB claimants or number of first payments (i.e.: $FP = \sum_{i,j} b_{ij}$) and the number of days/weeks/or months of unemployment for which
benefits are paid (i.e.: $CW = \sum_{i,j} d_{i,j}$). Because
EUB = (AB) x (CW) or, stated another way

$$EUB = (AB) \times (FP) \times \left(\frac{CW}{FP}\right)$$

where AB is the average benefit paid to all unemployed workers

$\left(\frac{CW}{FP}\right)$ is the average length of time of compensated
unemployment(10),

AB can easily be estimated from administrative records
once EUB, FP and CW are known.

Estimates of AB such as this, however, have the limitation of attributing any change in AB to changes in statutory benefits though, in fact, these may arise from the changing mix of unemployed (e.g. if the proportion of unemployed workers with an earnings-related supplement increases, then AB will also increase). This (compensation effect) problem cannot be overcome with available data. Changes in AB therefore cannot be automatically equated with changes in statutory benefits.

Trends in the real value of AB (in 1975 prices) during 1960-1980 are shown in Table 2. The general long-term picture is one of growth. AB growth was fairly moderate and in line with real wage developments in the 1960s (not in Italy, however). It speeded up in the 1970s, especially following the first oil crisis. This appears to have displaced upwards the long-term growth pattern and led to growth rates in AB which outpaced changes in real wages. This trend, however, did not continue in the latter years of the 1970s: AB growth rates slowed down in all countries examined and have even shown negative values in most recent years (i.e. in Canada, Germany, Italy, the United Kingdom and the United States)(11). This drop in the real value of AB can partly be ascribed to policy changes concerning benefit values to strengthen work incentives and to reduce government cost; i.e. adjustments in statutory benefits have been made at less frequent intervals, have been smaller than in earlier years and have not kept pace(12) with prices and wages (see Table 3). It also reflects, however, a change in the mix of the unemployed among whom the proportion of long-term unemployed, who are generally paid lower benefits, has increased(13).

C.   Average length of time of compensated unemployment

With the worsening of the employment situation, average and median duration of unemployment have shown a marked tendency to increase in most OECD countries since the early 1970s(14). The number of weeks of compensated unemployment has also shown a similar tendency. Table 4 shows trends in the average number of weeks of compensated unemployment. The data suggest a mixed pattern until the 1970s, e.g. a tendency to decrease in Japan and the United States and to increase in other countries. Thereafter, an upward trend is observed in all countries, with the lengthening in the second half of the 1970s in the number of weeks of unemployment for which benefits were paid ranging from just less than a week in Italy to just over five weeks in France.

The impact which longer spells of unemployment may have on EUB varies among Member countries. Table 5 provides an illustration of the additional cost which may be associated with a one-week change in duration of compensated unemployment. The estimates for six Member

196

Table 2

AVERAGE ACTUAL WEEKLY UNEMPLOYMENT BENEFIT, 1960-1980(a)
(At constant 1975 purchasing power. Six-year averages)

	1960–1965	1965–1970	1970–1975	1975–1980
Canada ($)	43.07	43.65 (+0.2)	72.73(b) (+8.9)	83.69 (+2.4)
Germany (DM)	–	153.60	195.80 (+4.7)	230.8 (+2.8)
Japan (Yen)	7 720	10 245 (+4.8)	14 629 (+6.1)	17 978(c) (+3.5)
Italy (Lire)	6 016	5 051 (-2.9)	7 079 (+5.8)	9 412 (+4.9)
United Kingdom (£)	10.20	15.18 (+6.9)	17.10 (+2.0)	16.40 (-0.7)
United States ($)	61.46	66.74 (+1.4)	70.84 (+1.0)	69.57 (-0.3)

a) Figures in brackets show the average annual percentage change from previous period six-year average.
b) Benefits were made taxable since 1972. The change in the net real value of benefit is then overstated.
c) Refers to 1975-1979.

Table 3

TRENDS IN AVERAGE ACTUAL UNEMPLOYMENT BENEFITS, PRICES AND WAGES, 1960–1980
(1970 = 100)

		1960	1965	1970	1973	1975	1978	1980
Canada								
	AB	64	70	100	195	242	313	345
	P	77	83	100	116	143	180	217
	W	58	70	100	128	168	227	260
Germany								
	AB	..	61(a)	100	138	166	179	264
	P	77	89	100	119	135	150	165
	W	44	69	100	134	160	190	212
Italy								
	AB	73	85	100	213	276	537	720
	P	69	86	100	124	172	268	372
	W	41	67	100	156	241	434	635
Japan								
	AB	31	55	100	157	250	323	335(b)
	P	..	..	100	125	172	211	219(b)
	W	31	50	100	163	229	295	317(b)
United Kingdom								
	AB(c)	34	62	100	118	185	237	380
	P	67	80	100	128	185	270	363
	W	..	69	100	141	209	310	357
United States								
	AB	65	74	100	117	140	166	216
	P	76	82	100	115	139	168	213
	W	67	78	100	121	148	183	215

a) Refers to 1966.
b) Refers to 1979.
c) Refers to Great Britain only.
AB = Average actual unemployment benefits (in current prices).
P = Consumer prices.
W = Monthly or hourly gross earnings.

Table 4

AVERAGE NUMBER OF WEEKS OF COMPENSATED UNEMPLOYMENT

	1960-1965	1965-1970	1970-1975	1975-1980
Canada	7.9	8.2	11.4	13.7
France	n.a.	n.a.	24.1	29.4(a)
Germany	8.9	10.0	10.5	12.7
Italy	16.0	17.2	21.3	21.5
Japan	14.9	14.8	15.19	20.1
United States	13.2	11.7	13.8	14.4

a) Refers to 1975-79.

Table 5

COST OF ONE ADDITIONAL WEEK OF UNEMPLOYMENT
(at 1980 benefit levels and number of beneficiaries)

	Additional expenditure (in millions)	as % of total 1980 UI expenditure
Canada ($)	334	7.6
Germany (DM)	727	9.0
Italy (Lire)	38 536	4.6
Japan (Yen)(a)	30 952	4.8
United Kingdom (£)	58	4.3
United States ($)(a)	724	7.6

a) At 1979 benefit levels and number of beneficiaries.

countries are based on 1980 benefit levels and the number
of beneficiaries. On average, the figures suggest that a
one-week increase in duration of compensated unemployment
could push up EUB by between 4 and 8 per cent of total
expenditure. Longer duration of compensated unemployment
then appears as a potentially important factor in the
growth of EUB.

D.   Size of the labour force, unemployment and number of
      unemployment insurance beneficiaries

     With unchanged eligibility criteria and unemployment
rates, an increasing labour force can a priori be expected
to be associated with larger numbers of beneficiaries. If
the unemployment rate were to increase as well, the number
of beneficiaries would then be expected to increase even
faster. Changes in the size of the labour force and unemployment, then, if associated together, may reinforce or
weaken each other's distinct effect upon the number of
beneficiaries.

     Trends in the size of the labour force, unemployment
and number of beneficiaries are shown in Table 6. Labour
force and unemployment figures come from the same data
source and are therefore comparable. Beneficiary statistics, however, are from administrative sources or sample
surveys that are not, in most instances, comparable with
the other two sets of data. Ratios of beneficiaries to
unemployed cannot then be derived and, if calculated,
would not be very meaningful given these heterogenei-
ties(15). Statistics can, however, be used to compare
trends in each set of figures in an attempt to appraise
the possible evolution in the beneficiaries-to-unemployed
ratios. This is done in Table 7 which compares percentage
changes in the numbers of beneficiaries and unemployed.

     The following conclusions can be drawn from the two
tables:

     . The ratio of beneficiaries to unemployed probably
       declined slightly in the second half of the 1960s
       (except in Japan), increased markedly in the first
       half of the 1970s (except in Germany), and de-
       clined in the late 1970s to levels close to the
       early 1960s (e.g. in Italy and the United States)
       or well below them (e.g. in Germany, Japan and the
       United Kingdom). These trends can be ascribed to
       a number of reasons. First, the rise in the "full-
       employment unemployment rate" (FEUR) has tended to
       depress the number of beneficiaries as initial
       payments have grown less fast than benefit exhaus-
       tions; i.e. more beneficiaries have been pushed
       out of EUB schemes (into assistance or left with-
       out income support) than new ones have entered
       into them. This explains trends in the late 1960s

Table 6

SIZE OF LABOUR FORCE, NUMBERS OF UNEMPLOYED WORKERS
AND BENEFICIARIES, 1960–1980
(six-year averages)

	1960–1965	1965–1970	1970–1975	1975–1980
a) Size of labour force (thousands)				
Canada	6 848	7 922	9 221	10 795
France	19 942	20 798	21 933	22 677
Germany	26 957	26 675	26 801	26 253
Italy	20 666	20 943	20 984	22 084
Japan	46 393	49 955	52 495	55 562
United Kingdom	25 635	25 446	25 427	25 220
United States	74 365	81 546	90 179	100 963
b) Unemployed workers (thousands)				
Canada	380	337	547	814
France	238	388	628	1 101
Germany	185	236	418	1 007
Italy	720	1 146	1 194	1 694
Japan	617	600	728	1 215
United Kingdom	361	450	678	1 350
United States	3 950	3 150	5 189	6 905
c) Beneficiaries (thousands)				
Canada	341	294	540	731
France	n.a.	n.a.	307	739
Germany	121	151	264	550
Italy	437	488	707	704
Japan	517	540	613	704
United Kingdom	250	287	369	585
United States	2 031	1 380	2 693	3 423

Table 7

RATIOS OF INDICES OF BENEFICIARIES
AND ALL UNEMPLOYED(a), 1960-1980
(1970 = 100)

	1960-1965	1965-1970	1970-1975	1975-1980
Canada	110.8	108.2	116.1	111.1
France	..	..	90.4(b,c)	104.1(b,c)
Germany	102.2	97.8	97.2	86.0
Italy	151.1	106.6	148.9	116.5
Japan	99.1	106.4	99.6	68.5
United Kingdom	117.5	108.3	92.3	73.6
United States	100.4	85.4	100.0	99.6

a) Measured by dividing the beneficiaries index by
the all unemployed index.   Six-year averages.
b) Refers to 1972-1975.
c) 1972 = 100.

and late 1970s.   Second, the number of beneficiaries is more responsive to cyclical fluctuations than to longer-term increases in the FEUR.
These cyclical downswings have the effect of
bringing closer the insured and the total unemployment rates(16) and thus of increasing the
proportion of insured unemployed among all unemployed workers.   This factor explains trends
in the early and mid-1970s.   There is, however,
a third cause which explains the bounce in the
value of the ratio of beneficiaries to total
unemployed in this period.   Namely, the changes
in eligibility conditions and longer duration
of payment of benefits which followed in many
Member countries the first oil shock.

. Contrary to a priori expectations, the expanding labour force does not seem to have, in
general, resulted in a greater number of beneficiaries for any given unemployment rate.
This can partly be ascribed to the fact that
unemployment has increasingly hit young people
and females, i.e. groups which are less or not
protected at all by UB systems compared to
prime-age males.

E.   Conclusions

The following general conclusions seem warranted:

- The behaviour of each factor has been changing throughout the period considered and so has its contribution to unemployment insurance spending.
- Changes in economic activity affect certain factors more than others (e.g. numbers of beneficiaries). Important lags are also observed (e.g. the duration of time of unemployment for which benefits are paid tends to respond to cyclical variations only after some time has elapsed).
- Cyclical influences and long-term trends tend to interact (e.g. changes in the insured unemployment rate and the growing share of youths and females in the labour force) so that the influence of various factors underlying changes in EUB changes over time (e.g. the effect upon EUB of the number of beneficiaries).
- The growth pattern of EUB changed dramatically with the first oil shock. Peak figures were reached in most Member countries around 1975-78. Since then, annual growth rates slowed down and even became negative. The new surge in unemployment since 1981 is, however, causing a new bounce in EUB.
- The unemployment rate aside, discretionary policy changes are of greatest importance in explaining EUB trends. Policies to improve the real value of benefits and towards uprating and adjustment of benefits for inflation had an important influence on the growth of EUB expenditure in the 1960s and until about the second oil shock. Less stringent eligibility criteria have also played a similar role since around the mid-1970s. Equally, in the late 1970s the need to check upon public expenditure growth meant closer examination of EUB. The policy changes which have followed (e.g. little or no increase in the real value of benefit or in the eligible population) have meant some moderation in the rate of growth of EUB.
- Policy considerations, important as they are, cannot, however, prevent changes in unemployment (in terms of number or duration) from being reflected in total EUB. Indeed, this is exactly what is currently happening with the new rise in unemployment. In spite of continuing lengthening of the average period during which unemployed workers are paid benefits (a very important factor underlying EUB), growth in EUB in 1981 and 1982 should turn out to be more contained than in the recent past. The reasons for this are tightening in eligibility and payment criteria and slow growth if not cuts in the real value of statutory unemployment benefits. In the late 1970s the relationship between EUB and a

1 per cent change in unemployment could be estimated at between 0.25 and 0.30. This is somewhat
below earlier OECD mid-1970s estimates of 0.30 to
0.35 and nearer to elasticity values prevailing in
the early 1970s(17). Given changes in unemployment
insurance benefit policy in the late 1970s, the
difference between these two elasticities gives,
perhaps, a measure of the possible impact which
more or less "generous" policies can have on EUB.

IV. AN UNEMPLOYMENT INSURANCE EXPENDITURE MODEL

A.   The model

At the simplest level, EUB can be thought of as being equal to the product of a number of constituent
parts. The numbers of parts and the factors appearing in
each of them can be differently established, as has been
the case in different studies(18). Since the purpose of
this study is to estimate the impact which policy changes
and economic variables can have on EUB for both past and
future periods, the following accounting identity, established earlier on in Section II is used as a basis for
the analysis:

EUB = (AB) x (FP) x (NW)

where AB is the actual average weekly benefit paid;
      FP the number of claimants to whom benefits
         are actually paid;
      NW (or, which is the same, CW/FP) is the
         average number of weeks during which bene-
         fits were paid, i.e. the ratio of total
         weeks compensated (CW) to the number of
         claimants (FP).

The question which needs to be addressed is to relate
these three constituent parts to their determinants. This
is the subject of the rest of this section.

To facilitate the integration of the EUB model into
larger econometric models, the choice of explanatory variables has been limited to those which appear in most econometric models.

i) Actual average weekly benefits paid (AB)

This can be regarded as a policy-controllable variable. A number of factors are identified in Figure 1,
Section II, as counting for improvements in the real value
of average benefits. In this analysis, however, the simplified hypothesis is made that AB tends to be determined
in relation to the general standard of living and adjusted

204

for changes in it. Good proxies for general living standards which can be used include per capita measures of GDP, private consumption or disposable income. GDP per capita (GDP/N) is the measure used in this study.

Policy considerations, however, also intervene and importantly influence AB. There are two reasons why this is so. First, they can affect views about the adequacy of benefits and lead to the gradual increase in replacement ratios. This process was apparent in the 1960s and early to mid-1970s, but seems to have reached an upper bound due to work disincentive considerations. The logarithm of the time variable (t), rather than time itself, is therefore used as the explanatory variable to dampen the rates of growth as time progresses. This implies that higher replacement ratios have increasingly been seen as unjustifiable in the light of the current economic recession. Second, policy considerations can intervene at irregular intervals to change the long-run relationship between AB and GDP/N. Upward displacements in this relationship have occurred in many Member countries, especially in the early 1970s. To take account of such events(19), dummy variables (db) are used in this analysis.

The regression equation for AB (ignoring the error term) is as follows:

$$AB = a_o + b_o \left(\frac{GDP}{N}\right) + c_o (\log t) + d_o (db)$$

with a_o, b_o, c_o and $d_o > 0$.

ii) <u>Number of claimants</u> (FP)

General economic conditions and, more specifically, the unemployment rate for the insured labour force, are the main determinants of the number of UB claimants. However, policy decisions as to eligibility criteria and length of time over which benefits are paid are also important.

In most Member countries the unemployment rate for the insured labour force is not available. What is available is the total unemployment rate, and a complication arises because the relationship between these two rates is likely to be non-linear. The exact form of this non-linearity is, however, difficult to predict. First, the difference between the two rates may tend to vary at high and low rates of unemployment. Second, insured unemployment rates may tend to be somewhat higher at given levels of unemployment when unemployment has been rising rather than falling, to the extent that some workers exhaust their benefits or lose eligibility. However, as unemployment rises, the labour force may become increasingly composed of workers with less permanent attachment to the labour force, such as youths and females. They are less likely to qualify for unemployment insurance, though unemployment falls disproportionately on them. The data up to 1980 suggest a widening gap between total and insured unemployed for exactly this latter reason. They also appear to imply an approximately logarithmic relationship of insured to total unemployment rates.

The regression equation used for FP is specified (omitting the error term) as follows:

$$FP = a_i + b_i (\log U) + c_i (\log t) + d_i (db)$$

$$\text{with } b_i > 0$$

$$a_i, c_i < 0$$

$$d_i \gtrless 0$$

where $\log U$ (U is the number of unemployed workers) is used as an approximation of the non-linear relationship of insured to total unemployment rates; $\log t$ for the increasing youth and female component in the labour force; and db for policy changes concerning coverage and eligibility. The expected sign for c_i is negative because labour force growth involves groups which are not covered by UI programmes[20]. The sign for d_i cannot be determined a priori depending on whether policy changes involve groups which are less or more exposed to employment fluctuations.

iii) Average number of weeks during which benefits were paid (NW)

This is again a variable which reflects changes in general economic conditions as well as policy changes concerning duration of payment of benefits.

As market conditions deteriorate, NW will first decrease, reflecting the inflow of new claimants, and then increase, as unemployed workers experience difficulties in finding new jobs and stay longer on benefits. Two variables can serve as regressors: changes in the number of unemployed workers (ΔU) lagged by one year to take account of the effects described above, and the unemployment rate (UR_t) as an indicator of the difficulties experienced by jobless persons in finding a new job. The relationship between NW and UR_t can be expected to be non-linear as unemployed persons intensify their efforts to find a new job and more exhaust their benefits. To control for policy changes concerning maximum duration of payment of benefits, a dummy variable is introduced. Given that the tendency has been for governments to extend the period of payment of benefits, the coefficient of this dummy variable can be expected to be positive.

The regression equation is specified (ignoring the error term) as follows:

$$NW = a_2 + b_2 \ (\Delta U_{t-1}) + c_2 \ (\log UR_t) + d_2 \ (db)$$

$$\text{with } a_2, \ b_2, \ c_2 \text{ and } d_2 \geqslant 0$$

The following is the complete model for EUB:

$$EUB = (AB) \times (FP) \times (NW)$$

$$AB = a_0 + b_0 \ (GDP/N) + c_0 \ (\log t) + d_0 \ (dp)$$

$$FP = a_1 + b_1 \ (\log U) + c_1 \ (\log t) + d_1 \ (db)$$

$$NW = a_2 + b_2 \ (\Delta U_{t-1}) + c_2 \ (\log UR_t) + d_2 \ (db)$$

B.   Regression results

AB, FP and NW data used to estimate the above three equations come from national sources and are described in the statistical annex. GDP, population and labour force data are from OECD files. The time period covered is 1960 to 1980. The estimation procedure used is OLS.

The regression results are presented in Table 8 and more fully in Section V. These are, in general, encouraging. The parameters signs are as expected, except for Italy in the AB and FP equations, and Japan in the FP equation. In the case of Italy, the negative sign for the time variable in AB can be explained by the fact that benefits remained constant in money terms over the 1960s and they were adjusted upwards at irregular intervals in the 1970s, thus declining in real value most of the time. Similarly, the positive sign for the time variable in the FP equation reflects the fact that, in practice, the unemployment insurance programme in Italy is a programme for older and long-term unemployed workers, other workers (i.e. the cyclically unemployed) mainly falling under the "Cassa integrazione guadagni" scheme. The positive slope, then, merely reflects the increasing presence of this group among the unemployed. No explanation could, at this stage, be found for the peculiar result obtained for Japan.

The general conclusions which can be drawn from the parameters estimates (Table 8) and the derived arc-elasticities (Table 9) are:

. general living standards have a positive though not always significant influence upon AB. All in all, political considerations appear as the most impor-tant factor in the determination of the level of benefits;

207

Table 8

REGRESSIONS RESULTS(a)

(time period: 1960–1980)

	Canada	Germany	Italy	Japan	United States
AB equation					
Const.			7 937.12(c)	2 135.07(c)	67.93(c)
GDP/N	0.00(b)		0.00(c)	0.00(c)	
T	21.63(c)		-2 990.78(c)	2 019.98(c)	4.77(c)
DM					3.83(b)
$\bar{R}^2$	.91	.81	.70	.98	.83
D.w	1.89	1.51	0.87	1.76	1.25
FP equation					
Const.	-3 820.92(c)	-4 954.75(c)		4 562.85(c)	-42 369.10(c)
U_L	1 069.03(c)	737.66(c)		-521.96(b)	5 899.13(c)
T	-254.71(c)		188.86(c)	195.35(c)	
DM			1 106.32(c)		
$\bar{R}^2$	.95	.89	.77	.33	.86
D.w	1.69	1.93	.70	1.33	1.51
NW equation					
Const.	15.44(c)	18.71(c)	27.70(c)	62.50(c)	24.02(c)
ΔU_{t-1}		0.00(c)			0.00(b)
UR_t	3.97(c)	1.81(c)	3.38(c)	10.92(c)	3.73(c)
DM					
$\bar{R}^2$	.86	.88	.76	.85	.82
D.w	1.60	1.77	1.57	.87	1.28

a) Terms which are not significant are not shown. For full regression results, see Annex.
b) Significant at 95 per cent.
c) Significant at 99 per cent.

GDP/N = gross domestic product per capita; T = time variable; DM = dummy variable.
U = numbers unemployed; ΔU_{t-1} = change in numbers unemployed lagged by one year; UR = unemployment rate.

Table 9

REGRESSION ESTIMATES OF ARC-ELASTICITIES
FOR GDP PER CAPITA AND UNEMPLOYMENT VARIABLES, 1975-1980
(Significant coefficients only)

	Canada	Germany	Italy	Japan	United States
Average benefits equation					
GDP/N	1.01		2.89	0.80	
Number of claimants equation					
U	0.38	0.33		-0.35	0.69
Number of weeks of compensated unemployment					
$\triangle U_{t-1}$		0.13			0.59
UR		0.14		0.53	0.00

. the number of claimants is highly responsive to
changing flows into unemployment (except in Italy
and Japan);
. duration of payments of benefits is positively influenced by inflows into unemployment and general
labour market conditions which affect unemployed
persons' probability of finding a new job (i.e.
outflows). These influences, however, tend to be
generally small or not significant. Policy
changes concerning maximum duration for payment of
benefits also appear to have had some effect,
though this is not clearly detectable given the
level of aggregation at which this model works.

While generally satisfactory, however, it is obvious
that the application of a common model to countries with
different institutional and socio-economic settings is
not ideal. Clearly, if the common model were to be modified to take specific national differences into account,
regression results would probably be improved.

C. Simulations

An attractive feature of the above EUB three-
equation model is that it makes it possible to conduct a
number of macro-simulations to provide indications as to

209

the possible influences on EUB of a number of changes in economic as well as policy variables such as:

. the unemployment rate;
. policy decisions concerning benefit levels and eligibility as well as duration of payment of benefits criteria.

The rest of this section presents the results of various illustrative simulations for Canada, Italy and the United States and, in fewer instances, Germany and Japan.

i) Simulated influence of policy changes in 1970-75(21) upon expenditure in the late 1970s

Estimates of the possible influence of policy changes in 1970-75 upon EUB in the late 1970s are presented in Table 10. The figures show by how much actual EUB in the second half of the 1970s exceeded, on average, simulated EUB without early 1970s policy changes. The data suggest that policy changes were a very important growth factor of EUB in Canada and Italy, where expenditure without policy changes could have been, on average, about half what it actually was. These changes, however, appear as having been less important in the United States where the additional cost they possibly caused can be estimated at, on average, about 2 per cent of actual expenditure.

The last two columns in Table 10 show estimates of additional public expenditure and total national resources devoted to unemployment insurance as a result of policy changes in the early 1970s. Among the three countries, Canada stands out as the nation where policy changes were most important.

ii) Simulated cost of uprating unemployment benefits in excess of changes in consumer prices and average earnings

As shown in Table 3, during the 1970s average benefits in most Member countries tended to rise faster than prices and earnings. (This, however, was not the case in the United States, where the real value of benefits has been falling since 1977). Obviously enough, this has meant that EUB was higher than it would have been, had benefits grown in line with prices or earnings. The additional cost thus incurred is shown in Table 11. The figures show that in all countries considered, except in the United States, EUB would have been lower than it actually was by:

. between 12 (in Japan) and 49 (in Italy) per cent, had benefits just maintained their real value;
. between 5 (in Japan) and 21 (in Canada) per cent, had benefits grown in line with average earnings.

210

Table 10

SIMULATED ADDITIONAL EXPENDITURE IN 1975-80
DUE TO POLICY CHANGES(a) IN 1970-75
(Additional expenditure as a per cent
of actual·expenditure - mean annual figures)

| | Additional expenditure as a per cent of | | |
	Actual expenditure	Total public expenditure	GDP
Canada	50.3	2.2	0.9
Italy	59.0	0.9	0.1
United States	2.0	0.0(b)	0.0(b)

a) Concerning benefit levels, eligibility and duration of payments of benefits.
b) Less than 0.05.

Policy decisions concerning the real value of benefits
were thus an important element in the growth of EUB. In
terms of public expenditure, however, the additional resources spent on increasing the real value of benefits
were less than half a percentage point, except in Canada
and Germany, where they represented more than one percentage point. Had these additional resources been saved,
general government financial deficits, as a percentage of
GDP, might have been lower by between 0.6 (in Canada) and
0.1 (in Japan) percentage points.

iii) Simulated additional cost due to increased numbers of weeks of compensated unemployment

The importance of changes in the number of weeks
claimants draw benefits as a factor of EUB growth is already shown in Section III(c). Table 12 shows simulations
of the additional costs to EUB in 1979 due to the lengthening in the period during which the unemployed claimed
benefits as compared with the average number of compensated weeks of unemployment during 1970-75.

The figures show that, in all countries examined,
except the United States where duration actually de-
creased, and Italy where it changed very little, longer
duration of compensated unemployment has implied an additional expenditure of between 11 (in Germany) and 28 (in
Japan) per cent of actual EUB.

211

Table 11

SIMULATED ADDITIONAL EXPENDITURE DUE TO 1970 AVERAGE UNEMPLOYMENT BENEFIT
RISING FASTER THAN CONSUMER PRICES OR AVERAGE EARNINGS, 1979
(Selected countries)

	Additional expenditure due to 1970 average benefit rising faster than:			
	Consumer prices		Average earnings	
	% of actual expenditure	% of total public expenditure	% of actual expenditure	% of total public expenditure
Canada	36.4	1.4	20.8	0.8
Germany	36.1	1.0	17.6	0.5
Italy	48.7	0.5	14.4	0.2
Japan	12.4	0.2	5.2	0.1
United States(a)	-5.0	-0.1	-11.4	-0.1

a) The minus sign for the United States denotes that average benefits rose less fast
than prices and earnings, thus actual expenditure was lower than it would have been had
benefits risen in line with prices or earnings.

Table 12

SIMULATED ADDITIONAL EXPENDITURE DUE TO CHANGES IN THE NUMBER OF WEEKS
OF COMPENSATED UNEMPLOYMENT(a), 1979
(Selected countries)

	Number of weeks of compensated unemployment in excess of 1970-75 average	Estimated additional cost		
		Total amount(b)	% of actual EUB	% of public expenditure
Canada	2.8	792	19.8	0.7
Germany	1.3	818	10.9	0.2
Italy	0.4	13 173	2.2	0.0(d)
Japan	5.8	179 521	27.6	0.5
United States(c)	-0.7	-507	-5.4	-0.0(d)

a) Changes are measured as deviations from 1970-75 average number of weeks of compensated unemployment.
b) National currencies, millions.
c) The minus sign for the United States denotes that duration of compensated unemployment in 1979 was below the 1970-75 average figure, thus, expenditure was below what it would have been had the number of weeks of compensated unemployment remained unchanged at the 1970-75 average level.
d) Less than 0.05.

213

iv) Reductions in EUB which would have resulted had the 1979 unemployment rate been reduced by selected percentage points

These simulations are presented in Table 13 and the graphs in Section V. The figures suggest expenditure reductions of different size in different countries, e.g. highest in the United States and lowest in Italy. Not only are changes in EUB positively related to reductions in the rate of unemployment, but they also tend to be proportionally greater the greater the size of the reduction in unemployment.

v) Additional expenditure resulting from unemployment rates in excess of the 1970, 1973 and 1975 rates

This information is presented in Table 14. The figures show the ratio of actual to simulated expenditure had the unemployment rate remained unchanged at its 1970, 1973 or 1975 value, respectively. Thus, for example in Canada, in 1978 the unemployment rate peaked reaching 8.4 per cent. This was 2.7 percentage points more than the 1970 unemployment rate. In terms of EUB this increase in unemployment can be estimated to have implied expenditure about 25 per cent in excess of what it would have been had the unemployment rate remained unchanged at 5.7 per cent. Similarly, in the United States the unemployment rate peaked in 1975 reaching 8.5 per cent, 3.6 percentage points more than in 1970. As a result actual EUB was about 82 per cent more than the simulated expenditure with a 4.9 per cent unemployment rate. In the case of Italy, actual expenditure also exceeds simulated expenditure but a much weaker relationship between EUB and unemployment is observed. This is for the reasons outlined earlier (i.e. short-term unemployment mainly results in payments of benefits out of the "Cassa integrazione guadagni" and not out of the UB fund).

On the whole, the additional EUB due to unemployment rates above those prevailing in the early 1970s was important: had unemployment stayed at its 1970 level, expenditure in 1979-80 would have been, on average, about 16, 13 and 18 per cent below its actual level in Canada, Italy and the United States. In terms of total public expenditure and gross domestic product, the simulated additional expenditure due to unemployment in excess of the 1970 rate ranged between 0.5 and 0.20 per cent in Canada, 0.07 and 0.03 per cent in Italy and 0.3 and 0.06 per cent in the United States.

Table 13

SIMULATED REDUCTIONS IN UNEMPLOYMENT INSURANCE
EXPENDITURE FOLLOWING SPECIFIED REDUCTION IN
THE UNEMPLOYMENT RATE – 1979
(Selected countries)

	Actual expenditure(a)	Simulated percentage reduction in expenditure with a per cent reduction in the unemployment rate of:		
		10%	20%	30%
		as a percentage of EUB		
Canada	4 393	– 5.9	–12.3	–19.3
Italy	611 067	– 4.0	– 8.4	–13.2
United States	9 406	–10.7	–22.2	–34.5

a) Current prices and national currencies

V. REGRESSION RESULTS AND SIMULATIONS

This section contains the following tables and graphs:

A. Regression results for Canada, Germany, Italy, Japan and the United States: Full equation results plus graphs with actual and predicted lines.

B. Simulations for Canada, Italy and the United States: graphs showing influence of a 10, 20 and 30 per cent reduction in unemployment upon:

  i) number of claimants;
 ii) numbers of weeks of compensated unemployment;
iii) expenditure on unemployment insurance benefit.

The graph for average insurance benefit is also shown, although this is assumed not to be affected by changes in unemployment.

Table 14

RATIO OF ACTUAL TO SIMULATED EXPENDITURE WITH UNEMPLOYMENT
RATES EQUAL TO 1970(A), 1973(B) OR 1975(C) LEVELS

	A	B	C
CANADA(a)			
1971	1.06		
1972	1.06		
1973		0.99	
1974		0.97	
1975		1.13	
1976		1.16	1.02
1977		1.24	1.10
1978		1.25	1.11
1979		1.18	1.05
1980		1.19	1.05
ITALY(b)			
1971	0.95		
1972	1.01		
1973	1.01		
1974	1.03	0.96	
1975	1.09	0.02	
1976	1.12	1.05	1.08
1977	1.12	1.05	1.09
1978	1.16	1.08	1.12
1979	1.14	1.07	1.11
UNITED STATES(c)			
1971	1.27		
1972	1.20		
1973		0.98	
1974		1.11	
1975		1.82	
1976		1.66	0.93
1977		1.53	0.86
1978		1.28	0.73
1979		1.18	0.67

a) Canadian unemployment rates used in simulations
were 5.7, 5.7 and 6.9 in the three years respectively.
b) Italian unemployment rates used were 5.4, 6.4 and
5.9 respectively.
c) U.S. unemployment rates used were 4.9, 4.9 and
8.5 respectively.

A. Regression Results

- Key to symbols:

GDP/N	:	gross domestic product per capita
U	:	numbers unemployed
$\triangle U_{t-1}$	:	change in numbers unemployed lagged by one year
UR	:	unemployment rate
T	:	time variable
DM	:	dummy variable
FP	:	number of claimants to whom benefits are paid
AB	:	average weekly benefit paid
NW	:	average number of weeks during which benefits are paid
* significant at 95 per cent		
** significant at 99 per cent		

- Figures in brackets under coefficients are t-statistics

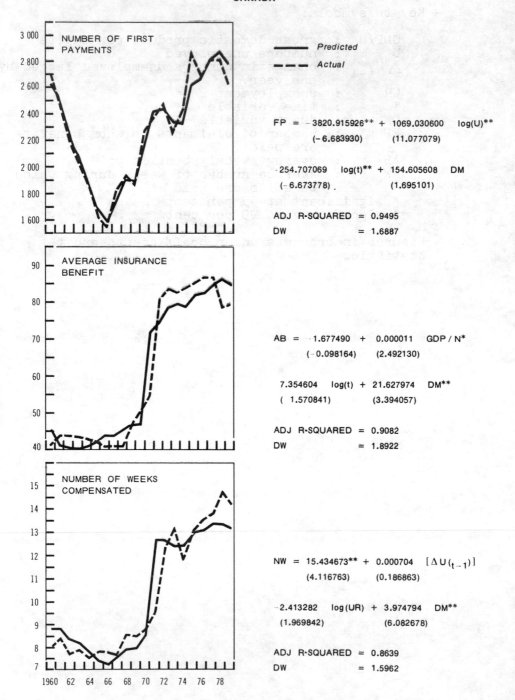

NUMBER OF FIRST PAYMENTS

Predicted
Actual

$$FP = -3820.915926^{**} + 1069.030600 \quad \log(U)^{**}$$
$$(-6.683930) \qquad (11.077079)$$

$$-254.707069 \quad \log(t)^{**} + 154.605608 \quad DM$$
$$(-6.673778) \qquad (1.695101)$$

ADJ R-SQUARED = 0.9495
DW   = 1.6887

AVERAGE INSURANCE BENEFIT

$$AB = -1.677490 + 0.000011 \quad GDP / N^{*}$$
$$(-0.098164) \qquad (2.492130)$$

$$7.354604 \quad \log(t) + 21.627974 \quad DM^{**}$$
$$(1.570841) \qquad (3.394057)$$

ADJ R-SQUARED = 0.9082
DW   = 1.8922

NUMBER OF WEEKS COMPENSATED

$$NW = 15.434673^{**} + 0.000704 \quad [\Delta U_{(t-1)}]$$
$$(4.116763) \qquad (0.186863)$$

$$-2.413282 \quad \log(UR) + 3.974794 \quad DM^{**}$$
$$(1.969842) \qquad (6.082678)$$

ADJ R-SQUARED = 0.8639
DW   = 1.5962

1960 62 64 66 68 70 72 74 76 78

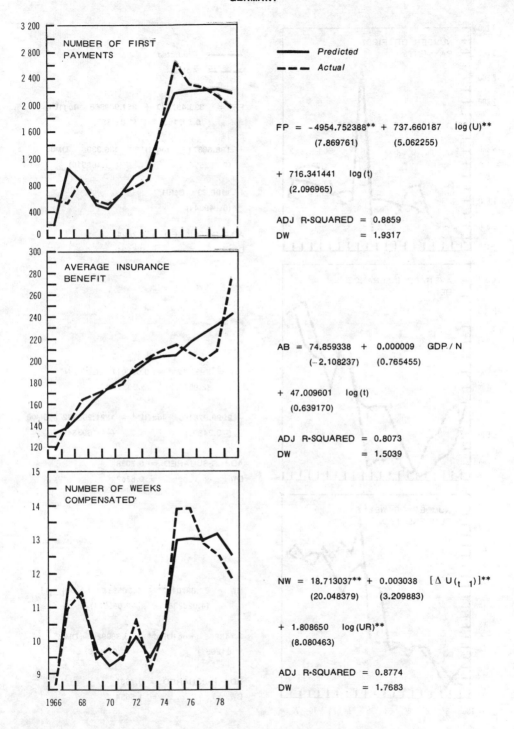

NUMBER OF FIRST PAYMENTS

$$FP = -4954.752388^{**} + 737.660187 \quad \log(U)^{**}$$
$$(7.869761) \qquad (5.062255)$$

$$+ 716.341441 \quad \log(t)$$
$$(2.096965)$$

ADJ R-SQUARED = 0.8859
DW = 1.9317

AVERAGE INSURANCE BENEFIT

$$AB = 74.859338 + 0.000009 \quad GDP/N$$
$$(-2.108237) \qquad (0.765455)$$

$$+ 47.009601 \quad \log(t)$$
$$(0.639170)$$

ADJ R-SQUARED = 0.8073
DW = 1.5039

NUMBER OF WEEKS COMPENSATED

$$NW = 18.713037^{**} + 0.003038 \quad [\Delta U_{(t-1)}]^{**}$$
$$(20.048379) \qquad (3.209883)$$

$$+ 1.808650 \quad \log(UR)^{**}$$
$$(8.080463)$$

ADJ R-SQUARED = 0.8774
DW = 1.7683

Predicted
Actual

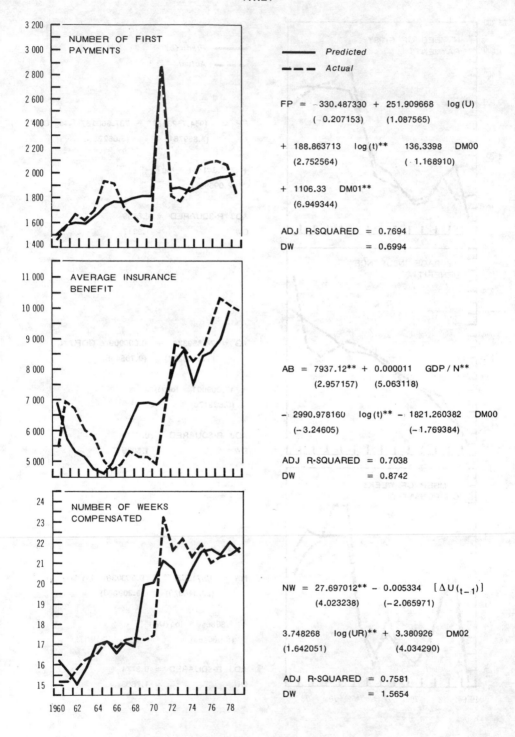

NUMBER OF FIRST PAYMENTS

Predicted

Actual

FP = -330.487330 + 251.909668   log (U)
      (-0.207153)   (1.087565)

+ 188.863713   log (t)** 136.3398   DM00
   (2.752564)   (-1.168910)

+ 1106.33   DM01**
   (6.949344)

ADJ R-SQUARED = 0.7694
DW   = 0.6994

AVERAGE INSURANCE BENEFIT

AB = 7937.12** + 0.000011   GDP / N**
     (2.957157)   (5.063118)

- 2990.978160   log (t)** - 1821.260382   DM00
   (-3.24605)   (-1.769384)

ADJ R-SQUARED = 0.7038
DW   = 0.8742

NUMBER OF WEEKS COMPENSATED

NW = 27.697012** - 0.005334 $[\Delta U_{(t-1)}]$
     (4.023238)   (-2.065971)

3.748268   log (UR)** + 3.380926   DM02
(1.642051)   (4.034290)

ADJ R-SQUARED = 0.7581
DW   = 1.5654

1960 62 64 66 68 70 72 74 76 78

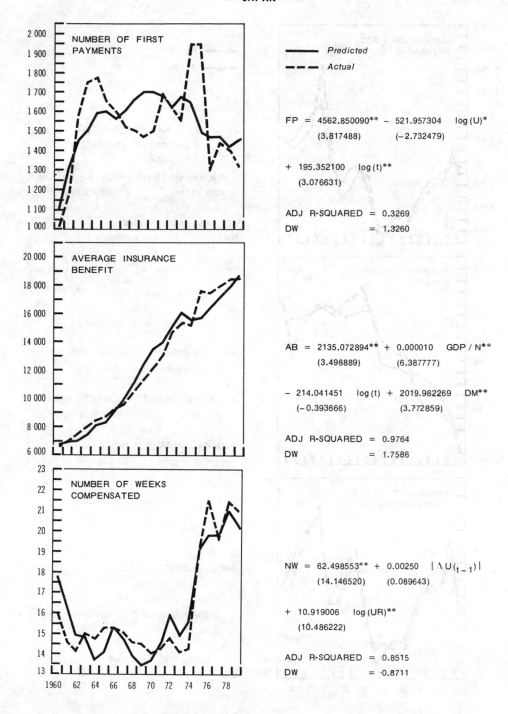

NUMBER OF FIRST PAYMENTS

— Predicted
--- Actual

$$FP = 4562.850090^{**} - 521.957304 \quad \log(U)^*$$
$$(3.817488) \qquad (-2.732479)$$

$$+ 195.352100 \quad \log(t)^{**}$$
$$(3.076631)$$

ADJ R-SQUARED = 0.3269
DW = 1.3260

AVERAGE INSURANCE BENEFIT

$$AB = 2135.072894^{**} + 0.000010 \quad GDP/N^{**}$$
$$(3.498889) \qquad (6.387777)$$

$$- 214.041451 \quad \log(t) + 2019.982269 \quad DM^{**}$$
$$(-0.393666) \qquad (3.772859)$$

ADJ R-SQUARED = 0.9764
DW = 1.7586

NUMBER OF WEEKS COMPENSATED

$$NW = 62.498553^{**} + 0.00250 \quad [\wedge U_{(t-1)}]$$
$$(14.146520) \qquad (0.089643)$$

$$+ 10.919006 \quad \log(UR)^{**}$$
$$(10.486222)$$

ADJ R-SQUARED = 0.8515
DW = -0.8711

221

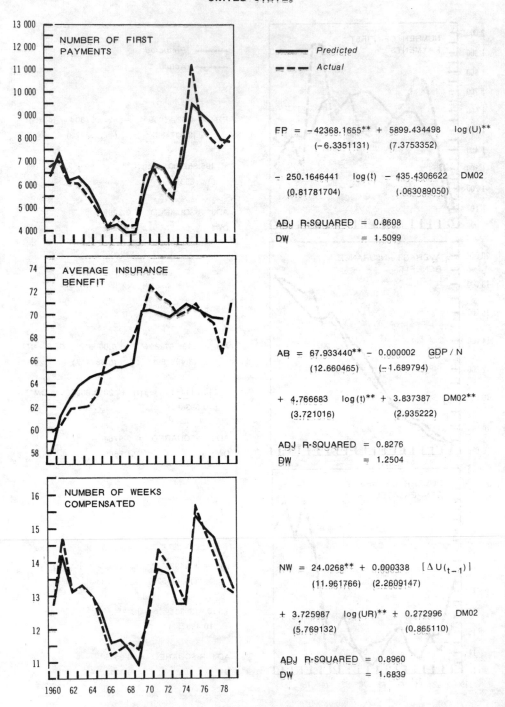

NUMBER OF FIRST PAYMENTS

— Predicted
--- Actual

$$FP = -42368.1655^{**} + 5899.434498 \quad \log(U)^{**}$$
$$\quad (-6.3351131) \quad (7.3753352)$$

$$- 250.1646441 \quad \log(t) - 435.4306622 \quad DM02$$
$$(0.81781704) \quad (.063089050)$$

ADJ R-SQUARED = 0.8608
DW = 1.5099

AVERAGE INSURANCE BENEFIT

$$AB = 67.933440^{**} - 0.000002 \quad GDP/N$$
$$(12.660465) \quad (-1.689794)$$

$$+ 4.766683 \quad \log(t)^{**} + 3.837387 \quad DM02^{**}$$
$$(3.721016) \quad (2.935222)$$

ADJ R-SQUARED = 0.8276
DW = 1.2504

NUMBER OF WEEKS COMPENSATED

$$NW = 24.0268^{**} + 0.000338 \quad [\Delta U_{(t-1)}]$$
$$(11.961766) \quad (2.2609147)$$

$$+ 3.725987 \quad \log(UR)^{**} + 0.272996 \quad DM02$$
$$(5.769132) \quad (0.865110)$$

ADJ R-SQUARED = 0.8960
DW = 1.6839

1960 62 64 66 68 70 72 74 76 78

B. Simulations

- Key to symbols:

    B = 0.0   dependent variable value with actual
                    unemployment rates

    B = 0.1 ⎞ as above but assuming reductions
    B = 0.2 ⎬ in actual unemployment rates
    B = 0.3 ⎠ of 10, 20 or 30 per cent respectively

CANADA

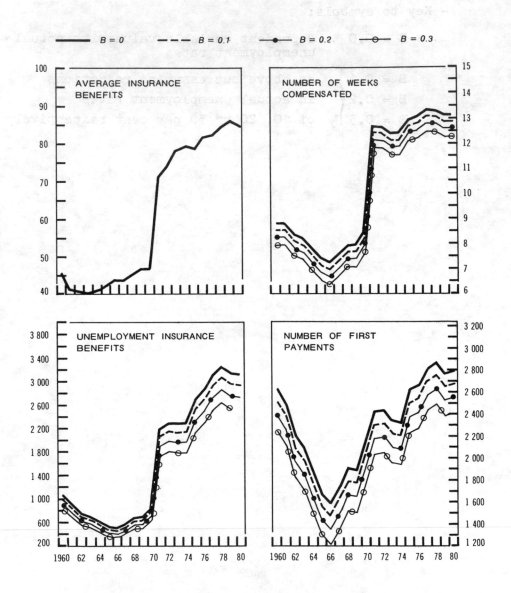

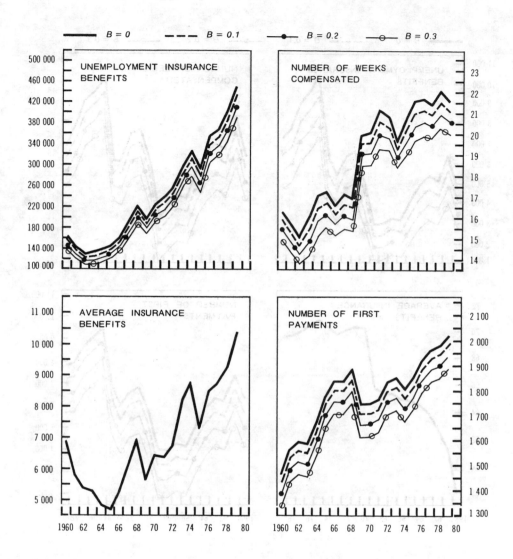

UNEMPLOYMENT INSURANCE BENEFITS

NUMBER OF WEEKS COMPENSATED

AVERAGE INSURANCE BENEFITS

NUMBER OF FIRST PAYMENTS

B = 0   B = 0.1   B = 0.2   B = 0.3

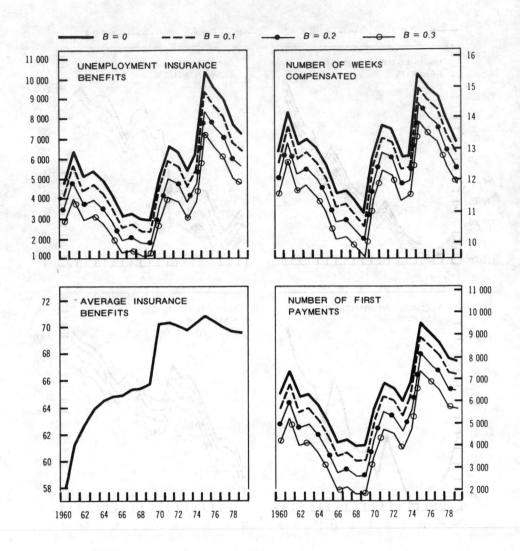

FOOTNOTES

1. For an assessment of the relative importance of various sources of income support for the unemployed, see Chapter I.

2. e.g. the total unemployment rate, the insured unemployment rate and the growing share in the labour force of those most vulnerable to unemployment such as youths and females.

3. e.g. for any given rate of unemployment, the number of beneficiaries can vary depending on how unemployment is distributed between the insured and the non-insured labour force.

4. Cyclical factors may, however, affect this relationship. See G.M. von Furstenberg, "Stabilisation Characteristics of Unemployment Insurance", Industrial and Labour Relations Review, vol. 29, Number 3, April 1976, pp. 363-376.

5. Among the countries examined, the only exception is France. In this country the relationship appears rather stable.

6. The overall picture presented above is similar to that applied by K. Judge to old age pensions: See "State Pensions and the Growth of Social Welfare Expenditure", Journal of Social Policies, No. 10, Part A, October 1981, pp. 503-530.

7. All figures are unweighted averages.

8. The following accounting identity provides the analytical framework for the analysis of these five factors: EUB = (EUB/BxD) x (B/U) x (U/LF) x (LF) x (D), where the first term is the average level of actual benefit per claimant (B) and average number of weeks of compensated unemployment (D); the second the ratio of beneficiaries to the unemployed (U); the third the unemployment rate; the fourth the size of the labour force (LF); and the fifth is the average duration of unemployment for insured unemployed.

9. See Annex.

10. i.e. the number of weeks of unemployment compensated during the year divided by the number of first payments. It may include more than a period of continuous unemployment. It excludes all unemployment for which no benefits were paid (e.g. waiting periods, disqualifications, etc.).

11. See Annex.

12. For instance, in the United Kingdom the real value of flat-rate unemployment benefit as an index with 1948 equal to 100 reached a peak in 1974 (equal to 188.3, 188.4 and 211.6 for a single person, couple and couple with two children respectively); it declined slightly afterwards and then increased again to reach a new peak in late 1976 (index equal to 209.3 for a couple with two children) in late 1977 (index equal to 188.4 and 188.9 for a single person and married couple respectively). Ever since it has been declining rapidly (index equal to 181.0, 181.2, 165.3 respectively). (House of Commons, Hansard, 24th June 1981, p. 113).

13. See OECD, The Challenge of Unemployment, Paris, 1982, pp. 37-38.

14. See OECD, The Challenge of Unemployment, op. cit., pp. 36-44.

15. In Canada, for example, the number of beneficiaries is a global number which also includes beneficiaries who have received sickness and maternity benefit and those who have done some part-time work during the period they have been paid benefit. The consequence is that in a number of instances beneficiaries exceed the unemployed. Statistics on regular UI beneficiaries can partly overcome these problems. Surveys of Consumer Finances, however, indicate that a great number of UI beneficiaries have not been actively looking for a job during the reference year on difficulties of deriving beneficiaries/unemployed ratios in France, see B. Grais, "La couverture du risque de chômage", Economie et Statistique, February 1977, pp. 59-60.

16. i.e. the unemployment rate for the insured labour force and the unemployment rate for the total labour force.

17. A. Mittelstadt, "Unemployment Benefits and Related Payments in Seven Major Countries", OECD Occasional Studies, July 1975, p. 8.

18. See, for instance, G.M. von Furstenberg, "Stabilisation Characteristics of Unemployment Insurance", op. cit. in note 4.

19. e.g. to take into account: the 1972 reform in Canada; the 1968 and 1973 benefit upratings in Italy; the 1974 reform in Japan; the 1966 introduction of the earnings-related supplement in the United Kingdom; and federal pressure by the Nixon Administration to boost state benefits which had the effect of 23 states increasing benefits in 1971.

20. The specification implies that FP equals zero for some $U > 0$. In this instance, all unemployed will come from the non-insured labour force and the insured unemployment rate only equals zero.

21. Concerning benefit levels, eligibility and duration of payment of benefits.

Annex

SELECTED UNEMPLOYMENT
COMPENSATION STATISTICS

GENERAL NOTES

The following time series, from 1960 to 1980, are shown in this paper:

I. Expenditure on cash transfers to unemployed workers

. total
. average per unemployed worker.

II. Selected unemployment insurance data on:

. average weekly unemployment insurance benefit paid;
. total and average number of weeks of unemployment compensated;
. number of first payments;
. number of beneficiaries.

Distinctions between insurance, assistance and other cash payments to the unemployed are difficult to establish. This is because no clear set of criteria is available and because programmes can present mixed insurance and assistance features at the same time. For the purpose of this analysis insurance benefits are those paid on the basis of a quid pro quo relationship (i.e. paid only to those who contribute, and out of specially constituted unemployment insurance funds). Assistance benefits include discretionary cash transfers which are normally means-tested. Other benefits include lump-sum payments, special programme benefits and benefits for workers on short-working hours.

Cash transfers to unemployed workers are defined according to United Nations guidelines on "Classification of the Functions of Government", i.e. as: "Payments under social insurance or other government schemes to individuals, including war veterans, for loss of income due to unemployment", but excluding administration, operation, support, etc. of unemployment compensation benefits. Income-tested assistance money is included if paid out of (i) schemes specifically established for unemployed workers (e.g. unemployment assistance benefits in Germany and New Zealand) (ii) general assistance schemes, if sums paid to unemployed workers are separately shown (e.g.

supplementary benefits in the United Kingdom). Also included are lump sum payments (e.g. compulsory redundancy pay), when their cost is met by governments. If, however, total payments are split between governments and employers, the employers' share is not included.

Because benefits are taxable in some countries, net payment figures are desirable for the purpose of international comparisons. These, however, are not available. The actual income support function of unemployment compensation programmes is, therefore, over-stated by gross transfer figures in countries where benefits are taxed (e.g. Canada and France).

I. EXPENDITURE ON CASH TRANSFERS TO UNEMPLOYED WORKERS

EXPENDITURE ON UNEMPLOYMENT COMPENSATION PROGRAMMES, CANADA, 1960–1980

dollars

Fiscal year	Unemployment insurance benefits (millions)	Unemployment assistance benefits	Other	Total		Total expenditure per unemployed worker	
				Current prices (millions)	1975 prices (millions)	Current prices	1975 prices
1960	482			482	893	1 081	2 001
61	494			494	915	1 060	1 963
62	409			409	744	1 049	1 907
63	394			394	704	1 053	1 881
64	344			344	604	1 062	1 863
65	312			312	538	1 114	1 921
66	295			295	492	1 175	1 959
67	353			353	569	1 193	1 923
68	438			438	674	1 223	1 882
69	499			499	734	1 378	2 027
70	695			695	993	1 460	2 086
71	891			891	1 238	1 665	2 313
72a	1 872			1 872	2 463	3 499	4 604
73a	2 004			2 004	2 474	3 891	4 804
74a	2 119			2 119	2 354	4 123	4 581
75a	3 144			3 144	3 144	5 975	5 975
76a	3 342			3 342	3 094	4 597	4 256
77a	3 885			3 885	3 601	4 599	3 965
78a	4 537			4 537	4 571	4 980	3 953
79a	4 008			4 008	2 904	4 783	3 466
80a	4 393			4 393	2 890	5 067	3 333

a) Benefits made taxable in 1972. Figures include special benefits to unemployed workers (i.e. sickness, maternity, retirement, fishing, training and those paid to persons outside Canada).

EXPENDITURE ON UNEMPLOYMENT COMPENSATION PROGRAMMES, FRANCE, 1960-1980

Francs

Calendar year	Unemployment insurance benefits (millions)	Unemployment assistance benefits (millions)	Other	Total Current prices (millions)	Total 1975 prices (millions)	Total expenditure per unemployed worker Current prices	Total expenditure per unemployed worker 1975 prices
1960	63	31		94	214	293	894
61	63	44		107	233	527	1 146
62	81	48		129	269	561	1 169
63	110	47		157	314	575	1 150
64	122	97		219	415	1 014	1 923
65	200	55		255	481	948	1 788
66	242	53		295	546	1 054	1 951
67	367	82		449	802	1 230	2 197
68	619	276		895	1 543	2 096	3 614
69	625	339		964	1 555	2 021	3 259
70	722	336		1 059	1 629	2 076	3 194
71	939	411		1 350	1 956	2 373	3 438
72	1 251	512		1 763	2 415	2 963	4 059
73	1 618	567		2 185	2 766	3 793	4 802
74	2 426	793		3 219	3 617	5 234	5 881
75	5 986	1 830		7 816	7 816	8 665	8 665
76	8 295	2 624		10 920	9 927	11 100	9 796
77	10 731	3 439		14 270	11 892	13 330	11 827
78	15 227	4 685		19 912	15 200	16 832	12 849
79	21 107	7 366		28 473	19 637	21 013	14 492
80	23 687	9 314		32 801	20 001	22 544	13 746

EXPENDITURE ON UNEMPLOYMENT COMPENSATION PROGRAMMES, GERMANY, 1960-1980

DM

Calendar year	Unemployment insurance benefits (millions)	Unemployment assistance benefits(a) (millions)	Other(b) (millions)	Total		Total expenditure per unemployed worker	
				Current prices (millions)	1975 prices (millions)	Current prices	1975 prices
1960	—	—	—	—	—	—	—
61	—	—	—	—	—	—	—
62	—	—	—	—	—	—	—
63	—	—	—	—	—	—	—
64	—	—	—	—	—	—	—
65	391	—	31	—	—	—	—
66	401	—	27	—	—	—	—
67	1 641	109	32	1 783	2 603	3 881	5 665
68	1 179	172	46	1 398	1 983	4 321	6 131
69	674	82	33	798	1 100	4 421	6 158
70	651	52	19	722	973	4 852	6 535
71	868	53	22	943	1 207	5 096	6 521
72	1 284	84	29	1 398	1 696	5 672	6 881
73	1 395	108	36	1 538	1 744	5 625	6 378
74	3 552	222	80	3 854	4 083	6 616	7 010
75	7 765	776	203	8 745	8 745	8 141	8 141
76	6 906	1 299	243	8 448	8 083	7 967	7 622
77	6 283	1 332	263	7 878	7 271	7 649	7 059
78	6 270	1 393	264	7 927	7 124	7 984	7 174
79	7 468	1 644	331	9 442	8 149	10 777	9 301
80	8 110	1 540	363	10 013	8 191	11 265	9 215

a) Assistance benefits paid after exhaustion of insurance benefits.
b) Assistance benefits paid independently from previous receipt of benefits. Financed by the federal budget.

EXPENDITURE ON UNEMPLOYMENT COMPENSATION PROGRAMMES, ITALY, 1960-1980

Lire

Calendar year	Unemployment insurance benefits (millions)	Unemployment assistance benefits	Other(a) (millions)	Total		Total expenditure per unemployed worker	
				Current prices (millions)	1975 prices (millions)	Current prices	1975 prices
1960	41 259		1 483	42 742	106 855	51 127	127 817
61	57 983		1 815	59 798	145 849	84 222	205 421
62	63 773		1 699	65 472	155 886	107 155	255 133
63	62 638		4 151	66 789	145 193	132 518	288 081
64	66 826		15 413	82 239	171 321	149 798	312 060
65	72 420		52 213	124 633	249 266	112 282	224 564
66	67 950		31 873	99 823	191 967	83 744	161 046
67	67 258		21 084	88 342	163 596	79 875	147 917
68	70 547		25 691	96 238	178 219	82 114	152 064
69	67 061		40 320	107 381	191 752	92 570	165 303
70	69 277		43 674	112 951	194 743	101 666	175 286
71	172 311		78 213	250 524	410 695	225 901	370 329
72	147 669		77 874	225 543	346 989	173 196	267 532
73	240 354		64 192	304 546	422 981	233 368	324 123
74	336 382		123 168	459 550	534 360	412 893	480 108
75	331 423		320 028	651 451	651 451	529 635	529 635
76	383 180		349 946	733 126	626 603	514 114	439 413
77	549 472		388 729	938 201	679 856	607 250	440 036
78	600 315		563 774	1 164 089	751 025	740 986	478 055
79	611 067		674 575	1 285 642	722 271	757 151	425 366
80	728 052		637 172	1 365 224	632 048	804 019	372 231

a) Benefits paid under the "Cassa integrazione guadagni" scheme.

239

EXPENDITURE ON UNEMPLOYMENT COMPENSATION PROGRAMMES, JAPAN, 1960–1980

Yen

Calendar year	Unemployment insurance benefits (1000 millions)	Unemployment assistance benefits	Other (1000 millions)	Total		Total expenditure per unemployed worker	
				Current prices (1000 millions)	1975 prices (1000 millions)	Current prices	1975 prices
1960	35		5	40	121	53 300	161 600
61	42		77	119	140	74 200	212 100
62	61		11	72	195	122 000	329 800
63	85		12	97	242	164 400	411 000
64	93		15	108	257	200 000	476 100
65	97		17	114	259	200 000	454 600
66	107		19	126	268	193 900	412 500
67	109		20	129	263	204 800	417 900
68	117		22	139	272	235 600	461 900
69	130		22	152	281	266 700	493 900
70	147		54	201	347	340 700	587 500
71	195		70	265	427	414 100	667 800
72	295		18	313	489	428 800	670 000
73	241		108	349	48	505 800	712 500
74	375		135	510	573	698 600	784 900
75	657		48	705	705	705 000	705 000
76	532		143	675	619	625 000	573 400
77	598		154	752	637	683 000	579 400
78	683		186	869	706	700 000	569 800
79	651		205	856	674	731 600	576 100
80				951	694		

EXPENDITURE ON UNEMPLOYMENT COMPENSATION PROGRAMMES, UNITED KINGDOM, 1960-1980

£

	Fiscal year data				Calendar year data			
Fiscal year (a)	Unemployment insurance benefits (millions)	Unemployment assistance benefits (b) (millions)	Other (c) (millions)	Total (millions)	Total		Total expenditure per unemployed worker	
					Current prices (millions)	1975 prices (millions)	Current prices	1975 prices
1960	34	23		57	62	172	190	528
61	41	22		63	60	158	210	550
62	70	32		102	88	226	217	556
63	70	37		107	133	332	268	670
64	50	30		80	87	212	249	608
65	55	28		83	84	195	281	653
66	85	32	29	146	110	244	391	870
67	130	65	40	235	230	500	457	994
68	132	79	48	259	262	546	483	1 007
69	135	80	34	249	246	482	475	931
70	158	95	41	294	280	518	504	934
71	250	155	61	466	410	695	566	960
72	219	191	47	457	511	798	634	991
73	182	150	31	363	341	494	593	859
74	227	200	48	475	471	581	869	1 073
75	473	388	107	961	827	827	955	955
76	582	578	95	1 255	1 273	1 088	956	817
77	605	729	82	1 466	1 473	1 091	1 016	752
78	660	755	89	1 504	1 493	1 023	1 032	707
79	681	767	113	1 561	1 484	894	1 104	665
80	1 328	1 186	278	2 792	2 241	1 141	1 343	684

a) Ending 31 March. The first year is 1.4.1960 to 31.3.1961.
b) Supplementary benefit to unemployed persons.
c) Redundancy pay. Includes only the cost of the Redundancy Final Rebate to Employers and Redundancy Fund guarantee payments.

EXPENDITURE ON UNEMPLOYMENT COMPENSATION PROGRAMMES, UNITED STATES, 1960-1980

Dollars

Calendar year	Unemployment insurance benefits (millions)	Unemployment assistance benefits	Other(a) (millions)	Total		Total expenditure per unemployed worker	
				Current prices (millions)	1975 prices (millions)	Current prices	1975 prices
1960	2 996		83	3 079	5 598	799	1 453
61	4 295		106	4 401	7 859	934	1 667
62	3 104		78	3 182	5 682	814	1 453
63	2 971		90	3 061	5 195	727	1 276
64	2 688		88	2 776	4 786	733	1 264
65	2 299		66	2 365	4 008	703	1 191
66	1 875		38	1 913	3 188	665	1 109
67	2 191		46	2 237	3 608	752	1 213
68	2 139		68	2 207	3 395	784	1 205
69	2 241		86	2 327	3 422	822	1 208
70	3 985		201	4 186	5 814	1 024	1 422
71	5 811		349	6 160	8 213	1 234	1 645
72	5 669		364	6 033	7 735	1 246	1 598
73	4 370		200	4 570	5 506	1 062	1 279
74	6 774		247	7 021	7 632	1 383	1 504
75	16 955		1 185	18 140	18 140	2 317	2 317
76	14 809		1 577	16 386	15 458	2 248	2 221
77	11 981		1 148	13 129	11 619	1 915	1 695
78	8 978		439	9 417	7 783	1 557	1 287
79	9 406		285	9 691	7 179	1 625	1 204
80	15 791		334	16 125	10 539	2 165	1 415

a) Includes veterans' unemployment benefits and special unemployment benefits (for 1975-1978 only).

II. SELECTED UNEMPLOYMENT INSURANCE DATA

CANADA

Year	Average weekly unemployment insurance benefit		Number of weeks compensated		Number of first payments (a)	Number of beneficiaries (b)
	Current $	1975 prices	Total (thousands)	Average	(thousands)	(thousands)
1960	22.32	41.31	21 592	8.00	2 700	430
1961	23.82	44.11	20 735	8.43	2 461	416
1962	24.17	43.95	16 928	7.72	2 192	340
1963	24.45	43.63	16 122	7.91	2 038	325
1964	24.57	43.10	14 017	7.54	1 860	282
1965	24.54	42.31	12 718	7.81	1 628	254
1966	24.52	40.87	12 041	7.78	1 548	234
1967	25.46	41.06	13 852	7.62	1 817	268
1968	26.57	40.88	16 488	8.55	1 928	313
1969	31.71	46.64	15 734	8.48	1 855	307
1970	35.08	50.12	19 817	8.77	2 261	385
1971	39.35	54.65	22 634	9.55	2 371	439
1972	61.79	80.85	30 461	12.33	2 470	582
1973	68.45	83.77	29 537	13.19	2 238	566
1974	74.89	82.73	28 461	11.80	2 410	558
1975	84.64	84.23	37 327	13.07	2 857	724
1976	92.89	85.51	36 190	13.53	2 678	701
1977	101.00	87.07	38 701	13.79	2 806	752
1978	109.71	87.07	41 355	14.72	2 809	803
1979	108.63	78.71	36 896	14.18	2 600	713
1980	120.92	79.57	36 333	13.15	2 762	703

a) Number of new cases of recorded unemployment among insured persons.
b) Average weekly number.

244

FRANCE

Year	Average weekly unemployment insurance benefit		Number of weeks compensated		Number of first payments	Number of beneficiaries (a)
	Current Francs	1975 prices	Total	Average		
			(thousands)		(thousands)	(thousands)
1960						
1961						
1962						
1963						
1964						
1965						
1966						
1967						
1968						
1969						
1970				25.1		
1971				23.4		
1972			12 963	27.0	480	248
1973			11 802	24.1	490	226
1974			13 789	23.1	597	264
1975			25 842	21.9	1 180	494
1976			32 462	28.6	1 135	621
1977			39 055	29.1	1 342	747
1978			46 402	31.3	1 482	887
1979			-	36.1	-	-
1980			49 435	-	-	945

a) Average daily figure.

GERMANY

I. Unemployment Insurance Data

Year	Average weekly unemployment insurance benefit		Number of weeks compensated		Number of first payments (thousands)	Number of beneficiaries (a) (thousands)
	Current DM	1975 prices	Total (thousands)	Average		
1960			9 124	7.84	1 164	175
61			6 207	7.88	788	119
62			5 484	8.54	642	105
63			6 584	9.29	709	126
64			5 521	9.60	575	106
65			5 047	9.95	507	97
66	79	117	5 041	8.63	584	97
67	98	144	6 672	10.96	521	320
68	115	164	10 007	11.47	872	192
69	121	169	5 483	9.43	581	105
70	130	175	4 998	9.77	512	96
71	139	178	6 282	9.38	670	120
72	160	194	8 183	10.64	769	157
73	179	203	8 008	9.07	882	154
74	198	210	18 330	10.21	1 795	352
75	215	215	36 835	13.88	2 653	707
76	216	207	32 088	13.90	2 308	615
77	216	194	49 399	12.85	2 260	557
78	233	209	26 909	12.53	2 147	516
79	318	275	23 384	11.82	1 978	448
80	343	280	23 682	11.17	2 120	454

a) Average weekly number.

GERMANY

II. Unemployment Assistance Data (a)

Year	Average weekly unemployment insurance benefit		Number of weeks compensated		Number of first payments (thousands)	Number of beneficiaries (b) (thousands)
	Current DM	1975 prices	Total (thousands)	Average		
1960			2 669	11.86	225	51
61			1 242	11.09	112	24
62			878	10.97	80	17
63			832	10.02	83	16
64			783	10.73	73	15
65			638	10.46	61	12
66	51	76	529	10.80	49	10
67	75	110	1 891	12.12	156	36
68	76	108	2 762	16.06	172	53
69	72	101	1 467	15.77	93	28
70	74	100	888	13.25	67	17
71	86	110	803	12.55	64	15
72	102	124	1 050	13.46	78	20
73	113	128	1 190	14.51	82	23
74	136	144	2 091	14.62	143	40
75	165	165	5 749	16.86	341	110
76	178	170	8 564	20.39	420	164
77	186	171	8 529	21.06	405	163
78	202	181	8 189	19.78	414	157
79	279	241	6 985	18.43	379	134
80	294	241	6 339	18.48	343	121

a) Includes only assistance benefits paid after exhaustion of income benefits.
b) Average weekly number.

ITALY

Year	Average weekly unemployment insurance benefit		Number of weeks compensated		Number of first payments	Number of beneficiaries(a)
	Current Lire	1975 prices	Total (thousands)	Average	(thousands)	(thousands)
1960	2 177	5 443	22 095	15.2	1 457	363
1961	2 849	6 949	23 754	15.2	1 565	390
1962	2 828	6 733	26 282	15.8	1 665	432
1963	2 786	6 057	26 245	16.3	1 608	431
1964	2 800	5 833	27 875	16.5	1 689	458
1965	2 541	5 082	33 290	17.2	1 934	547
1966	2 457	4 725	33 262	16.8	1 921	530
1967	2 639	4 887	29 735	17.2	1 734	489
1968	2 878	5 330	28 603	17.3	1 655	470
1969	2 884	5 150	27 131	17.2	1 577	446
1970	2 975	5 129	27 148	17.4	1 559	446
1971	2 996	4 911	67 094	23.3	2 875	1 103
1972	4 375	6 731	39 362	21.6	1 820	647
1973	6 347	8 815	39 407	22.2	1 772	648
1974	7 449	8 662	40 097	21.3	1 885	659
1975	8 225	8 225	45 012	21.9	2 059	740
1976	10 007	8 553	43 845	21.0	2 085	721
1977	12 962	9 393	44 698	21.3	2 099	735
1978	15 970	10 303	43 854	21.4	2 054	721
1979	17 948	10 083	39 722	21.7	1 835	653
1980	21 409(b)	9 912(b)	39 675(b)	21.8(b)	1 800(b)	652(b)

a) Secretariat's estimate. Average monthly number.
b) Provisional figures.

248

JAPAN

| Year | Average weekly unemployment insurance benefit | | Number of weeks compensated | | Number of first payments | Number of beneficiaries(a) |
	Current Yen	1975 prices	Total (thousands)	Average	(thousands)	(thousands)
1960	2 171	6 579	16 232	16.06	1 011	374
1961	2 440	6 971	17 021	14.59	1 167	397
1962	2 776	7 503	22 085	14.10	1 566	517
1963	3 216	8 040	26 297	15.01	1 752	612
1964	3 565	8 488	26 162	14.73	1 776	613
1965	3 844	8 736	25 291	15.30	1 653	590
1966	4 350	9 255	24 519	15.29	1 604	579
1967	4 721	9 635	22 993	15.10	1 523	543
1968	5 332	10 455	21 973	14.59	1 506	524
1969	6 101	11 298	21 318	14.51	1 470	504
1970	7 012	12 090	21 002	14.04	1 496	499
1971	8 075	13 024	24 099	14.26	1 690	569
1972	9 380	14 656	24 033	14.83	1 621	570
1973	11 040	15 333	21 863	14.14	1 546	521
1974(b)	13 452	15 115	27 864	14.32	1 946	648
1975(b)	17 556	17 556	37 410	19.19	1 949	870
1976(b)	19 052	17 479	27 907	21.55	1 295	649
1977(b)	21 201	17 967	28 208	19.55	1 443	656
1978(b)	22 626	18 395	30 186	21.47	1 406	702
1979(b)	23 484	18 491	27 735	21.04	1 318	645
1980(b)						

a) Average monthly number.
b) From 1974 onward: total and average number of weeks compensated are Secretariat estimates.

GREAT BRITAIN

Year	Average weekly unemployment insurance benefit(a)		Number of weeks compensated		Number of first payments	Number of bene- ficiaries(b)
	Current £	1975 prices	Total	Average		(thousands)
1960	3.1	8.6				192
61	3.3	8.7				185
62	3.8	9.7				257
63	4.0	10.0				363
64	4.6	11.2				199
65	5.6	13.0				167
66	6.2	13.8				187
67	6.9	15.0				333
68	7.8	16.3				307
69	8.2	16.1				287
70	9.1	16.9				306
71	9.8	16.6				412
72	10.5	16.4				431
73	10.7	15.5				247
74	16.5	20.4				253
75	16.8	16.8				436
76	22.0	18.8				477
77	20.9	15.5				561
78	21.6	14.8				537
79	24.6	14.8				477
80	34.6(c)	17.7(c)				709

a) Total expenditure on unemployment insurance benefits divided by 52 and by the number of recipients of unemployment benefits, with and without supplementary allowance.
b) Department of Health and Social Security's estimates of the number of unemployed beneficiaries on a selected day in each quarter.
c) Secretariat's estimate.

UNITED STATES

Year	Average weekly unemployment insurance benefit(a)		Number of weeks compensated(a)		Number of first payments (a)	Number of Insured unemployed(b)	
	Current $	1975 prices	Total (thousands)	Average	(thousands)	State programmes (thousands)	All programmes (thousands)
1960	32.87	59.76	85 630	12.7	6 754	1 908	2 071
1961	33.80	60.36	104 217	14.7	7 067	2 290	2 994
1962	34.56	61.71	79 325	13.1	6 073	1 783	1 946
1963	35.28	61.89	80 137	13.3	6 041	1 806	1 973
1964	35.96	62.00	71 380	13.0	5 498	1 605	1 753
1965	37.19	63.03	58 813	12.2	4 813	1 328	1 450
1966	39.76	66.27	46 547	11.2	4 139	1 061	1 129
1967	41.25	66.53	52 902	11.4	4 619	1 005	1 270
1968	43.43	66.82	48 660	11.6	4 197	1 111	1 187
1969	46.17	67.90	47 923	11.4	4 212	1 101	1 177
1970	50.34	69.92	78 838	12.3	6 397	1 805	2 070
1971	54.02	72.03	95 400	14.4	6 627	2 150	2 608
1972	56.76	72.77	81 108	14.0	5 780	1 848	2 192
1973	59.00	71.08	71 205	13.4	5 328	1 632	1 793
1974	64.25	69.84	97 803	12.7	7 715	2 262	2 558
1975	70.23	70.23	175 332	15.7	11 160	3 986	4 937
1976	75.16	70.91	127 425	14.9	8 560	2 991	3 846
1977	78.79	69.73	113 244	14.2	7 985	2 655	3 308
1978	83.67	69.15	100 961	13.3	7 564	2 359	3 645
1979	89.67	66.42	106 101	13.1	8 074	2 434	2 592
1980	98.92	64.65	149 020	14.9	10 001	3 350	3 837

a) State programmes only.
b) Average weekly number.

III. DATA SOURCES

CANADA
: Statistics Canada, Canadian Statistical Review, Historical Summary and subsequent issues. The average number of weeks compensated ($\bar{a}$) is, when not available, implicitly estimated from data on the number of first payments (FP) and the number of total weeks compensated (CW) i.e.:

$$\bar{a} = CW/FP$$

FRANCE
: Centre d'étude des revenus et des coûts; UNEDIC and INSEE, Données Sociales, 1981 edition.

GERMANY
: Federal Institute of Labour, Nuremberg. The average number of weeks compensated ($\bar{a}$) is implicitly derived by dividing the average number of beneficiaries (B) by the number of first payments (FP), times the number of weeks in a year, i.e.:

$$\bar{a} = B \times 52/FP$$

ITALY
: Relazione sulla situazione economica del paese, various issues. The average number of beneficiaries (B) is a Secretariat's estimate based on annual count figures of number of first payments (FP) times the average number of weeks compensated ($\bar{a}$), divided by the number of weeks in a year, i.e.:

$$B = \bar{a} \times FP/52$$

JAPAN
: Ministry of Labour, Yearbook of Labour Statistics, various years. Duration data have been estimated from data on the number of first payments and number of weeks compensated. See Canada above for methodology.

UNITED KINGDOM
: Central Statistical Office, Annual Abstract of Statistics, various issues; Department of Health and Social Security, Social

UNITED KINGDOM
(cont'd)

Security Statistics, various issues; and Department of Employment, Yearbook of Labour Statistics. Supplementary benefit figures are only available for Great Britain (that is, they exclude Northern Ireland). United Kingdom estimates are derived by multiplying Great Britain supplementary benefit figures by the ratio of United Kingdom to Great Britain expenditure on unemployment insurance benefit. Calendar year figures for total expenditure are derived by multiplying total United Kingdom expenditure for each financial year by the ratio of calendar (published in Central Statistical Office, National Income and Expenditure, various issues) to financial year expenditure on unemployment benefit.

UNITED STATES

U.S. Department of Labor, Employment and Training Administration, Handbook of Unemployment Insurance Financial Data, 1938-76, Washington, 1978, and updates; Economic Report of the President, Washington, 1981; and U.S. Chamber of Commerce, Survey of Current Business.

OECD SALES AGENTS
DÉPOSITAIRES DES PUBLICATIONS DE L'OCDE

ARGENTINA – ARGENTINE
Carlos Hirsch S.R.L., Florida 165, 4° Piso (Galeria Guemes)
1333 BUENOS AIRES. Tel. 33.1787.2391 y 30.7122

AUSTRALIA – AUSTRALIE
Australia and New Zealand Book Company Pty. Ltd.,
10 Aquatic Drive, Frenchs Forest, N.S.W. 2086
P.O. Box 459, BROOKVALE, N.S.W. 2100

AUSTRIA – AUTRICHE
OECD Publications and Information Center
4 Simrockstrasse 5300 BONN. Tel. (0228) 21.60.45
Local Agent/Agent local :
Gerold and Co., Graben 31, WIEN 1. Tel. 52.22.35

BELGIUM – BELGIQUE
Jean De Lannoy, Service Publications OCDE
avenue du Roi 202, B-1060 BRUXELLES. Tel. 02/538.51.69

BRAZIL – BRÉSIL
Mestre Jou S.A., Rua Guaipa 518,
Caixa Postal 24090, 05089 SAO PAULO 10. Tel. 261.1920
Rua Senador Dantas 19 s/205-6, RIO DE JANEIRO GB.
Tel. 232.07.32

CANADA
Renouf Publishing Company Limited,
2182 ouest, rue Ste-Catherine,
MONTRÉAL, Qué. H3H 1M7. Tel. (514)937.3519
OTTAWA, Ont. K1P 5A6, 61 Sparks Street

DENMARK – DANEMARK
Munksgaard Export and Subscription Service
35, Nørre Søgade
DK 1370 KØBENHAVN K. Tel. +45.1.12.85.70

FINLAND – FINLANDE
Akateeminen Kirjakauppa
Keskuskatu 1, 00100 HELSINKI 10. Tel. 65.11.22

FRANCE
Bureau des Publications de l'OCDE,
2 rue André-Pascal, 75775 PARIS CEDEX 16. Tel. (1) 524.81.67
Principal correspondant :
13602 AIX-EN-PROVENCE : Librairie de l'Université.
Tel. 26.18.08

GERMANY – ALLEMAGNE
OECD Publications and Information Center
4 Simrockstrasse 5300 BONN Tel. (0228) 21.60.45

GREECE – GRÈCE
Librairie Kauffmann, 28 rue du Stade,
ATHÈNES 132. Tel. 322.21.60

HONG-KONG
Government Information Services,
Publications/Sales Section, Baskerville House,
2/F., 22 Ice House Street

ICELAND – ISLANDE
Snaebjörn Jónsson and Co., h.f.,
Hafnarstraeti 4 and 9, P.O.B. 1131, REYKJAVIK.
Tel. 13133/14281/11936

INDIA – INDE
Oxford Book and Stationery Co. :
NEW DELHI-1, Scindia House. Tel. 45896
CALCUTTA 700016, 17 Park Street. Tel. 240832

INDONESIA – INDONÉSIE
PDIN-LIPI, P.O. Box 3065/JKT., JAKARTA, Tel. 583467

IRELAND – IRLANDE
TDC Publishers – Library Suppliers
12 North Frederick Street, DUBLIN 1 Tel. 744835-749677

ITALY – ITALIE
Libreria Commissionaria Sansoni :
Via Lamarmora 45, 50121 FIRENZE. Tel. 579751/584468
Via Bartolini 29, 20155 MILANO. Tel. 365083
Sub-depositari :
Ugo Tassi
Via A. Farnese 28, 00192 ROMA. Tel. 310590
Editrice e Libreria Herder,
Piazza Montecitorio 120, 00186 ROMA. Tel. 6794628
Costantino Ercolano, Via Generale Orsini 46, 80132 NAPOLI. Tel. 405210
Libreria Hoepli, Via Hoepli 5, 20121 MILANO. Tel. 865446
Libreria Scientifica, Dott. Lucio de Biasio "Aeiou"
Via Meravigli 16, 20123 MILANO Tel. 807679
Libreria Zanichelli
Piazza Galvani 1/A, 40124 Bologna Tel. 237389
Libreria Lattes, Via Garibaldi 3, 10122 TORINO. Tel. 519274
La diffusione delle edizioni OCSE è inoltre assicurata dalle migliori librerie nelle
città più importanti.

JAPAN – JAPON
OECD Publications and Information Center,
Landic Akasaka Bldg., 2-3-4 Akasaka,
Minato-ku, TOKYO 107 Tel. 586.2016

KOREA – CORÉE
Pan Korea Book Corporation,
P.O. Box n° 101 Kwangwhamun, SÉOUL. Tel. 72.7369

LEBANON – LIBAN
Documenta Scientifica/Redico,
Edison Building, Bliss Street, P.O. Box 5641, BEIRUT.
Tel. 354429 – 344425

MALAYSIA – MALAISIE
University of Malaya Co-operative Bookshop Ltd.
P.O. Box 1127, Jalan Pantai Baru
KUALA LUMPUR. Tel. 51425, 54058, 54361

THE NETHERLANDS – PAYS-BAS
Staatsuitgeverij, Verzendboekhandel,
Chr. Plantijnstraat 1 Postbus 20014
2500 EA S-GRAVENHAGE. Tel. nr. 070.789911
Voor bestellingen: Tel. 070.789208

NEW ZEALAND – NOUVELLE-ZÉLANDE
Publications Section,
Government Printing Office Bookshops:
AUCKLAND: Retail Bookshop: 25 Rutland Street,
Mail Orders: 85 Beach Road, Private Bag C.P.O.
HAMILTON: Retail Ward Street,
Mail Orders, P.Q. Box 857
WELLINGTON: Retail: Mulgrave Street (Head Office),
Cubacade World Trade Centre
Mail Orders: Private Bag
CHRISTCHURCH: Retail: 159 Hereford Street,
Mail Orders: Private Bag
DUNEDIN: Retail: Princes Street
Mail Order: P.O. Box 1104

NORWAY – NORVÈGE
J.G. TANUM A/S Karl Johansgate 43
P.O. Box 1177 Sentrum OSLO 1. Tel. (02) 80.12.60

PAKISTAN
Mirza Book Agency, 65 Shahrah Quaid-E-Azam, LAHORE 3.
Tel. 66839

PHILIPPINES
National Book Store, Inc.
Library Services Division, P.O. Box 1934, MANILA.
Tel. Nos. 49.43.06 to 09, 40.53.45, 49.45.12

PORTUGAL
Livraria Portugal, Rua do Carmo 70-74,
1117 LISBOA CODEX. Tel. 360582/3

SINGAPORE – SINGAPOUR
Information Publications Pte Ltd,
Pei-Fu Industrial Building,
24 New Industrial Road N° 02-06
SINGAPORE 1953, Tel. 2831786, 2831798

SPAIN – ESPAGNE
Mundi-Prensa Libros, S.A.
Castelló 37, Apartado 1223, MADRID-1. Tel. 275.46.55
Libreria Bosch, Ronda Universidad 11, BARCELONA 7.
Tel. 317.53.08, 317.53.58

SWEDEN – SUÈDE
AB CE Fritzes Kungl Hovbokhandel,
Box 16 356, S 103 27 STH. Regeringsgatan 12,
DS STOCKHOLM. Tel. 08/23.89.00
Subscription Agency/Abonnements:
Wennergren-Williams AB,
Box 13004, S104 25 STOCKHOLM.
Tel. 08/54.12.00

SWITZERLAND – SUISSE
OECD Publications and Information Center
4 Simrockstrasse 5300 BONN. Tel. (0228) 21.60.45
Local Agents/Agents locaux
Librairie Payot, 6 rue Grenus, 1211 GENÈVE 11. Tel. 022.31.89.50

TAIWAN – FORMOSE
Good Faith Worldwide Int'l Co., Ltd.
9th floor, No. 118, Sec. 2,
Chung Hsiao E. Road
TAIPEI. Tel. 391.7396/391.7397

THAILAND – THAILANDE
Suksit Siam Co., Ltd., 1715 Rama IV Rd,
Samyan, BANGKOK 5. Tel. 2511630

TURKEY – TURQUIE
Kültur Yayinlari Is-Türk Ltd. Sti.
Atatürk Bulvari No : 77/B
KIZILAY/ANKARA. Tel. 17 02 66
Dolmabahce Cad. No : 29
BESIKTAS/ISTANBUL. Tel. 60 71 88

UNITED KINGDOM – ROYAUME-UNI
H.M. Stationery Office,
P.O.B. 276, LONDON SW8 5DT.
(postal orders only)
Telephone orders: (01) 622.3316, or
49 High Holborn, LONDON WC1V 6 HB (personal callers)
Branches at: EDINBURGH, BIRMINGHAM, BRISTOL,
MANCHESTER, BELFAST.

UNITED STATES OF AMERICA – ÉTATS-UNIS
OECD Publications and Information Center, Suite 1207,
1750 Pennsylvania Ave., N.W. WASHINGTON, D.C.20006 – 4582
Tel. (202) 724.1857

VENEZUELA
Libreria del Este, Avda. F. Miranda 52, Edificio Galipan,
CARACAS 106. Tel. 32.23.01/33.26.04/31.58.38

YUGOSLAVIA – YOUGOSLAVIE
Jugoslovenska Knjiga, Knez Mihajlova 2, P.O.B. 36, BEOGRAD.
Tel. 621.992

Les commandes provenant de pays où l'OCDE n'a pas encore désigné de dépositaire peuvent être adressées à :
OCDE, Bureau des Publications, 2, rue André-Pascal, 75775 PARIS CEDEX 16.
Orders and inquiries from countries where sales agents have not yet been appointed may be sent to:
OECD, Publications Office, 2, rue André-Pascal, 75775 PARIS CEDEX 16.

67306-01-1984

OECD PUBLICATIONS, 2, rue André-Pascal, 75775 PARIS CEDEX 16 - No. 42813 1984
PRINTED IN FRANCE
(81 84 03 1) ISBN 92-64-12561-2